The Mystical

Initiations

of Freedom

The Path to Self-Mastery, vol 9

The Mystical Initiations of Freedom

KIM MICHAELS

Copyright © 2019 Kim Michaels. All rights reserved. No part of this book may be used, reproduced, translated, electronically stored or transmitted by any means except by written permission from the publisher. A reviewer may quote brief passages in a review.

MORE TO LIFE PUBLISHING

www.morepublish.com

For foreign and translation rights,
contact info@ morepublish.com

ISBN: 978-87-93297-50-0

The information and insights in this book should not be considered as a form of therapy, advice, direction, diagnosis, and/or treatment of any kind. This information is not a substitute for medical, psychological, or other professional advice, counseling and care. All matters pertaining to your individual health should be supervised by a physician or appropriate health-care practitioner. No guarantee is made by the author or the publisher that the practices described in this book will yield successful results for anyone at any time. They are presented for informational purposes only, as the practice and proof rests with the individual.

For more information: *www.ascendedmasterlight.com* and *www.transcendencetoolbox.com*

CONTENTS

Introduction 7

1 | Introducing the Seventh Ray 11

2 | Introducing Saint Germain 15

3 | Freedom beyond symbols 21

4 | You are an artist sculpting with pure energy 31

5 | Invoking the artistic mindset 53

6 | Is anything on earth real? 73

7 | Invoking a realistic sense of what is real 91

8 | Loving your Divine plan more than a daydream 109

9 | Invoking Love for my Divine plan 137

10 | Welcome to reality simulator earth 177

11 | Invoking a new sense of reality 197

12 | The way you see things co-creates those things 223

13 | Invoking the vision of how I co-create 249

14 | Overcoming the things that take your peace 285

15 | Invoking manifestation through surrender 311

16 | When matter and you do not matter 343

17 | Invoking freedom from the self that matters 363

INTRODUCTION

This book is part of the series *The Path to Self-Mastery*. The purpose of the series is to give you a complete course for knowing and passing the mystical initiations of the seven spiritual rays. The books in the series form a progression, and it is recommended that you start by working through the books for the first six rays before progressing to this book.

The purpose of this book is to teach you about the characteristics of the Seventh Ray, which will show you how to find greater freedom and also manifest better material circumstances for yourself. If you are new to ascended master teachings, you will benefit greatly from reading the first book in the series, *The Power of Self,* because it gives a general introduction to the spiritual path as it is taught by the ascended masters. This will give you a good foundation for taking greater advantage of the teachings in this book.

This book is designed as a workbook in order to help you better integrate and apply the teachings. You will get the best results if you give the invocation that corresponds to the chapter you are studying. It is recommended that you give a specific invocation once a day for nine days and then study part of the corresponding dictation before or after giving the invocation. Each evening, make calls to be taken to Saint Germain's retreat, called the Cave of Symbols, in the etheric realm over Wyoming, United States.

You give an invocation by reading it aloud, thereby invoking high-frequency spiritual energy. For more information about invocations and how to give them, please see the website: *www.transcendencetoolbox.com*. You can also purchase a recording of the invocations and give them along with the recording. The recording is available on *www.morepublish.com*.

In order to learn more about the ascended masters and how they give dictations, see the website *www.ascendedmasterlight.com*. If you are not familiar with the concepts of the fall and of fallen beings, please read *Cosmology of Evil*. That book gives a profound yet easily understood explanation of why there are some beings who have no respect for the free will (or lives) of human beings. It explains why they are willing to do anything in order to control us or destroy those who will not be controlled.

The purpose of the books in *The Path to Self-Mastery* series is to take you from the 48th to the 96th level of consciousness. As Saint Germain will explain, there are still some levels of consciousness to go through before you are ready to ascend at the 144th level. To help you go through the initiations of these levels, the ascended masters have provided a number of books, as Saint Germain will mention. The books can be purchased at *www.morepublish.com* or from major booksellers. These books are:

My Lives With Lucifer, Satan, Hitler and Jesus

Healing Your Spiritual Traumas

Introduction

Fulfilling Your Divine Plan

Fulfilling Your Highest Spiritual Potential

Making Peace with Being on Earth

1 | INTRODUCING THE SEVENTH RAY

Color of the Seventh Ray: Violet
Corresponding chakra: Seat of the soul or innocence chakra
Elohim of the Seventh Ray: Arcturus and Victoria
Archangel and Archeia of the Seventh Ray: Zadkiel and Amethyst
Chohan of the Seventh Ray: Saint Germain
Decrees for the Seventh Ray: 7.01 Decree to Elohim Arcturus, 7.02 Decree to Archangel Zadkiel, 1.03 Decree to Saint Germain.

Pure qualities of the Seventh Ray

Traditionally, the Seventh Ray qualities are seen as freedom, forgiveness and justice. A deeper understanding is that the Seventh Ray is the seat of your playfulness, your willingness to approach life according to Jesus' statement: "Unless you become as a little child, ye shall in no way enter the kingdom."

When you embody the pure Seventh Ray qualities, you feel that you live in a world that is basically good, and you are here to express yourself and play with what is available. You are not worried or anxious about life or the future, and you trust that Spirit will protect you and that the Mother will nurture you. You feel a sense of bubbling freedom and a desire to experience what the world has to offer and to add to it through your own creative expression. You feel holy innocence.

Perversions of the Seventh Ray

The primary perversion of the Seventh Ray qualities is a tendency to take life very seriously. This can be expressed as a perversion of both freedom and justice, which combines into the sense that you live in a world where everything is a struggle, perhaps even a struggle against a force that is unjustly seeking to take away your freedom.

Take the old saying: "Laugh at the devil, and he runs away from you." There is a truth here, in the sense that if you take something too seriously, you give it power over you. Of course, one might say that there are many things in the world that *are* seeking to limit your freedom and that *are* unjust, so does that mean you should not take them seriously? There is a balance where one realizes the truth in another statement by Jesus: "Be ye wise as serpents, harmless as doves." There is a fine balance between being naive to the temporary conditions in the world and taking them so seriously that you think you cannot feel free until they are changed.

The extreme perversion of the Seventh Ray is the epic mindset where one thinks the world is locked in an epic battle between good and evil, meaning that anything can be justified in the fight to destroy evil. This leads to complete insensitivity

1 | Introducing the Seventh Ray

towards life, which has led to some of the worst examples of human cruelty. As with everything else, insensitivity towards others comes from an insensitivity towards oneself.

When you have perverted the Seventh Ray qualities, you tend to think that the problems in the world exist because other people do not take them as seriously as you do. As you overcome this imbalance, you realize that the conditions are still here because people take them too seriously, thus thinking the conditions of the material world have power over their spirits. In reality, we are all spiritual beings, and one of our ultimate tasks on earth is to demonstrate that we will not allow material conditions to limit our Spirits and their expression in this world. Allowing our higher selves to express themselves through us is the key to freedom, and it is the playfulness of the divine man-child, who knows he or she is one with the Father—and with God all things are possible.

2 | INTRODUCING SAINT GERMAIN

There is, of course, no such thing as a typical Chohan. Yet if you thought the previous six Chohans were difficult to grasp, you will find that no one is as enigmatic as Saint Germain. Even among ascended masters, he is considered somewhat of a marvel, and he is truly a being of great depth, even mystery. How could it be otherwise for the master who embodies the Seventh Ray of Freedom, and who on top of that serves as the Hierarch of the Age of Aquarius?

Saint Germain ascended on May 1st, 1684. No sooner had he ascended, than he asked for and received a dispensation to take on a body and appear as the "Wonderman of Europe." This was a somewhat enigmatic figure, whose existence is nevertheless well documented. He appeared to the heads of state of several European countries over a period of more than a century. His desire was to unite Europe into one nation, but since the kings of Europe were too trapped in their ego games, his endeavor did not succeeded. Instead, he was instrumental in inspiring and sponsoring the

Founding Fathers of America, inspiring that nation to become a bulwark for freedom against the totalitarian expansion that he foresaw might have taken away freedom and have delayed his vision for a Golden Age for centuries.

Saint Germain was embodied as Francis Bacon, who was instrumental in writing the Shakespearean plays and thereby bringing the English language to a higher state, in which it is especially suited for expressing complex spiritual concepts. It is said that Saint Germain was Merlin, at the court of King Arthur. Yet he wants us to understand that although there was a physical figure inspiring the Arthurian legends, they are to be seen as myths and not to be taken too literally. To say that Saint Germain was exactly as the legends portray Merlin is a misnomer.

Saint Germain works in several etheric retreats, one is the Great Divine Director's retreat, the Rakoczy Mansion over Transylvania. His primary retreat is the Cave of Symbols, located in the etheric realm over Table Mountain in the American state of Wyoming. However, there are 17 places in Wyoming named Table Mountain so there is not much point in going looking for the physical entrance, even though you can find descriptions of people who supposedly did enter this way.

However, Saint Germain makes it clear that such descriptions were given for people in a different time, who needed something more concrete. His retreat is, of course, etheric, meaning that it does not have a physical entrance through which anyone who finds it can enter. You will enter only by raising your consciousness through the path offered by the first six Chohans. Thinking you can go to a physical location and Saint Germain will automatically appear to you is, of course, an ego game. By the time you reach the level of Saint Germain, you should have left these more obvious ego games behind you—for Saint Germain has little time for them.

Of course, people who come to Saint Germain's retreat are not free of ego games, and the primary one they must deal with is the desire to force Saint Germain himself into a little mental box created by their egos. Many spiritual students have grand expectations of how Saint Germain should behave and how he should treat them with great fanfare. Saint Germain is an expert in shattering all such mental boxes. After all, which mental box created by the ego could possibly hold the God of Freedom?

There are even many students who have a mental image of Saint Germain based on ascended master teachings. Yet in embodying the Flame of Freedom, Saint Germain has no fixed form, and he has no sense of obligation or even what people call honor or dignity. He is completely free to appear and to express himself in any way he wants, and he takes some joy in taking on the exact appearance that most disappoints people's expectations. In fact, he finds a childlike joy in taking on an appearance that is so far beyond people's expectations that they do not even recognize him, sometimes mistaking him for one of the servants at the retreat, occasionally even subjecting him to verbal abuse, contempt or ridicule.

It is quite common that beginning students enter Saint Germain's retreat and receive guidance from him, but they do not recognize him. Only when they – through their guidance – have shed some of their expectations and mental boxes, will they be so free that they can recognize Saint Germain by vibration regardless of his outer appearance. This, of course, is one of the primary goals of Saint Germain, namely to help you build the discernment that can see through any outer appearance and discern between reality and unreality based on vibration alone. You will never find freedom by taking on an appearance; you will find freedom only in becoming one with the vibration of Freedom, the Flame of Freedom, even the

God Flame of your own I AM Presence. What is the ego but an appearance? It has no reality to it, but it insists that you and your creative expression must conform to its appearance. When you stop projecting an appearance upon Saint Germain, you will also stop projecting an appearance upon the real you, and this is the key to your freedom. You may have chosen to express yourself a certain way in the past, even for many past lifetimes, but there is no cosmic law that says you have to continue to express yourself the same way or even be bound by past choices. Only when you can make a choice that is completely unaffected by any and all past choices, can you be truly free to meet Saint Germain the way he wants you to meet him: as an equal.

Saint Germain has a very distinct vibration, which is very high and very quick. It is hard to grasp Saint Germain, for he will not come down in vibration to meet you—*you* must come up to meet him. When you do, you find in Saint Germain an incredible Presence that deeply inspires you to realize, just how much more we can be than what we have come to see ourselves as here on earth. Truly, Saint Germain is beyond this world, and he wants *us* to get beyond this world. For as he likes to say: "We have yet other worlds to conquer."

The first world you must conquer is your Self, and Saint Germain is the most inspiring guide you could ever find—when you find him. How do you find Saint Germain? Well, to start, stop looking for him to have a specific appearance. Then, stop looking for him outside yourself. If you can allow Saint Germain complete freedom as to how he expresses himself, you will eventually begin to give yourself that same freedom. *That* is when you will discover Saint Germain, as he expresses himself through your heart flame. And that is when you will truly know freedom. As Saint Germain likes to say:

2 | Introducing Saint Germain

Saint Germain I AM, and I am free.
Why are you not free?
Because you are not me.
Yet the truth you might see
is that you can become me.

3 | FREEDOM BEYOND SYMBOLS

Saint Germain I AM, and I come with a momentum of the Seventh Ray of freedom that is little known and little understood, even to ascended master students, and that is the momentum of victory. Truly, when you have gone through the initiations of the six rays, you have built a momentum. You know you can pass your tests, you know that whatever we, the Chohans, throw at you, you are able to deal with it, to step back, to look at yourself, to overcome anything in your psychology that stands in your way and then to surrender, to let go. In letting go, you begin to feel a new energy rising within you, and that is the momentum of victory on the Seventh Ray of Freedom.

Truly, when you realize that you are more than anything in this world – when you realize that you are more than any sense of self you have built through all of your embodiments – how can you fail to realize, that you can overcome, transcend and be free from any condition on earth, and any condition in your own psychology? How can you, then, fail to feel this bubbling joy of victory coming up from the depth of your being?

Meeting Saint Germain face to face

That is, then, when you and I can meet, and I can appear to you, stand before you, not as this God-like figure high above you, but I can stand before you and look at you as an equal. You can accept me as an equal, and we can therefore share in a moment of oneness, total oneness, of knowing that we have united in freedom!

For we are both god-free beings. I am a unique individual; you are a unique individual. I am not requiring you to be something you are not, and you are not afraid that I will require you to be something you are not. That is, indeed, when we can transcend into a new awareness where we both go beyond the student-teacher relationship. We, indeed, unite in that Flame of Freedom whereby you, as the one in embodiment, become an open door for giving that Flame of Freedom to all that you meet, the Flame of Freedom that I AM and that I am willing to stream through you when we attain that oneness. This, then, is the vision of your potential when you attain some mastery on the seven rays.

A special opportunity to attain freedom

Surely, those of you who have gone through these initiations of the first six rays, you have made mighty strides towards this ultimate victory of freedom. I am sure you realize that from the moment you were born, and, of course, going back many lifetimes on this planet, the culture and the fallen beings, and

3 | Freedom beyond symbols

even well-meaning human beings (such as your parents and teachers and siblings) have done almost everything possible to hammer down your creative drive and your creative freedom. They have made you so afraid to express yourself that most people dare not even be creative. They have even put upon you that your creativity should live up to a standard predefined by some institution or authority on earth.

How can freedom be predefined? Creativity is the unknown – is that which has never before been seen – so how can creativity follow a predefined standard? It simply cannot be done, my beloved. Thus, you will never be truly free until you dare to go beyond all of the man-made standards, even those that have been created based on a valid spiritual teaching. Even students of the ascended masters have created a standard for themselves and each other, and in many cases they built even an organizational culture that limited the creativity of the members. This, of course, will not get you to the point of knowing the freedom of victory on the Seventh Ray.

How can you know victory when you think you have to blindly follow an outer standard—that is not the Christ-standard but a standard based on the consciousness of anti-christ? This, of course, will never lead you to freedom, and it will never lead you to victory.

Visiting the Cave of Symbols

As you use the invocations in this book, you will be taken, if you are willing, to my spiritual retreat, called the Cave of Symbols—no matter where it is located. It has been said in the past that it was located over a mountain called Table Mountain in the state of Wyoming in the United States, but can there really be a physical location that can confine the Retreat of Freedom?

Nay, for the Retreat of Freedom is more than anything else a state of consciousness that is not localized. It is non-local, and therefore if you think you can go to a certain physical location and sit there and meditate on me and I will appear to you, you are, of course, mistaken. You can meditate on me in consciousness, but you must be willing to shift your consciousness. You see my beloved, I will not come to you; I will not come down to a certain level of human consciousness. When you come to the initiations of the Seventh Ray, you must come up, for that is what you have been prepared to do by the first six rays.

The mistic chamber

Come up into freedom! Thus, if you are willing to use these invocations to come up higher in consciousness, you will indeed be allowed to enter the Cave of Symbols. In my retreat I will take you to a special place where you go into a chamber, and the chamber has a special construction. When you are inside of it, it seems like the chamber has no solid walls; they are all like a mist.

The mist can sometimes be seen as having extremely fine particles of light that sparkle, but nevertheless there seems to be no solid wall that you can feel. If you attempt to go in one direction in this chamber, the mist will move in front of you, and you will never come to a wall, you will never come to a border, you will never come to a limitation. This is at first a very challenging initiation for many people, for they have been so used to defining themselves based on limitations, based on boundaries that they had not set for themselves.

What do you do when you come to the initiation of freedom? You have to face the test of letting go of all the earthly boundaries that define your sense of self. You have to ultimately be willing to define yourself based not on anything on earth, but based exclusively on your I AM Presence and the individuality locked in your Presence and causal body.

The concept of "no-self"

In fact, you even have to come to the point where you no longer define your "self," for you are not seeing your self as being a self. You, in fact, attain the state of consciousness that by some eastern teachers has been described as "no-self." The concept of "no-self," however, is (or at least can be) difficult to grasp for people in a linear, dualistic state of consciousness. What you face in my retreat in the mystic chamber, "the mist-ic chamber," that has mystical properties is precisely that you cannot define yourself based on any conditions from the outside.

The only way to pass this initiation without actually going mad is that you stop defining your sense of self. You are just an open door who from moment to moment carries out the impulses from the Presence. In fact, you do not even carry them out, you let them flow through you without any preconceived sense of what *should* or *should not* be expressed, or what *should* or *should not* happen.

You are the open door for the impulses from the Presence to stream through you unhindered, and you are open in the sense that no matter what the reaction is from other people or from the material world, you are still the open door. You do not judge, you do not analyze, you do not evaluate, you simply are that open door, nothing more.

This is the test you face in the chamber of the mist that moves in front of you so there are no boundaries that you can grasp. This is an initiation that you will be given, in the beginning, only for a very short period of time, for most people cannot handle it for very long. It is somewhat similar to the sensory deprivation that some people expose themselves to on earth, and it can be a difficult initiation.

The mirror of symbols

You will be exposed to it for a very brief moment in the beginning, and then I will immediately take you to another chamber, a chamber that has a mirror that does not show your physical body or your etheric, mental or emotional body. It shows you a symbol, and this symbol depicts the current limitation that holds back your freedom. In the beginning, you will be allowed to see only one limitation at a time, and then you will be taken into another chamber where you can work on this limitation.

This chamber, the third chamber, could be visualized almost like being inside one of these amethyst crystals, geodes, that are hollow and the inside is like the crystalline structure of the amethyst. In this particular chamber your violet flame decrees will be multiplied and reflected back to you by the different surfaces of the crystals so that you have an extreme multiplication. This will help you consume the symbols you have seen, the symbols that depict the blocks you have to the freedom flowing through you.

You see, in reality everything is created out of symbols. This is a teaching we have not given yet to any organization, but which we will give in the not-too-distant future when we deem that the time is right. The reality is that in your three higher bodies – your identity, mental and emotional body – you form symbols, geometric forms and structures. These are the ones that are then impressed upon the Ma-ter light, impressed upon elemental life, and they depict them as physical circumstances. These symbols can be very complex, very intricate, depending on the complexity found in your subconscious mind. When you are in this chamber of the amethyst crystals, you have a unique opportunity to invoke the violet flame, based on the momentum built on the first six rays, and then have it multiplied by the crystalline structure to consume these symbolic structures in your subconscious mind, in the levels of your subconscious mind.

Seeing the symbol for your outer self

When you have consumed a certain portion, you can go back to the mirror chamber, see another one and then as you gradually purify yourself, go back to the mistic chamber and again experience how long you can stay in freedom before you confront another momentum, another unresolved structure in your subconscious mind. When you come in contact with something – be it fear or whatever – you then go into the mirror chamber. You now see a symbol for that unresolved substance, and then you go back into the amethyst chamber to resolve it, to consume it with the violet flame.

The goal is, of course, that you come to the point where you can stand in the mirror chamber and you can see not only a specific belief, a specific limitation, but you can actually see the symbol for the outer personality and individuality that you have built over many lifetimes. The individuality that you think you are because you have seen yourself and life through that perception filter for so long that many people even think that this is their God-given, divine individuality. They even think this is what is anchored in the I AM Presence. I tell you, it is not! It is entirely man-made. It is made by you, and it is made in response to the conditions you have encountered in the material universe for thousands if not millions, of embodiments. Therefore, it is very old, very ingrained, and many people are very attached to it because they feel it is a wonderful individuality and personality.

This is precisely what Christ talked about when he said that unless you were willing to lose your life for his sake, you should not find eternal life. This is the "life," the outer personality, the worldly personality, that must die before you become the Living Christ. You cannot let it die as long as you are identified with it, as long as you are attached to it, and as long as you do not see that it limits you, but you think that this is who you are and who you are meant to be.

True self-awareness

When you can stand there and look in the mirror and see this symbol and see that it is just a symbol – it is not who you are – then you have a foundation for going back into the crystal chamber, invoking intense calls to the violet flame to consume it, then going back in the mistic chamber. Now, when you are not attached to this structure, then you can stand to be in the chamber of the mist, for now you need no structure in order to maintain a sense of self-awareness.

You can remain for as long as you like in the pure awareness that most of you can only glimpse in short glimpses when you are in the body and looking at everything through the filter of the body. Surely, as you become able to endure this pure awareness for longer and longer periods of time, you will feel in your waking awareness less attachment to anything in this world, a greater sense of freedom. This will build this sense of victory that no matter what limitations you are facing in this embodiment or from past lifetimes, you know you can transcend them all, for they are nothing but symbols. *You* are not a symbol—you are *real!*

You are a God-free Being! You are an extension of the Creator's Being! You are my equal in every way, for I too am an extension of the Creator's Being! In the deepest reality, I am not the Saint Germain you have come to know through the many past ascended master teachings and organizations. I too am not a symbol, and what has been expressed in words and images is just a symbol. I AM a God-free Being of pure awareness, and when you see yourself as that and see me as that, then we are one, then we have that unity, then we are totally equal. *That* is when you have won your freedom, and I have taken you as far as I can take you as the Chohan of the Seventh Ray.

The supreme joy of the Chohans

This is my supreme joy: to stand there and experience that oneness. You are not standing in front of me, for we are blending our pure awareness together in knowing, in gnosis, in complete oneness! That is the ultimate victory for you and the ultimate reward for me, and the joy of seeing a student who has gone all the way on the seven rays, and therefore is ready to graduate and move on to the Maha Chohan and the Eighth Ray, and move on to the Buddha and other masters on the higher rays.

Indeed, this is the joy of all of the Chohans. Of course, I am not so selfish that when you come to this point of victory, I am going to enjoy your victory all alone. You will find that the other six Chohans are there, and the Maha Chohan is there and indeed we can all share in that oneness. Every time we of the eight Chohans raise up one lifestream to that ultimate victory, there is such a multiplication and outpouring that we all share in it. We all become more and that allows us to have more momentum to help the unascended people on earth.

That is why, as Jesus said, "And I, if I be lifted up from the earth, shall draw all men unto me." We the Chohans desire to draw all men unto us, and when we have drawn *you* unto us, you will also desire to draw all other men and women unto you, the you that you now are. This is the you that is victorious, for you have passed the initiations. You have been faithful over a few things, and now you will be ruler over many things.

Thus, I truly commend those who have been faithful to use these teachings and invocations to the seven rays. If you have not yet given them all, it is never too late. Go back and start over and then build up that momentum. Truly, what we have given you with these books is a scientific formula that when applied with a necessary surrender, *will* produce the promised result. It will not do it in a *mechanical* way, it will do it in a *creative* way, for you must be willing to see and to surrender the symbols that are not you.

If you are willing, then the results will be manifest! Many of you who have used the first six books will know this already, for you have experienced transformation. Thus, I say: "Accept the inner knowing that this book of the Seventh Ray can bring your ultimate victory."

Then, surrender into that victory and do not resist the victory! Do not let the ego or the forces of this world or the prince of this world whisper in your ear that you are not worthy or that it is not possible! My beloved, accept that victory is possible, and then surrender into that victory, the Victory that I AM and that you are also—when you accept that I AM!

4 | YOU ARE AN ARTIST SCULPTING WITH PURE ENERGY

I AM the Ascended Master Saint Germain, and it is my great joy to give you this first installment in the levels of initiation that you go through under me in my retreat, which has been called the Cave of Symbols. Let me begin by talking about this retreat.

You may be familiar with previous ascended master dispensations and teachings that talk about this retreat in more detail. You may have seen pictures of how there is supposedly great halls that have various occult or esoteric symbols that supposedly have some special significance. If you know these symbols, you will be able to precipitate anything you want. This, of course, is a teaching that was given for a lower level of consciousness than the teachings we are giving today. Therefore, we had to appeal to what people wanted at that level of consciousness. The previous Chohans have done everything they could to help you rise above that level of consciousness so you are now ready for a higher teaching.

The true meaning of symbols

What does it truly mean that my retreat is the cave of "symbols?" Well, in order to understand this, let me reach back to something that was taught by the ancient Greek philosopher Plato quite a number of years ago. Plato said that beyond the physical, material world there is a higher realm, a realm of what he called "ideal forms." These ideal forms could also be said to be symbols. It was the interaction of these ideal forms in the higher world that determined what would be manifest in the physical realm and what form things would take here in the physical realm. This is a more accurate description of the Cave of Symbols but we can, of course, go further today.

We have given you teachings that you have a physical body but beyond that you have an emotional, mental and identity body. How do you co-create? Well, we have taught you that you receive light and energy from your I AM Presence. As this energy passes through the three higher bodies, it takes on the forms of whatever structures, images, symbols, forms you have in those three higher bodies. This is truly a representation of the co-creative process.

What Plato called the "world of ideal forms" was to some degree the spiritual realm, the ascended realm, but it could also very well be said to be your three higher bodies. You have certain forms in the three higher bodies. In your three higher bodies you may indeed have certain forms that are more ideal, more pure, more elaborate, more detailed than what is actually manifest in the physical realm. The reality is that most people have a certain ideal form, ideal image, ideal symbol in their three higher bodies. The question now becomes: "Why can they not manifest that in the physical realm?"

People with a self-centered vision

You will know, when you look at humankind, that people are at many, many different levels of consciousness. The majority of human beings on this earth are at a much lower level than the consciousness you are at when you start this course [This book], at least if you have followed the instructions by the other six Chohans. You will look at many people on earth and you can see that what they actually have in their three higher bodies is not necessarily what Plato would call an ideal form. They have a very limited vision, they have some very distorted images and ideas. Nevertheless, you will see that most people actually have higher forms in their three higher bodies than what is manifest in the physical, material realm, at least in their personal lives.

The question becomes: "What is it that prevents people from manifesting the forms they have in their higher bodies at the physical level?" This is a question that could be said to be as relevant for a person with the lowest level of consciousness as for an ascended master student at your level of consciousness. Now of course, if you go to the very lowest level of consciousness, you will see that there are actually some people there who are able to manifest something in the physical that is very close to the forms they have in their three higher bodies. Unfortunately, what they have in their three higher bodies is very, very low, very distorted forms, very impure. You can actually see some people at a low level of consciousness who have a certain higher vision, for example, a king who wants to manifest a certain palace. He may be able to envision this palace and he may actually be able to bring into physical manifestation something that is very close to what he is envisioning. Unfortunately, this is, of course, an entirely self-centered vision. In order to actually build that palace, it requires the slave labor of tens of thousands of people.

You see here that there are some people who are able to formulate a vision in their three higher bodies and bring it into physical manifestation. It may not be a destructive vision. You cannot say that some of these elaborate palaces, that you find in most nations in the world, are necessarily ugly or distorted. Some of them can be quite beautiful from a certain earthly perspective. Nevertheless, when you see how they were actually brought about, you see that the people who originally envisioned these palaces did have a very low, very self-centered, very self-focused level of consciousness. In order to manifest their vision, it required the slave labor of tens of thousands of people.

You are seeing here that at a lower level of consciousness, you have some people that are actually capable of bringing forth a vision into physical manifestation, but, number one, the vision is self-centered and, number two, the way they bring it about is also self-centered.

How a golden age can be manifest

The question now becomes for you as an ascended master student: "Is this what you want to accomplish?" Are you somehow thinking that by following this course, I will give you some secret formula, some secret symbol, that will allow you to manifest anything you desire? You see my beloved, at the first level of initiation in my retreat you are, of course, facing the combination of the First Ray of Will and Power with the Seventh Ray of Freedom. When you look at the history of humankind, you can see that there are actually people who have had a considerable momentum of will and power but they have been completely unbalanced when it comes to freedom. In other words, in order for the one king to manifest his will, he had to use his power to take away the freedom of tens of thousands of people in order to build that palace, that stone structure.

This, of course, is not what I am going to teach you in this course. I am in no way going to teach you how to use your willpower to override the free will of other people, whether it be one person or tens of thousands of people. Do you understand, my beloved, that we of the ascended masters, as we have now said many times, have absolute respect for free will? You may say from a certain perspective that it is my goal to manifest a Golden Age on earth. In that Golden Age no one will be lacking the basic necessities of life and no one will be suffering. Yes, that is my goal, my beloved, but how can I accomplish this goal? I do not envision that a Golden Age will be manifest by a limited number of powerful kings and emperors or other kinds of leaders who are having some vision but who are manifesting that vision by forcing, by manipulating, by overtaking the free will of their underlings. This is not how I envision the manifestation of my Golden Age.

Now, I know that you will say: "Well, this is obvious to me." Is it equally obvious to you that I do not intend to manifest the Golden Age by having a limited number of spiritual people, who may have a benign intent, override the will of the majority of the population? We have talked about the top 10 percent, the 80 percent of the population in the middle and the 10 percent that are the bottom. Naturally, the fallen beings in embodiment and those whose minds are taken over by the fallen consciousness, form the lowest 10 percent. They are very often using force to bend the will of the 80 percent of the population to their schemes. There are ascended master students who have thought that being part of the top 10 percent means that you are supposed to bend the will of the 80 percent, based on your higher vision and your higher intent.

We have attempted to make something very clear to you, especially by the teachings we have given on the primal self, the avatars coming to earth and how you can fulfill your Divine plan, fulfill your highest spiritual potential. We have attempted with these teachings to make it very clear that we do not want you to override or force the will of the majority. This is not how I intend to manifest my Golden Age. This means that at the end of this course, I will have taken you, if you follow my instructions and are willing to come up through these seven initiations, to the 96th level of consciousness.

The crucial initiation at the 96th level

We have said before that at the 96th level of conscious, you face a crucial initiation. At the 96th level you will have reached some level of mastery of bending matter with your mind. Therefore, you face the crucial initiation: "Will you step up to the higher level of Christhood where you seek to raise the whole? Or will you start descending to the lower level where you are using your mastery to bend the will of other people, to force the will of other people?" This is a crucial initiation. Naturally, it is my aim that you will pass this initiation and move on to the level of Christhood.

That is why I am talking about it right at the onset because it is important for me to set the tone for these levels of initiations that you will go through at my retreat. You should know that we have raised you to a much higher level of consciousness than you were at when you started this course. This means that I need to address what Nada talked about when she talked about the daydreams that spiritual students can have. There is actually a very pervasive, very persuasive daydream that many ascended masters students have, and it is that as you move higher on the path, the initiations become easier and easier. There are many spiritual students, New Age students, ascended master students, who dream that one day they will have passed some critical initiation and then it will be all easy from there. They will be home free. This, of course, is completely unrealistic. This is not how the path of initiation works.

How the path of initiation works

Now, we can take different approaches to this. We can say that at the 48th level of initiation, you are looking at life through the filter of a certain number of illusions that you have taken on. Therefore, the initiation that takes you from the 48th to the 49th level requires you to see beyond the illusions you currently have, come up one step higher by shedding the illusion that is the primary illusion for the 48th level. In a sense, we could say that the initiation you face at the 96th level is very similar. You are still looking through the considerable number of illusions you have left between the 96th and the 144th level. You are still having to look at your situation, look at the initiation, through those illusions and the illusions are still blinding you.

Of course, you can say that at the 96th level you do not have nearly as many illusions as you have at the 48th level. At the 48th level, what makes it difficult to see the initiation you are facing at that level is not all of the illusions that are above the 48th level, it is the illusion you have at your current level that makes it difficult to pass that initiation. Again, at the 96th level it is not so that all of the illusions you have passed up until that level now make it easier for you to pass the initiation at that level. It is not so that what makes it difficult for you to pass the initiation is all the illusions above your level. It is the illusion at your current level that makes it difficult to pass that initiation. It is no easier to see through that illusion at the 96th level than it is at the 48th level. Nor will it be any easier to see through the illusion at the 144th level than it is at other levels. You see my beloved, whatever level you are at, the illusion at that level is as difficult as it is on any other level. Therefore, it is meaningless to think that it becomes easier as you move along on the path.

Now, we may say that from a certain perspective the illusion you face at the 48th level is much more direct, much more obvious, much more clear-cut, much more easy to see in terms of defining what is the right thing to do and the not right thing to do at that level. This is in a sense true. At the lower levels of consciousness, there is a certain contrast between "right and not-right" in terms of passing the initiation. You cannot see that contrast at the 48th level. You can easily see it at the 96th level but at the 96th level you cannot see so easily the difference between passing the initiation and not passing the initiation.

In a sense, we could say that the illusions become more subtle as you go to the higher levels. It becomes more difficult to define what is the right choice and the not-so-right choice at the higher levels than it is at the lower levels. You need to let go of this daydream that when you reach the 96th level, it will be all easy from there. You need to be willing to face the initiation at each of the seven levels I present to you and not have this hope that one day I will give you some ultimate formula that will make everything easy and that will allow you to manifest whatever you want.

The balance of free will

You see, as Nada has already touched upon several times in her discourses, there is a crucial need to balance your individual will with the will of other people and with the overall vision for the planet. You may say: "I am an ascended master student and I want to help manifest the Golden Age of Saint Germain." This is an honorable and constructive desire to have. You need to consider, as Nada also talked about, how you can have these internal spirits that are based on either the compensatory mechanism or other mechanisms where *you* are having a vision of what Saint Germain's Golden Age means that is not actually in alignment with *my* vision. I even talked about this in my introduction that I gave after Nada's discourses where I want you to empty your mind of all these daydreams of how you think the Golden Age will be, and how you think it will be manifest.

What is it you want to help manifest? Is it the Golden Age as *I* see it? Or is it the Golden Age as *you* see it—perhaps based on some of the popular images that are floating around in the collective consciousness? These are, quite frankly, in many cases based on how the fallen beings would envision a golden age, which means they envision it with themselves in control. The fallen beings have a vision of the golden age where there are a few leaders who will manifest these very elaborate, very sophisticated societies by forcing the will of the majority. Some of these fallen beings honestly believe that this will be for people's own good because they do not believe that people are capable of even knowing what they want or holding a vision of a better society. This, of course, is not *my* vision.

My vision is to manifest a golden age based on raising the collective consciousness so that the majority of the people on earth will have a vision of a better society. They will have, truly, an inner knowing, an inner acceptance, that such a society can be manifest, and *is* manifest and is in the process of being manifest. This is what you already see in many of the more developed nations in the world where people have come very, very far in the last, say 100 years, in terms of accepting what material affluence is possible for their nations. You can see that these people's great grandparents could not at all have believed and accepted that the current society was a possibility. They would have considered it a far-flung Utopian pipe dream.

My vision is to raise up the people and how do we do this? We do it, not by forcing them but by having the top 10 percent raise your vision so that you, by being in embodiment, by being part of the collective consciousness, pull up on the majority. Not that you force them to see but that you make it possible for them to see. Then, they will begin to see and accept a higher vision. What does it, then, take for you to (so to speak) align your will with the will of Saint Germain? Well, it takes that you recognize here that there never was a situation for you as a co-creator where you could manifest anything you wanted without considering that you were part of a greater whole.

Individual will and a greater will

We have given you teachings that some of you are avatars that came to earth from a natural planet. We have said that on a natural planet, matter is less dense and it is far easier for you to have a vision in the higher levels of your mind and to manifest that vision in the physical. Yet, we have also said that on a natural planet you are not in the duality consciousness. Therefore, you do not suffer from the illusion of separation that makes you think that you are a separate individual living among other separate individuals. You do not suffer from the illusion that what you do to others does not affect yourself. You know you are part of a whole. This is also what the original inhabitants of the earth knew before the fallen beings came here.

Now, there is a difference between an avatar and the original inhabitants, in the sense that many of the original inhabitants have not developed as strong of an individuality as avatars who came to earth from a natural planet. That is why you see that the 80 percent of the population on earth are very much influenced by the collective consciousness. That is why we are talking about raising up the collective consciousness and then these individuals, who are part of the 80 percent, will be able to grasp the vision that is first held by the top 10 percent. Of course, some among the top 10 percent are the original inhabitants who have grown to that level. The point I am making here is that when you came as an avatar, you did not come here with the vision that you would be some kind of all-mighty leader who would force the will of the population.

You came here with the vision that you would help inspire other people. You also came here with the knowledge, with the experience, that on a natural planet you are not exercising your co-creative abilities in a vacuum as if no one else mattered. Your co-creative abilities are exercised based on your will but that will is not a separate will. It is a will that is aligned with the whole, with a greater vision—first of all with your I AM Presence. You may say: "How can a new co-creator on a natural planet align its will with an over-all vision when it has a point-like sense of identity?" Well, it cannot but it can align its individual will with the will of its I AM Presence. When you do this, your I AM Presence will be in alignment with the whole, with the overall vision for that planet. Therefore, you are not exercising your will in contradiction to the will of other co-creators around you. This is a very important thing to keep in mind at this level.

You also need to recognize that even though we have said it is easier to manifest what you want on a natural planet, it is still not so that you can have any vision you want and manifest it. Even on a natural planet, there are certain, what we might call "conditions," for how you can exercise your co-creative abilities. Now, some would say these are limitations but I prefer not to use this word for a specific reason.

Aligning your lower will to your higher will

Therefore, I want to give you the vision that on a natural planet, you are not creating in a vacuum. You are an artist and I use this word because I want to compare it to a type of artist that you know from earth, namely a sculptor. A sculptor is not working with air that can be formed into any form; a sculptor is working with a specific material. This means that when you consider co-creating a sculpture, you have to first use your will power to make a choice as to which material you are going to use. Now, even in ancient times, sculptors had a variety of materials that they could use. They could use clay. Clay is a very soft material that you can very easily form into almost any shape. If you are very impatient and want to see something manifest very quickly, you use clay. The thing is, clay is not something that will last for a long time. Even if you burn it, it has a limited life expectancy.

Once you become more experienced as a sculptor, you might say that the ease of manifesting something becomes less

4 | *You are an artist sculpting with pure energy*

important to you. Now, you want to manifest something that has a longer life span, and that means you need to choose a more durable material. You could choose limestone, for example. More difficult to form than clay but also more durable, still not the most durable material, not the most beautiful material. Granite is much more durable but also very difficult to shape. Marble is easier to shape than granite and has, most people would say, a greater beauty, a greater hue, a greater shine.

You see here that one of the daydreams that many spiritual students have, as I said, is that they can compensate for the loss (that they felt when they encountered the fallen beings for the first time and were put down by them) by acquiring some magical ability. They dream of manifesting something that is so spectacular that people cannot deny it, they cannot ignore it. When you consider that you are on planet earth and that matter has a certain density on earth, you can see very quickly that this is simply not a realistic dream. Therefore, I need you (at this very first level), and I know I have asked you to do this before, but I still need you to make a conscious decision to let these far-flung daydreams die, to just let them go. Because what you want to do at this level, is you want to use your willpower to choose what material you are going to use to manifest your work of art.

Now, you may say: "But do I have a clear vision of what to manifest?" I would say: "Yes, you did have a clear vision when you made your Divine plan of what you wanted to manifest in this lifetime." It is not a matter of you sitting here with your current level of consciousness, your current vision, and deciding with your outer mind what you want to manifest. It is a matter of you making a decision with your conscious mind that you want to align your conscious mind with the higher will that was used to formulate your Divine plan and with the higher will of Saint Germain and his vision for his Golden

Age. This is what I need you to do at this level. I need you to consider this. I need you to consider these dreams you might have and any desire you may have, any vision you may have of wanting to force the will of the people on earth, even for their own good.

Seeing yourself as an artist

I need you to make a shift in the mind where you begin to see yourself as an artist and your life as a work of art. This is something that for many of you will require a major adjustment because so far you have seen your life in other ways. Some of you have had in your mind a specific field of human endeavor that you either want to go into, or that you have gone into, or that you dream about going into of where you can give some service to society. It may be politics, it may be education, it may be science, it may be economics, it may be the media, it may be any number of things. It may be the family, raising a family, raising your children, it may be many things. You have tended to look at life through a certain filter based on this area that you are focused on. You have in many cases tended to look at, what are the practical ways of how this area works. For example, in politics, how does politics work? What does it take to be in the political field? What would it take, for example, to become an elected official?

You have, in many cases, looked at this, as this messenger, for example, did when he was a teenager. He had a vision of going into politics in his native Denmark and becoming a Prime Minister. My beloved, I tell you that given his attainment from past lives, if he had dedicated his attention to this, he could have become a Prime Minister of Denmark but this was not the highest vision of his Divine plan. Fortunately, he was able to look at the area of politics and he was able to see that politics is an area of compromise. You cannot look at the higher principles, the higher vision of what really should be manifest. You need to look at what is possible in any given political situation. You often need to make trade-offs and compromises in order to get into a position of power. He saw that he was not willing to compromise and therefore he decided not to pursue a career in politics.

I know that there are many of you who have done the same thing in your area. You have looked at the mechanics of how things work in that field. You have realized that there are certain things that you are not willing to do, certain compromises you are not willing to make, and, therefore, you have become discouraged. I am not here telling you to do what this messenger did and abandon that field of interest. It may very well be that for most of you, it is in your Divine plan to pursue that area of interest. However, in order to really bring forth what you want to bring forth in your Divine plan, you need to overcome this sense of discouragement, this sense that the mechanics of how you manifest something on earth are so difficult, so distorted, so unbalanced that you either do not want to deal with the area at all, or that you do not see how you can manifest something higher in that area.

Avoiding discouragement

You understand that Nada said that discouragement is the sharpest tool in the devil's tool kit. The fallen beings have done everything they could to pervert any area of human endeavor on this planet, precisely for the point that those who are beginning to have a level of Christ discernment will look at this area, see the perversion, see the imbalances, see the compromises and become so discouraged that they do not even try to make a difference. You see my beloved, how most spiritual students have this push-pull, these two polarities? On the one hand, you have the daydream of how you would like to manifest something really significant. On the other hand, you have this discouragement of feeling that there is nothing you could realistically do that would make a difference. Do you see how one of these polarities plays into the other?

The fact that you see the compromises and the difficulties makes you discouraged, but that propels you (in order to be able to stand living on the planet) to go into the daydream of thinking that there is some magical formula, some magical esoteric symbol, that will allow you to cut through all the compromises and still manifest some spectacular, miraculous result. Do you see how many of you have been torn between these two and how finding an ascended master teaching did not necessarily make this easier? We give you a vision of what should be possible, we are putting on you that you are the ones who can make it happen. Yet, you still see what Master MORE, in a previous dictation said was "the gap," the gap between the teaching and your state of consciousness, your normal life and what you think is actually possible for you to manifest.

It is my desire with these seven levels of initiations to help you overcome that gap, to close the gap so that there is no gap between the teaching we are giving you and what you can realistically see you can manifest in your life. However, I am not going to do this by giving you a magic wand. I am going to do this by helping you shift your consciousness.

4 | You are an artist sculpting with pure energy

Choosing your artistic medium

The first shift I am asking you to make is this: shifting your approach to life into an artistic approach. Of course, I aim to give you seven levels of this, but at this first level it means that you need to choose which artistic medium you want to use. What is the artistic medium you want to use in bringing forth your creation? Well, which medium is there on earth? You will say: "Well, there is matter, everything is matter." I would say: "Is that so?"

We have already given teachings about this where we have taken you through these levels. You can look at the macroscopic level where everything supposedly is matter. Then, you can go to the level of molecules, the level of atoms, the level of subatomic particles, the level of pure energy waves. You can see that everything is not matter because matter is an interference pattern, a very complex interference pattern, of energy waves. What is the medium of creation? Is it matter or is it energy? Or is it perhaps an even finer substance than what people normally call energy?

You see, what the world of science calls energy is something like electricity or sunlight but this is still a – somewhat, at least – physical substance. There is a finer energy, which is the emotional energy, the mental energy, the identity-level energy and the spiritual-level energy. These are finer levels of energy. There is a way to look at this as if these are not even energies as you see them on earth. They are simply little on-and-off signals. It is almost like you can envision on a television or computer screen where there is a little diode that is either on or off. When it is on, it can take on different colors and the many diodes together form the image.

Now my beloved, when you are watching your television and you are seeing, for example, a movie about war, do you think that what you see on the television screen is actually real people who are running around shooting each other? Of course, you do not because you know that what you are seeing on the television screen is only an image. When you, then, look away from the television screen or perhaps even look at the television itself, look at the wall behind the television, the pictures that are hanging on that wall, you look outside your window and there are either other buildings or fields and trees. When you look at all this, that you supposedly call the "real world," what are all of these things you are seeing? Are they real things made out of matter or are they really like the images you see on the television screen where there is some little unit that is either turned on or turned off, and many of these units form a complex pattern that in your mind is translated to a picture on the wall?

Why it is difficult to manifest what you want

My beloved, why is there a gap between what you can envision and what you can manifest? It is because if you are trying to manifest something based on the symbols, the forms that are already in the material world, then you will encounter the full opposition and resistance, not only from the collective consciousness but from matter itself.

Matter itself becomes solidified into a form. We might say that you have energy that is completely fluid and can take on any form, but then a symbol, an image, is superimposed upon that energy. Now, it is lowered into the material realm where it becomes what you call matter, and that matter is locked into that form, locked into that matrix.

Seeking to override that matrix is a resistance because once the energy has taken on a certain form, there is a certain resistance to changing it. This is not necessarily a malicious resistance but when an elemental being has taken on the form of a tree, it is impregnated upon that elemental to maintain that image. Therefore, there is a certain resistance, even from nature, even from anything in the physical, towards changing it. That is why I need you to begin this shift and I will, of course, talk more about this in coming lessons.

I need you to realize consciously here that as an artist on planet earth, you are facing a very, very difficult task because matter is dense. There is tremendous resistance. The collective consciousness is dense, you are not creating under ideal conditions. Therefore, you need to be very, very careful in choosing the medium in which you are creating your sculpture. I assure you that you do not want to choose the medium of matter, the medium of macroscopic forms and then try to manifest something at that level.

This is where many of the people who have followed these courses of precipitation, of mind over matter, have failed to get the results they desired. They have started at the physical level with a desire, often based on compensation. They have started at the physical level, then they have decided with the outer mind: "I want to manifest this beautiful house." Then, they have attempted (whether they knew about the three higher levels of the mind or not) to use the mind's power to somehow project this out into the universe and have it come back to them as a physical manifestation. I am not saying this cannot be done for simple things like getting a house, but for the things that are in your Divine plan, this is not a constructive approach.

You cannot start with the forms that are already in the physical and try to somehow make them better or perfect them. You might say, as an ascended master student, that you decide with your conscious mind: "I want to manifest a beautiful house." Now, you create the highest vision you can come up with of this house. Now, you focus on your identity mind. You project that image into the identity mind from the conscious mind and then you envision that the light of your I AM Presence flows through that image, flows into the mental then into the emotional and then into the physical. Then, you think that, based on what we have told you, now your creation should be manifest in the physical when you have gone through these steps. What I am telling you is that while this is possible, this is not Christhood.

Choosing your starting point

Christhood is that you do *not* start with the physical. You do *not* start at the level of the physical with conditions as they currently are and try to envision how they could be made better. Christhood is that you say: "Conditions in the physical are not ideal. Why are they not ideal? Because someone had a limited vision, a vision that sprang from duality, a vision that may have sprung from the fallen consciousness and they were projecting that image onto the pure energy. Therefore, if we are to truly change things in the physical, we need to reach up for a higher vision. We need to free our minds from these constraints of what is already manifest so that we cannot be closed-minded but we can be open to receiving a higher vision from above."

My vision of the Golden Age is higher than what most people on earth can fathom. Therefore, it is not a matter of taking what is there already and making it more beautiful or more elaborate or more sophisticated. I talked about people, ascended master students, who dreamed about having beautiful cities with gold in the streets and golden buildings. They looked at some of the Greek temples and the more beautiful buildings that you have on earth today and they projected in their minds that there were cities that had even wider boulevards than you have today, even larger buildings than you have today and they were golden, covered in gold.

That is not my vision for how the cities in the Golden Age will be. My vision is very, very different. What I am saying is this: If you start with what is already manifest and use that as your foundation for what you can co-create, then you are setting yourselves up for great difficulty and great resistance. You may be able to manifest something this way but it will not be what you envisioned in your Divine plan. It will not be your highest potential, it will not be Christhood. Christhood is to go beyond status quo, not to make status quo more elaborate and therefore more entrenched.

I need you to make this shift. I need you to begin to make this shift of seeing yourself as an artist but you are not sculpting from matter. You are not taking a block of stone and chiseling away until you have a sculpture. You are sculpting by using pure energy, the finer energy in the higher identity realm, which we have sometimes called the etheric realm to indicate that this is an energy that is beyond the physical.

You are starting with an empty space, a blank slate, a clean white page. These are the on-off signals that are the smallest units of energy available in your unascended sphere. You are starting with this blank screen and you are going to reach up for a vision of what was in your Divine plan. Then, you are going to – when you have that vision – superimpose that upon the blank screen, bring it down through the identity, mental, emotional level into the physical.

It is not a vision based on what you see around you right now. It is not a vision based on what *is* manifest, but what *could be* manifest—if your vision is free from what is already manifest.

5 | INVOKING THE ARTISTIC MINDSET

In the name I AM THAT I AM, Jesus Christ, I call to my I AM Presence to flow through the I Will Be Presence that I AM and give this invocation with full power. I call to Saint Germain to help me adopt the artistic mindset of seeing that matter is an illusion because everything is made from finer energies. Help me overcome all belief that matter can limit my creative expression, including …

[Make personal calls]

Part 1

1. I am an artist and my entire life is a work of art.

> O Saint Germain, you do inspire,
> my vision raised forever higher,
> with you I form a figure-eight,
> your Golden Age I co-create.
>
> **O Saint Germain, what love you bring,**
> **it truly makes all matter sing,**
> **your violet flame does all restore,**
> **with you we are becoming more.**

2. The medium in which I create my work of art is not matter. I sculpt by using energy, the energy that originates in the spiritual realm and then flows into my identity body, then into my mental body, then into my emotional body and then into physical manifestation.

> O Saint Germain, what Freedom Flame,
> released when we recite your name,
> acceleration is your gift,
> our planet it will surely lift.
>
> **O Saint Germain, what love you bring,**
> **it truly makes all matter sing,**
> **your violet flame does all restore,**
> **with you we are becoming more.**

3. I receive my creative energy directly from my I AM Presence, and nothing on earth is more important to me than to maintain and expand this connection.

5 | Invoking the artistic mindset

> O Saint Germain, in love we claim,
> our right to bring your violet flame,
> from you Above, to us below,
> it is an all-transforming flow.
>
> **O Saint Germain, what love you bring,**
> **it truly makes all matter sing,**
> **your violet flame does all restore,**
> **with you we are becoming more.**

4. As the pure energy flows through the three higher bodies, it takes on the forms of whatever structures, images, symbols, forms I have in those three higher bodies. This is how the co-creative process works.

> O Saint Germain, I love you so,
> my aura filled with violet glow,
> my chakras filled with violet fire,
> I am your cosmic amplifier.
>
> **O Saint Germain, what love you bring,**
> **it truly makes all matter sing,**
> **your violet flame does all restore,**
> **with you we are becoming more.**

5. The circumstances that are manifest in my life right now are a product of the light taking on the form of the images I hold in my three higher bodies. The only realistic way to change my physical circumstances is to refine those images.

> O Saint Germain, I am now free,
> your violet flame is therapy,
> transform all hang-ups in my mind,
> as inner peace I surely find.
>
> **O Saint Germain, what love you bring,**
> **it truly makes all matter sing,**
> **your violet flame does all restore,**
> **with you we are becoming more.**

6. My work as an artist is not a matter of acquiring some magical ability to change matter. My work is to refine the images in my mind, and then matter *will* conform to those new images.

> O Saint Germain, my body pure,
> your violet flame for all is cure,
> consume the cause of all disease,
> and therefore I am all at ease.
>
> **O Saint Germain, what love you bring,**
> **it truly makes all matter sing,**
> **your violet flame does all restore,**
> **with you we are becoming more.**

7. As a true artist, I am not seeking to acquire some secret formula, some secret symbol, that will allow me to manifest anything my outer self desires.

> O Saint Germain, I'm karma-free,
> the past no longer burdens me,
> a brand new opportunity,
> I am in Christic unity.

5 | *Invoking the artistic mindset*

**O Saint Germain, what love you bring,
it truly makes all matter sing,
your violet flame does all restore,
with you we are becoming more.**

8. As a true artist, I have absolute respect for free will, and I give up any desire to manifest better circumstances, or even Saint Germain's Golden Age, by forcing the will of other people.

O Saint Germain, we are now one,
I am for you a violet sun,
as we transform this planet earth,
your Golden Age is given birth.

**O Saint Germain, what love you bring,
it truly makes all matter sing,
your violet flame does all restore,
with you we are becoming more.**

9. As a true artist, I am stepping up to the higher level of Christhood where I seek to raise the whole. I give up all of my daydreams, especially the one about having passed some critical initiation and then it will be all easy from there and I will be home free.

O Saint Germain, the earth is free,
from burden of duality,
in oneness we bring what is best,
your Golden Age is manifest.

**O Saint Germain, what love you bring,
it truly makes all matter sing,
your violet flame does all restore,
with you we are becoming more.**

Part 2

1. As a true artist, I want my act of manifestation to be based on the highest possible vision, and I know this vision is not found in my outer self. As the foundation for my creative efforts, I reach for the vision that I built into my Divine plan before coming into this embodiment.

O Saint Germain, you do inspire,
my vision raised forever higher,
with you I form a figure-eight,
your Golden Age I co-create.

**O Saint Germain, what love you bring,
it truly makes all matter sing,
your violet flame does all restore,
with you we are becoming more.**

2. My outer self cannot fathom Saint Germain's vision for his Golden Age. Therefore, I want to connect to the mind of Saint Germain and receive *his* true vision.

O Saint Germain, what Freedom Flame,
released when we recite your name,
acceleration is your gift,
our planet it will surely lift.

5 | Invoking the artistic mindset

> **O Saint Germain, what love you bring,**
> **it truly makes all matter sing,**
> **your violet flame does all restore,**
> **with you we are becoming more.**

3. I recognize that there is never a situation as a co-creator where I can manifest anything I want without considering that I am part of a greater whole. I knew this when I created my Divine plan, and therefore this is the vision upon which I want to build my artistic work.

> O Saint Germain, in love we claim,
> our right to bring your violet flame,
> from you Above, to us below,
> it is an all-transforming flow.

> **O Saint Germain, what love you bring,**
> **it truly makes all matter sing,**
> **your violet flame does all restore,**
> **with you we are becoming more.**

4. I am an artist, a sculptor, and I choose the material for my sculpture based on my desire to create something of lasting value. I do not choose the lower energies that are already in the physical spectrum.

> O Saint Germain, I love you so,
> my aura filled with violet glow,
> my chakras filled with violet fire,
> I am your cosmic amplifier.

> **O Saint Germain, what love you bring,**
> **it truly makes all matter sing,**
> **your violet flame does all restore,**
> **with you we are becoming more.**

5. I choose the pure energies coming from my I AM Presence, and I gain access to them by raising my outer will to be in alignment with the greater will that I used to formulate my Divine plan, the will that is one with the whole, one with Saint Germain's vision for the Golden Age.

> O Saint Germain, I am now free,
> your violet flame is therapy,
> transform all hang-ups in my mind,
> as inner peace I surely find.

> **O Saint Germain, what love you bring,**
> **it truly makes all matter sing,**
> **your violet flame does all restore,**
> **with you we are becoming more.**

6. I give up all unrealistic dreams of manifesting something that is so spectacular that people cannot deny it. I accept that I am on planet earth and that matter has a certain density.

> O Saint Germain, my body pure,
> your violet flame for all is cure,
> consume the cause of all disease,
> and therefore I am all at ease.

5 | Invoking the artistic mindset

> **O Saint Germain, what love you bring,**
> **it truly makes all matter sing,**
> **your violet flame does all restore,**
> **with you we are becoming more.**

7. I am making a conscious decision to let these far-flung daydreams die, to just let them go. I use my willpower to choose to manifest my work of art based on the vision in my Divine plan of what I want to manifest in this lifetime.

> O Saint Germain, I'm karma-free,
> the past no longer burdens me,
> a brand new opportunity,
> I am in Christic unity.

> **O Saint Germain, what love you bring,**
> **it truly makes all matter sing,**
> **your violet flame does all restore,**
> **with you we are becoming more.**

8. As a true artist, it is not a matter of me using my current level of consciousness, my current vision, and deciding with my outer mind what I want to manifest.

> O Saint Germain, we are now one,
> I am for you a violet sun,
> as we transform this planet earth,
> your Golden Age is given birth.

> **O Saint Germain, what love you bring,**
> **it truly makes all matter sing,**
> **your violet flame does all restore,**
> **with you we are becoming more.**

9. I am making the decision with my conscious mind that I want to align myself with the higher will that was used to formulate my Divine plan and with the higher will of Saint Germain and his vision for the Golden Age.

> O Saint Germain, the earth is free,
> from burden of duality,
> in oneness we bring what is best,
> your Golden Age is manifest.
>
> **O Saint Germain, what love you bring,**
> **it truly makes all matter sing,**
> **your violet flame does all restore,**
> **with you we are becoming more.**

Part 3

1. I am making a shift in my mind, and I see myself as an artist. I am willing to make the adjustment and give up other ways that I have so far looked at myself and my life.

> O Saint Germain, you do inspire,
> my vision raised forever higher,
> with you I form a figure-eight,
> your Golden Age I co-create.
>
> **O Saint Germain, what love you bring,**
> **it truly makes all matter sing,**
> **your violet flame does all restore,**
> **with you we are becoming more.**

2. I will look at the areas of life where I have had a special interest. I will realize that I have often looked at the mechanics of how things work in that field. I have realized that there are certain things that I am not willing to do, certain compromises I am not willing to make, and, therefore, I have become discouraged.

> O Saint Germain, what Freedom Flame,
> released when we recite your name,
> acceleration is your gift,
> our planet it will surely lift.

> **O Saint Germain, what love you bring,**
> **it truly makes all matter sing,**
> **your violet flame does all restore,**
> **with you we are becoming more.**

3. As an artist, I will let go of this discouragement and instead look for creative ways to bring forth what I want to bring forth in my Divine plan.

> O Saint Germain, in love we claim,
> our right to bring your violet flame,
> from you Above, to us below,
> it is an all-transforming flow.

> **O Saint Germain, what love you bring,**
> **it truly makes all matter sing,**
> **your violet flame does all restore,**
> **with you we are becoming more.**

4. I let go of all sense of discouragement, the sense that the mechanics of how I manifest something on earth are so

difficult, so distorted, so unbalanced that I do not see how I can manifest something higher in that area.

> O Saint Germain, I love you so,
> my aura filled with violet glow,
> my chakras filled with violet fire,
> I am your cosmic amplifier.
>
> **O Saint Germain, what love you bring,**
> **it truly makes all matter sing,**
> **your violet flame does all restore,**
> **with you we are becoming more.**

5. As a true artist, I see the need to overcome the push-pull, between the daydream of how I would like to manifest something really significant and the discouragement of feeling that there is nothing I could realistically do that would make a difference.

> O Saint Germain, I am now free,
> your violet flame is therapy,
> transform all hang-ups in my mind,
> as inner peace I surely find.
>
> **O Saint Germain, what love you bring,**
> **it truly makes all matter sing,**
> **your violet flame does all restore,**
> **with you we are becoming more.**

6. I see that the compromises and the difficulties make me discouraged, and that propels me into the daydream of thinking that there is some magical formula, some magical esoteric

5 | Invoking the artistic mindset

symbol, that will allow me to cut through all the compromises and still manifest some spectacular, miraculous result.

> O Saint Germain, my body pure,
> your violet flame for all is cure,
> consume the cause of all disease,
> and therefore I am all at ease.

> **O Saint Germain, what love you bring,**
> **it truly makes all matter sing,**
> **your violet flame does all restore,**
> **with you we are becoming more.**

7. As a true artist, I see no gap between the vision in my Divine plan and what I can realistically see myself manifest in my life. I will manifest my higher vision, not by finding a magic wand but by shifting my consciousness.

> O Saint Germain, I'm karma-free,
> the past no longer burdens me,
> a brand new opportunity,
> I am in Christic unity.

> **O Saint Germain, what love you bring,**
> **it truly makes all matter sing,**
> **your violet flame does all restore,**
> **with you we are becoming more.**

8. I am shifting my approach to life into an artistic approach by consciously acknowledging that matter is not matter. I look beyond the macroscopic level to the level of molecules, the level of atoms, the level of subatomic particles, the level of pure energy waves.

O Saint Germain, we are now one,
I am for you a violet sun,
as we transform this planet earth,
your Golden Age is given birth.

**O Saint Germain, what love you bring,
it truly makes all matter sing,
your violet flame does all restore,
with you we are becoming more.**

9. As a true artist, I see that everything is not matter because matter is an interference pattern, a very complex interference pattern, of energy waves. My medium of creation is the finer energy, which is the emotional energy, the mental energy, the identity-level energy and the spiritual-level energy.

O Saint Germain, the earth is free,
from burden of duality,
in oneness we bring what is best,
your Golden Age is manifest.

**O Saint Germain, what love you bring,
it truly makes all matter sing,
your violet flame does all restore,
with you we are becoming more.**

Part 4

1. As an artist, I do not see these finer levels of energy as energies, but as on-and-off signals. When they are on, they take on different colors and the many diodes together form an image.

5 | Invoking the artistic mindset

It is only my senses that make these signals seem like things made of matter.

> O Saint Germain, you do inspire,
> my vision raised forever higher,
> with you I form a figure-eight,
> your Golden Age I co-create.

> **O Saint Germain, what love you bring,**
> **it truly makes all matter sing,**
> **your violet flame does all restore,**
> **with you we are becoming more.**

2. As an artist, I know that what I see with my senses is not a real world made of separate things. The "real world" is not real things made out of matter, they are like the images on a television screen where there is some little unit that is either turned on or turned off, and many of these units form a complex pattern that in my mind is translated to a picture.

> O Saint Germain, what Freedom Flame,
> released when we recite your name,
> acceleration is your gift,
> our planet it will surely lift.

> **O Saint Germain, what love you bring,**
> **it truly makes all matter sing,**
> **your violet flame does all restore,**
> **with you we are becoming more.**

3. As an artist, I see that there is a gap between what I can envision and what I can manifest because I have been trying to

manifest something based on the symbols, the forms that are already in the material world.

> O Saint Germain, in love we claim,
> our right to bring your violet flame,
> from you Above, to us below,
> it is an all-transforming flow.

> **O Saint Germain, what love you bring,**
> **it truly makes all matter sing,**
> **your violet flame does all restore,**
> **with you we are becoming more.**

4. As an artist, I realize consciously that on planet earth, I am facing a difficult task because matter is dense and there is a resistance to change. The collective consciousness is dense, so I am not creating under ideal conditions.

> O Saint Germain, I love you so,
> my aura filled with violet glow,
> my chakras filled with violet fire,
> I am your cosmic amplifier.

> **O Saint Germain, what love you bring,**
> **it truly makes all matter sing,**
> **your violet flame does all restore,**
> **with you we are becoming more.**

5. As an artist, I am careful in choosing the medium in which I am creating. I do not want to choose the medium of matter, the medium of macroscopic forms and try to manifest something at that level. I will not start with the forms that are already in the physical and try to make them better.

5 | Invoking the artistic mindset

O Saint Germain, I am now free,
your violet flame is therapy,
transform all hang-ups in my mind,
as inner peace I surely find.

**O Saint Germain, what love you bring,
it truly makes all matter sing,
your violet flame does all restore,
with you we are becoming more.**

6. Christhood is that I do *not* start at the level of the physical with conditions as they currently are and try to envision how they could be made better. Christhood is knowing that to truly change things in the physical, I need to reach up for a higher vision. I need to free my mind from these constraints of what is already manifest so that I am open to receiving a higher vision from above.

O Saint Germain, my body pure,
your violet flame for all is cure,
consume the cause of all disease,
and therefore I am all at ease.

**O Saint Germain, what love you bring,
it truly makes all matter sing,
your violet flame does all restore,
with you we are becoming more.**

7. I am making the shift of seeing myself as an artist but I am not sculpting from matter. I am sculpting by using pure energy, the finer energy in the higher identity realm.

O Saint Germain, I'm karma-free,
the past no longer burdens me,
a brand new opportunity,
I am in Christic unity.

**O Saint Germain, what love you bring,
it truly makes all matter sing,
your violet flame does all restore,
with you we are becoming more.**

8. As an artist, I am starting with an empty space, a blank slate, a clean white page. These are the on-off signals that are the smallest units of energy available in my unascended sphere.

O Saint Germain, we are now one,
I am for you a violet sun,
as we transform this planet earth,
your Golden Age is given birth.

**O Saint Germain, what love you bring,
it truly makes all matter sing,
your violet flame does all restore,
with you we are becoming more.**

9. I am starting with this blank screen and I am reaching up for a vision of what is in my Divine plan. Then, I am superimposing that upon the blank screen, bringing it down through the identity, mental and emotional level into physical manifestation. It is not a vision based on what *is* manifest, but what *will be* manifest—as my vision is free from what is already manifest.

O Saint Germain, the earth is free,
from burden of duality,
in oneness we bring what is best,
your Golden Age is manifest.

**O Saint Germain, what love you bring,
it truly makes all matter sing,
your violet flame does all restore,
with you we are becoming more.**

Sealing:

In the name of the Divine Mother, I fully accept that the power of these calls is used to set free the River of Life, so it can outpicture the perfect vision of Christ for my own life, for all people and for the planet. In the name I AM THAT I AM, it is done! Amen.

6 | IS ANYTHING ON EARTH REAL?

I AM the Ascended Master Saint Germain, and for this second installment of the work you are doing at my retreat, I desire you to consider in your conscious mind: "What is real and what is *not* real?" Now, of course, philosophers have for centuries had various discussions and debates amongst themselves about the nature of reality, about what *can* be considered real and what *cannot* be considered real. Let me give this a more practical slant.

The reality simulator room

When you attend my retreat at this level, I have a special room where you can go. The room is a room that is not just circular but it is like a sphere inside, this means that you are seeing all the way around whatever is projected on the inside of the walls of this room. These walls form a screen upon which I can project any image whatsoever. Now, the important point of this exercise is that as you go into this room – and I know, of course, you are not in your physical body, you are in your identity body – you experience that you are inside a real world.

There is nothing that allows you to distinguish that you are not in a real world. In the beginning of this exercise you are thinking, you are feeling, you are experiencing that you are inside a real world. As we move further along in the exercise, we teach you that there are various ways whereby you, just with the power of your mind, can affect what is projected on the inside of the sphere. In other words, you realize that you are in a world that is not as real as it appeared to you when you entered it. It is not completely real in the sense that it is created by some outside force that has nothing to do with your mind. It is not real in the sense that you often consider the "real world" on earth where you think that this world cannot be influenced by the powers of your mind.

You learn gradually that you can actually use the powers of your mind to influence what seems like a real world. Now, I need you, as you are doing the exercises for this lesson, to ponder this with your conscious mind. Naturally, I am not interested in having you come to the conclusion that nothing in the physical octave is real. There are people, even some spiritual students, who have suddenly come to doubt that anything in the physical world is real and they can often go through an identity crisis and even end up in a mental institution. This, of course, is not what I desire to see for you. Therefore, we will consider what it means whether something is real or not.

What does reality mean?

The division I want to create here is that you know very well, as an ascended master student, that you are not living in a world that is exclusively inhabited by human beings. You are not alone, you are with seven billion other human beings on the planet, but you also know that there are other types of beings in the world in which you live. There are ascended masters, there are Elohim, there are angels and archangels and there is the Creator at the top of the pyramid. The distinction I want to make is this: What has been created by beings who are at a higher level of consciousness than human beings, is real. In other words, what has been created by the ascended masters, by the Elohim is real in the sense that it is not within the powers of the human mind to influence this.

We have given you many teachings about the creation of the universe, the creation of the different spheres. We have said that planet earth was created by seven spiritual beings, called the Elohim. They came together, used their co-creative powers to create this planet. They created it in a purer, in a higher, state than what you see today. When it comes to the original creation of the Elohim, the original matrix that the Elohim defined for earth, we will say for this exercise that this is real. This has reality to it. You can go to even higher levels. There are, of course, many ascended beings that are beyond the level of the Elohim that created the earth. There are different spheres that go all the way up to the Creator.

Nevertheless, the point here is simply this: There are certain things in the universe in which you live, even in the physical octave, that are created by beings who are in an ascended state of consciousness. In other words, they are permanent beings, they are not in duality, they do not see themselves as separate beings, they are one with the whole. They have created certain structures in the world that you live in, and for the purpose of this exercise, we will define these structures as real. There are certainly aspects of the earth that are real based on this definition. There is a certain reality to the planet itself and to some of the features and characteristics that the planet has.

How earth became what it is today

However, we now need to define that there is a distinction to be made because you know that the earth is not in its original state, in its pristine state. It is not in the same state in which it was created by the Elohim. What this means is that we need to consider how the planet has come to be in its current situation, in its current state. We have explained to you that this has happened over a very, very long time span. We have explained that when the planet was originally created, several life-waves of co-creators descended to earth. They also ascended from earth and while they were on earth, they actually built on to the foundation created by the Elohim and made the planet even more beautiful, even more detailed. They co-created the earth.

We have also explained that there came a turning point where more and more of the lifestreams that embodied on earth at that time started to go into the state of duality and separation. They gradually started a downward spiral and this has led to the current situation. These life-waves, these lifestreams, de-created the earth by taking it down from the level of the Elohim, so the earth is now quite far below that state.

What you recognize here is that when we define that what has been created by ascended beings is real, then we also need to say that that which has been de-created by unascended beings is unreal in comparison. This means that many of the current conditions and characteristics that you see on earth are unreal according to this definition. Of course, we could have other definitions of what is real and unreal, but based on this definition, we need to say that most of the conditions you see on earth today, are unreal.

What is unreal can be changed

Why is it important to make this distinction? Well, it is because you can, then, gradually begin to shift your attitude, the way you look at life, and realize that many of the limitations you see around you, many of the limitations you have come up against since you first came into embodiment on earth and certainly in this lifetime, are not real in an ultimate sense. While it is important to make this distinction, you could say from a purely practical standpoint: "The distinction is not very important because whether current conditions on earth are real or unreal, they are still here and I am still affected by them." This is, of course, perfectly true, but is it true that a practical consideration is really the only one that can be applied or the highest one that can be applied?

You see, my beloved, as you have grown up, both in this lifetime and in previous lifetimes, you have been programmed to accept that what is currently here on earth is real. You have been programmed by your parents, by your family, by the people in your society, even by the institutions in your society, to accept that current conditions are real. They represent a real world, which means that you do not have the powers of your mind to change these conditions. This is the belief that I need you to begin to question.

How something is created

For this purpose, we need to take a very simple step. We need to ask ourselves (as we have given teachings on before) how anything has ever been created. Now, we have said before that only the Creator has the power to create, so to speak, out of nothing. Philosophers and scientists have for a long time debated this "creation out of nothing" and they have come to various conclusions. The fact of the matter is that the Creator has the power to create the world in which you live, to define the parameters for it and to, out of its own Being, create the substance. In other words, before the Creator starts creating, there is nothing. There is no world, there is not even the void in which anything can be created.

There is, you could say, not necessarily "nothing" because we have taught you about something called the Allness. Nevertheless, compared to the things that are defined in your universe, there is "no thing" when the Creator starts creating. Yet all other beings in the realm that you live in, in the world of form you live in, are co-creators. They do not create out of nothing. They create based on what the Creator has created.

How do you co-create? You co-create by forming images, matrices, in your mind. Whatever your mind is like, depending on the level of co-creator you are, you form images in your mind and then you project those images onto the basic substance that the Creator has created in order to give you something out of which you can co-create. We have for practical purposes called it the Ma-ter Light. You are forming an image in your mind, in your case through the four levels of your mind, and you are projecting it upon the Ma-ter Light.

Now, we can say that even the Elohim, when they created the earth, they co-created this way. They formulated images in their minds, projected it onto the Ma-ter Light and over time,

6 | Is anything on earth real?

through certain rhythmic repetitions, the Elohim manifested the earth. It was not created in the way people normally understand creation, in the sense that there was some kind of physical matter that the Elohim could use to create earth.

The earth was manifested in the sense that the Elohim first created an image of the earth in the identity realm. This image was complex, it was based on all seven of the spiritual rays, with each Elohim representing one ray. They had this image, they formulated it gradually, they reinforced it, they caused it to vibrate at a certain level (a certain rate, we might say, a certain frequency) and then it was this vibration that they used to push their matrix into the mental realm. Here, they added onto the matrix, they made it more detailed through the mental level and then they finally caused it to vibrate at another level and they pushed it into the emotional level. Again at the emotional level, they worked on the matrix making it more detailed, making it, in a sense, more energetic and then, again, they intensified the vibration of the matrix until they pushed it into the physical.

Now, you are going to say, perhaps, based on what you were taught in this lifetime: "Where does that leave the process of evolution?" It does not exclude evolution because what the Elohim pushed into the physical was not a fully formed planet in the sense that it had all the life-forms on it that you see today or that you have seen in the past. What they pushed into the physical was, however, a planet that had not exactly the current size but at least had the basic matrix that you see on a planet, even on the earth today. It was, as I said, somewhat different but it was pushed into the physical. It did not appear gradually in the physical. It was not so that cosmic dust gradually collected and formed the earth. The earth in its basic matrix was pushed into the physical realm and appeared literally out of "nowhere," if you look at the process from the level of the physical senses. When the basic matrix for the earth was pushed into the physical, then a gradual process of evolution started, also directed by the Elohim. That gradual process then, over a very, very long timespan, produced an earth that was inhabitable for the first waves of lifestreams.

Matter is not real

What I am giving you here is a sense that is very important. Even what I have labeled as real is still created by a mind or, in this case, seven minds. You can see that in today's world you have a certain materialistic philosophy, which says that there is nothing outside the material world. This philosophy also says that your mind is a product of the material processes in your brain. Your thoughts, your feelings are the products of material processes in your brain. This means that, according to the materialist philosophy, the mind is not actually real—only matter is real. The reason it is important to consider this is that you could not have grown up in the modern world without having been affected by this. There is a very strong beast, we might say, in the collective consciousness that actually believes that only what has physical substance has reality.

What I am trying to show you here is that, in reality, there is no matter. Matter does not actually exist as a separate substance because matter was created by mind. Matter is a creation of mind. You see, what the materialists want you to believe (because this is what they believe, most of them, except the ones who are fallen beings and who are merely using the materialist philosophy to manipulate people) is that there was a process that brought matter into existence. Once matter was brought into existence, it will continue to exist indefinitely or at least for a very long time. In other words, matter has some

6 | Is anything on earth real?

kind of reality that exists independently of mind. What these materialists want you to believe is that your mind can only be subjective but that matter is objective. Matter has an objective existence that is independent of mind.

The reason it is important to consider this illusion is that it has, of course, been generated by the fallen beings. It has been generated for a very specific purpose and that is to disempower the population. The entire purpose of the materialist philosophy is to make people believe that their minds do not have the power to change matter. Therefore, once the earth is in a certain state, once matter has reached a certain density, there is nothing that human beings can do about it. This is just the way it is because the current conditions were created by impersonal, objective laws of nature that no human power can change.

You can go to the other polarity, namely traditional religion and you can see that they actually have a similarly disempowering philosophy. They tell you that the entire world was created by God, even the Almighty God. Of course, this means that current conditions that you see on earth were created by the Almighty Creator. This, again, means that the human mind, even the collective mind, has no power to change this.

You see that you have grown up in a society that, although it has two polarities that seem to be opposites, they are actually the same in terms of disempowering you. They spread a philosophy that says that humankind does not have the power to change current conditions on earth. Such a philosophy can only come from the fallen beings. That is why you need to consider it very carefully. You need to start questioning why you believe in this, whether it is real or not, until you come to that conclusion – not based on an intellectual reasoning but based on an inner intuitive experience – that it is not real. How will you come to that conclusion? Because when you attend my retreat, you experience that neither traditional religion nor materialistic science is real. Their conclusions, their philosophies, are not real. All you need to do is draw this into the conscious mind so that you experience, in an intuitive flash, the reality here. Some of you have already done this, I realize, but nevertheless, there is nothing wrong at all with having a mystical experience several times where you gradually reinforce this sense that they are not right when they tell you that mind cannot influence matter.

Why mind can influence matter

Why is it that mind can influence matter? Well, because from the very beginning, the entire material universe was created by mind. It was created by the minds of the Elohim and other spiritual beings. Ever since the earth went into a downward spiral, many of the conditions you currently see on earth were created by mind, namely the collective mind of humankind. This collective mind was to a very large degree misled and manipulated by the fallen beings after they started embodying here. You now have this downward spiral where the collective consciousness, directed by the fallen beings, has gradually taken the earth to a lower and lower level. This has many ramifications, including conflicts, natural disasters, and many imbalances in nature. First of all, it has the effect of densifying matter. Matter was less dense – whereby I mean it vibrated at a higher vibration – before the downward spiral started than it is now. Why is this important? Because the denser the matter, the more difficult it becomes for the mind to change matter.

You understand what the fallen beings have done? They have literally instituted a process whereby they misled and manipulated humankind into lowering the collective consciousness and thereby densifying matter. What has this done for the fallen beings? Well, they are the ones who have an unlimited willingness to manipulate, control, destroy and kill other human beings in a physical manner. Therefore, the denser the matter, the easier it is for the fallen beings to take control over humankind. Because the denser the matter, the less people are able to resist them by the powers of the mind and this means people are, then, left to resist only through physical means. Here, the fallen beings can always gain the advantage because they are willing to do what the original inhabitants of the earth are not willing to do and what avatars coming to earth are not willing to do. Neither of these groups are willing to kill unlimited numbers of people in order to, for example, advance a certain empire or political ideology or religion. The fallen beings are willing to do this and they are also willing to kill individuals who oppose them. Therefore, they can gain the upper hand.

When matter is less dense, when people are more aware of the powers of their minds, then the fallen beings do not have the same opportunities for gaining control. Literally, what the fallen beings have done is they have managed to lower matter to the current density. What they are now trying to do with their philosophies of both religion and materialism is that they are trying to make humankind accept that matter could never be raised in vibration, that the current conditions could never be fundamentally changed because: "That's just the way things are and there is nothing we can do about it. Certainly, there is nothing we can do about it by the power of the mind."

Deprogramming yourself

This, my beloved, is a very, very persuasive consciousness that has been forced upon this planet for such a long time now (at least religion) that it has affected the collective consciousness to such a degree that you cannot grow up here without being affected by it. What you need to do now is to start de-programming yourself from the programming you received as you were growing up, both in this and previous lifetimes. This is not something that is going to be done overnight. I am not asking for you to think that there can come a point where, "poof!" and you are suddenly free of this consciousness. Well, of course there will, but it is not going to happen in five minutes. I need you to work on this, and I need you to realize that you have internal spirits that believe in this programming and it will take some time for you to unravel them.

Nevertheless, I need you to make this shift here in your conscious mind where you begin to realize that there is a division to be made when you consider material conditions on earth. First of all, there are certain conditions that the human mind does not have the power to change. Just to make it simple, when the Elohim created the earth, it was round. It is not within the power of the human mind to change the earth to a different shape even if all people on the planet used the powers of their minds to try and make the earth an oval rather than a sphere—it could not be done. They cannot override this basic matrix.

However, many other conditions on earth, including, as I said, the density of matter (which I know is difficult for you to envision but it is nevertheless true) could be changed by the powers of the mind. It is important to begin to make this shift where you basically begin to realize, you begin at least to ponder, that any condition you encounter could potentially be changed by the powers of the mind. The question you now need to ponder is: "What mind are we talking about?"

The individual and the collective mind

Here, we need to make a distinction between the individual mind and the collective mind. I have said that the current density of matter was created over a long period of time by the collective mind that includes all human beings in embodiment on the planet, not only at any given time but over this long time span. Where do you stand as an individual in terms of overriding this? Well, of course, as an individual, you do not have the power to override the collective mind of all human beings.

You see what I am trying to get you to here? I am trying to get you to the realization that I am walking a very delicate balance. On the one hand, I need to help you start questioning what you were brought up with. I need you to start realizing that matter is a creation of the mind. At the same time, I also need to have you *not* switch into these delusions of grandeur, that Nada was talking about, where so many spiritual and New Age people, including ascended master students, believe that one day they could get the power of mind where they could just snap their fingers and create some miraculous change on earth.

I need you to have optimism but a realistic sense of optimism, where you do not build an expectation that you can do more than you can actually do as an individual. If you do allow yourself to go into these unrealistic expectations, then you will set yourself up for disappointment. There are books and courses out there that claim that in a few short chapters or in a matter of days they can teach you how to precipitate, for example, money or gold out of thin air. All of the people who buy these books or take these courses end up being disappointed because they cannot fulfill this expectation.

I am trying here, at the second level, to have you use the Second Ray of Wisdom to build a realistic expectation of what actually can be done. You need to recognize here that current conditions on earth are created by the collective mind. As an individual, you cannot override the collective mind. You do not have that power. Therefore, it is not realistic of you to build the expectation that you can acquire some kind of power of the mind that will override the collective consciousness. This would be against the Law of Free Will for one thing, and therefore this is not Christhood.

Realistic expectations

You see my beloved, the fallen beings have in a certain way acquired certain powers that, at least to some degree, can force or override the mind of the collective. That was how Adolf Hitler managed to get a majority of the German population to support him. Nevertheless, no Christed being would do this—obviously. Therefore, you see that as a Christed being, as a person who is on the path of Christhood, you are not even interested in acquiring the powers to manipulate the collective mind or even the single mind of another person. This is not what you are about. You therefore need to make the realistic assessment of saying: "What can I focus on? What can I focus on as my expectation of what I can get out of following these steps of initiation under Saint Germain?"

Here is my suggestion. As you move closer and closer to the 144th level of consciousness, there does come a phase where you begin to have the powers of the mind where you can actually, at least in a localized manner, override the density of matter. If you look at the arguments that are out there, you will see, for example, that many materialists go to great length to deny the miracles of Jesus. You can even see some Christians who deny, or at least largely ignore, the miracles

6 | Is anything on earth real?

performed by Jesus. However, there is significance in what Jesus did. Some of the miracles (not all of the ones recorded in the scriptures but some of them) were indeed real in the sense that he did perform this where he managed to override the density of matter. For example, changing one substance into another, calming a storm, walking on water, so forth and so on. This was because Jesus was close to the 144th level of consciousness. You recognize, of course, that this course is meant to take you to the 96th level of consciousness and there is still quite a ways from the 96th to the 144th level. It is not realistic of you, at this point, to build the sense that when you reach the 96th level, you will be able to perform the miracles that Jesus could perform. It just is not realistic, my beloved.

However, what did you see Jesus do when he performed these so-called miracles, which were not truly miracles but simply an application of natural law and the powers of the mind? Well, what he did was that he either healed people on an individual level or he performed miracles that did not manipulate the minds of other people. When Jesus turned water into wine, he changed the physical substance—he did not change the mind. He worked on a physical substance, not on the minds of other people. When he walked on water, he did not change the minds of the disciples but he did, of course, allow Peter to rise to a higher level of consciousness so that Peter could walk with him on the water. Peter could not maintain that consciousness and started sinking and this shows you, actually, that there is little value in artificially raising a person's consciousness.

This is why we are giving you a very gradual course that gradually raises your consciousness based on your own work, based on an inner building of attainment instead of temporarily bringing you into a euphoric state of mind that simply cannot be sustained. What Jesus did with Peter was to actually demonstrate that a person at a lower level of consciousness can be temporarily raised but it really has no effect whatsoever, as you saw Peter denying Jesus three times after his trial, despite the fact that he had been given that experience.

What I need you to do at this second level is build a realistic expectation of what you can do when you have finished this course. What I would like to suggest here is that you, first of all, realize that many of the dreams that people have – whether it is ascended master students or other New Age people or even normal people – could not be fulfilled within the parameters of the Law of Free Will. If you have a dream that would involve many other people changing their lives, or their behavior or their state of mind, then that dream is not within the parameters of the Law of Free Will. Unless you could *inspire* them to do this, but many, many people have dreams where, for example, they will have the powers to make people fall over by the power of the spirit so that people see that you have this great power and therefore you are this special person. Well, this is not lawful according to free will. You will see that Jesus did not do this except on certain occasions where the conditions were very different.

What you realize here is that you need to adjust your expectations so that you are not setting yourself a goal that would involve the manipulation of other people's free will. If you do so, you will, of course, make karma and this is what can actually bring you to that point where, at the 96th level of consciousness, you will fail that crucial initiation I talked about. You will seek to increase your own power rather than seeking to raise the whole.

What I would like you to consider here is that you want to set a goal for yourself that is realistic based on conditions as they are on earth, based on your inability to override the collective consciousness. It is also lawful, based on the consideration of the Law of Free Will, so that you are not trying to manipulate the minds of other people. This means that at this stage of your path, I am asking you to actually focus on a goal that relates primarily to yourself, a goal that does not require other people to change their minds, lives or behavior in order to fulfill your goal.

I am also asking you to consider what you could do to help advance my Golden Age. Now, I have said here that the crucial initiation at the 96th level is whether you will stay focused on yourself or whether you will start focusing on the whole. What I am guiding you towards here is the realization that you need to define a goal for yourself that does not require you to exercise power over other people. At the same time, it is not so focused on your own personal situation and conditions but has some importance for the whole. I am asking you to, at this point, consider that there are two elements of co-creation.

The two aspects of co-creation

The alpha aspect of co-creation is that you manifest something directly as a physical substance that (as I said about the Elohim), pretty much appears out of "nowhere." There was no physical substance before, now there is a physical planet. This is precipitation. I also ask you to consider that the omega aspect of co-creation is that you take conditions as they are on earth and you improve upon them.

You can see, for example, that even though there has been a downward spiral for a long time that densified matter and brought society to a lower and lower level, that downward spiral has been reversed. For some time, civilization has been in an upward spiral where there have been many improvements of living conditions. This is essentially why you have the luxury of sitting here, reading a book. You have time to read that book, instead of spending all your waking hours slaving in the fields and falling asleep as soon as you come back to your place of rest.

Things have been improved and how has this happened? Well, it has happened primarily because some people have been able to tune in to the ascended realm and bring forth ideas of how to improve some condition of life on earth. The alpha of co-creation is direct precipitation. The omega of co-creation is bringing ideas from the ascended realm into the physical.

I am asking you to, first of all, set a goal for yourself so that at the end of this course, you will be in a state of mind where you can receive ideas from me or another ascended master of your choice, ideas that relate to some area of life where you have a special interest. In other words, it is not a matter of manifesting riches out of thin air – that is not your goal at this point – but to bring forth an idea. Now, I am also asking you to consider another goal for yourself and that is to change your personal situation in life so that there is no conflict between your spiritual life and your practical, everyday, physical life. This is actually something I will talk more about in my next installment, but I want to give you the idea here that as a goal for this course:

- Become the open door for ideas from the ascended masters to improve some aspect of life.

- Bring harmony between your spiritual and your practical life.

This, then, is what I desire to give you for this installment, and I look forward to speaking to you again, giving you the next step up.

7 | INVOKING A REALISTIC SENSE OF WHAT IS REAL

In the name I AM THAT I AM, Jesus Christ, I call to my I AM Presence to flow through the I Will Be Presence that I AM and give this invocation with full power. I call to Saint Germain to help me have the inner knowing of what is real and what is unreal. Help me adopt realistic goals for my co-creative efforts, including …

[Make personal calls]

Part 1

1. What has been created by ascended beings is real. What has been de-created by unascended beings is unreal.

O Saint Germain, you do inspire,
my vision raised forever higher,
with you I form a figure-eight,
your Golden Age I co-create.

**O Saint Germain, what love you bring,
it truly makes all matter sing,
your violet flame does all restore,
with you we are becoming more.**

2. Many of the current conditions and characteristics on earth are unreal, and what is unreal can be changed.

O Saint Germain, what Freedom Flame,
released when we recite your name,
acceleration is your gift,
our planet it will surely lift.

**O Saint Germain, what love you bring,
it truly makes all matter sing,
your violet flame does all restore,
with you we are becoming more.**

3. Many of the limitations around me, many of the limitations I have come up against since I first came into embodiment on earth and in this lifetime, are not real in an ultimate sense.

O Saint Germain, in love we claim,
our right to bring your violet flame,
from you Above, to us below,
it is an all-transforming flow.

**O Saint Germain, what love you bring,
it truly makes all matter sing,
your violet flame does all restore,
with you we are becoming more.**

4. As I have grown up, both in this lifetime and in previous lifetimes, I have been programmed by my parents, family, the people in my society, even by the institutions in my society, to accept that current conditions are real.

O Saint Germain, I love you so,
my aura filled with violet glow,
my chakras filled with violet fire,
I am your cosmic amplifier.

**O Saint Germain, what love you bring,
it truly makes all matter sing,
your violet flame does all restore,
with you we are becoming more.**

5. I have been programmed to believe current conditions represent a real world, which means that I do not have the powers of my mind to change these conditions. I am now questioning this belief.

O Saint Germain, I am now free,
your violet flame is therapy,
transform all hang-ups in my mind,
as inner peace I surely find.

> O Saint Germain, what love you bring,
> it truly makes all matter sing,
> your violet flame does all restore,
> with you we are becoming more.

6. I co-create by forming images, matrices, in my mind, through the four levels of my mind, and projecting them upon the Ma-ter Light.

> O Saint Germain, my body pure,
> your violet flame for all is cure,
> consume the cause of all disease,
> and therefore I am all at ease.

> O Saint Germain, what love you bring,
> it truly makes all matter sing,
> your violet flame does all restore,
> with you we are becoming more.

7. Even what I have labeled as real is still created by a mind because mind always comes before the physical manifestation.

> O Saint Germain, I'm karma-free,
> the past no longer burdens me,
> a brand new opportunity,
> I am in Christic unity.

> O Saint Germain, what love you bring,
> it truly makes all matter sing,
> your violet flame does all restore,
> with you we are becoming more.

7 | Invoking a realistic sense of what is real

8. I consciously reject the materialist philosophy that my thoughts, my feelings are the products of material processes in my brain. I reject the beast in the collective consciousness that believes that only what has physical substance has reality.

> O Saint Germain, we are now one,
> I am for you a violet sun,
> as we transform this planet earth,
> your Golden Age is given birth.

> **O Saint Germain, what love you bring,**
> **it truly makes all matter sing,**
> **your violet flame does all restore,**
> **with you we are becoming more.**

9. In reality, there is no matter. Matter does not exist as a separate substance because matter was created by mind. Matter is a creation of mind.

> O Saint Germain, the earth is free,
> from burden of duality,
> in oneness we bring what is best,
> your Golden Age is manifest.

> **O Saint Germain, what love you bring,**
> **it truly makes all matter sing,**
> **your violet flame does all restore,**
> **with you we are becoming more.**

Part 2

1. I reject the materialist claim that matter has a reality that exists independently of mind. I reject the claim that my mind can only be subjective but that matter has an objective existence that is independent of mind.

> O Saint Germain, you do inspire,
> my vision raised forever higher,
> with you I form a figure-eight,
> your Golden Age I co-create.
>
> **O Saint Germain, what love you bring,**
> **it truly makes all matter sing,**
> **your violet flame does all restore,**
> **with you we are becoming more.**

2. I reject the materialist claim that the mind does not have the power to change matter. I reject the claim that once the earth is in a certain state, once matter has reached a certain density, there is nothing we can do about it.

> O Saint Germain, what Freedom Flame,
> released when we recite your name,
> acceleration is your gift,
> our planet it will surely lift.
>
> **O Saint Germain, what love you bring,**
> **it truly makes all matter sing,**
> **your violet flame does all restore,**
> **with you we are becoming more.**

3. I reject the religious claim that current conditions on earth were created by the Almighty Creator, and therefore the human mind, even the collective mind, has no power to change this.

> O Saint Germain, in love we claim,
> our right to bring your violet flame,
> from you Above, to us below,
> it is an all-transforming flow.

O Saint Germain, what love you bring,
it truly makes all matter sing,
your violet flame does all restore,
with you we are becoming more.

4. This disempowering philosophy can only come from the fallen beings. I know, based on an inner intuitive experience, that it is not real.

> O Saint Germain, I love you so,
> my aura filled with violet glow,
> my chakras filled with violet fire,
> I am your cosmic amplifier.

O Saint Germain, what love you bring,
it truly makes all matter sing,
your violet flame does all restore,
with you we are becoming more.

5. Neither traditional religion nor materialistic science is real. Their conclusions, their philosophies, are not real. I draw this knowing into my conscious mind so that I experience its reality in an intuitive flash.

> O Saint Germain, I am now free,
> your violet flame is therapy,
> transform all hang-ups in my mind,
> as inner peace I surely find.
>
> **O Saint Germain, what love you bring,**
> **it truly makes all matter sing,**
> **your violet flame does all restore,**
> **with you we are becoming more.**

6. Mind can influence matter because, from the very beginning, the entire material universe was created by mind. Ever since the earth went into a downward spiral, many conditions were created by mind, namely the collective mind of humankind.

> O Saint Germain, my body pure,
> your violet flame for all is cure,
> consume the cause of all disease,
> and therefore I am all at ease.
>
> **O Saint Germain, what love you bring,**
> **it truly makes all matter sing,**
> **your violet flame does all restore,**
> **with you we are becoming more.**

7. This collective mind has created a downward spiral that has had the effect of densifying matter. The denser the matter, the more difficult it becomes for the mind to change matter.

> O Saint Germain, I'm karma-free,
> the past no longer burdens me,
> a brand new opportunity,
> I am in Christic unity.

7 | Invoking a realistic sense of what is real

**O Saint Germain, what love you bring,
it truly makes all matter sing,
your violet flame does all restore,
with you we are becoming more.**

8. The fallen beings have instituted a process whereby they misled and manipulated humankind into lowering the collective consciousness and thereby densifying matter. The denser the matter, the easier it is for the fallen beings to take control over humankind.

O Saint Germain, we are now one,
I am for you a violet sun,
as we transform this planet earth,
your Golden Age is given birth.

**O Saint Germain, what love you bring,
it truly makes all matter sing,
your violet flame does all restore,
with you we are becoming more.**

9. The denser the matter, the less people are able to resist the fallen beings by the powers of the mind and this means people are left to resist only through physical means. Here, the fallen beings can always gain the advantage because of their unlimited willingness to kill.

O Saint Germain, the earth is free,
from burden of duality,
in oneness we bring what is best,
your Golden Age is manifest.

O Saint Germain, what love you bring,
it truly makes all matter sing,
your violet flame does all restore,
with you we are becoming more.

Part 3

1. The fallen beings have managed to lower matter to the current density. With their philosophies of both religion and materialism, they are trying to make humankind accept that matter could never be raised in vibration, that the current conditions could never be fundamentally changed.

O Saint Germain, you do inspire,
my vision raised forever higher,
with you I form a figure-eight,
your Golden Age I co-create.

O Saint Germain, what love you bring,
it truly makes all matter sing,
your violet flame does all restore,
with you we are becoming more.

2. I am now de-programming myself from the programming I received as I was growing up, both in this and previous lifetimes.

O Saint Germain, what Freedom Flame,
released when we recite your name,
acceleration is your gift,
our planet it will surely lift.

**O Saint Germain, what love you bring,
it truly makes all matter sing,
your violet flame does all restore,
with you we are becoming more.**

3. I realize that I have internal spirits that believe in this programming and I am willing to let them die.

O Saint Germain, in love we claim,
our right to bring your violet flame,
from you Above, to us below,
it is an all-transforming flow.

**O Saint Germain, what love you bring,
it truly makes all matter sing,
your violet flame does all restore,
with you we are becoming more.**

4. I am making the shift in my conscious mind where I realize there is a division to be made when considering material conditions on earth. There are certain conditions that the human mind does not have the power to change. Many other conditions, including the density of matter, can be changed by the powers of the mind.

O Saint Germain, I love you so,
my aura filled with violet glow,
my chakras filled with violet fire,
I am your cosmic amplifier.

> O Saint Germain, what love you bring,
> it truly makes all matter sing,
> your violet flame does all restore,
> with you we are becoming more.

5. Any condition I encounter could potentially be changed by the powers of the mind. I recognize I do not have – and do not *want* – the power to override the collective mind.

> O Saint Germain, I am now free,
> your violet flame is therapy,
> transform all hang-ups in my mind,
> as inner peace I surely find.

> O Saint Germain, what love you bring,
> it truly makes all matter sing,
> your violet flame does all restore,
> with you we are becoming more.

6. I let go of all internal spirits that have delusions of grandeur, wanting the power of mind to create some miraculous change or manifestation.

> O Saint Germain, my body pure,
> your violet flame for all is cure,
> consume the cause of all disease,
> and therefore I am all at ease.

> O Saint Germain, what love you bring,
> it truly makes all matter sing,
> your violet flame does all restore,
> with you we are becoming more.

7. I have a realistic sense of optimism where I do not build an expectation of doing more than I can actually do as an individual. I let go of the spirits that have unrealistic expectations.

> O Saint Germain, I'm karma-free,
> the past no longer burdens me,
> a brand new opportunity,
> I am in Christic unity.

> **O Saint Germain, what love you bring,**
> **it truly makes all matter sing,**
> **your violet flame does all restore,**
> **with you we are becoming more.**

8. I recognize that current conditions are created by the collective mind. As an individual, I cannot override the collective mind. It is not realistic to build the expectation that I can acquire a power of the mind that will override the collective consciousness.

> O Saint Germain, we are now one,
> I am for you a violet sun,
> as we transform this planet earth,
> your Golden Age is given birth.

> **O Saint Germain, what love you bring,**
> **it truly makes all matter sing,**
> **your violet flame does all restore,**
> **with you we are becoming more.**

9. As a Christed being, as a person who is on the path of Christhood, I am not interested in acquiring the powers to manipulate the collective mind or even a single mind of another person.

O Saint Germain, the earth is free,
from burden of duality,
in oneness we bring what is best,
your Golden Age is manifest.

**O Saint Germain, what love you bring,
it truly makes all matter sing,
your violet flame does all restore,
with you we are becoming more.**

Part 4

1. I am making a realistic assessment, and I am setting a goal that does not involve the manipulation of other people's free will. I am seeking to raise the whole, not increase my own power.

O Saint Germain, you do inspire,
my vision raised forever higher,
with you I form a figure-eight,
your Golden Age I co-create.

**O Saint Germain, what love you bring,
it truly makes all matter sing,
your violet flame does all restore,
with you we are becoming more.**

2. I am focusing on a goal that relates primarily to myself, a goal that does not require other people to change their minds, lives or behavior in order to fulfill my goal.

7 | Invoking a realistic sense of what is real

O Saint Germain, what Freedom Flame,
released when we recite your name,
acceleration is your gift,
our planet it will surely lift.

**O Saint Germain, what love you bring,
it truly makes all matter sing,
your violet flame does all restore,
with you we are becoming more.**

3. I am focusing on what I could do to help advance Saint Germain's Golden Age by tuning in to the ascended realm and bringing forth ideas of how to improve some condition of life on earth.

O Saint Germain, in love we claim,
our right to bring your violet flame,
from you Above, to us below,
it is an all-transforming flow.

**O Saint Germain, what love you bring,
it truly makes all matter sing,
your violet flame does all restore,
with you we are becoming more.**

4. I am setting a goal for myself so that at the end of this course, I will be in a state of mind where I can receive ideas from an ascended master that relate to an area of life where I have a special interest.

> O Saint Germain, I love you so,
> my aura filled with violet glow,
> my chakras filled with violet fire,
> I am your cosmic amplifier.
>
> **O Saint Germain, what love you bring,**
> **it truly makes all matter sing,**
> **your violet flame does all restore,**
> **with you we are becoming more.**

5. I am setting a goal for myself to change my personal situation so that there is no conflict between my spiritual life and my practical, everyday, physical life.

> O Saint Germain, I am now free,
> your violet flame is therapy,
> transform all hang-ups in my mind,
> as inner peace I surely find.
>
> **O Saint Germain, what love you bring,**
> **it truly makes all matter sing,**
> **your violet flame does all restore,**
> **with you we are becoming more.**

6. I accept that manifesting these goals is completely realistic, even with the current conditions on earth and the current density of matter.

> O Saint Germain, my body pure,
> your violet flame for all is cure,
> consume the cause of all disease,
> and therefore I am all at ease.

> **O Saint Germain, what love you bring,**
> **it truly makes all matter sing,**
> **your violet flame does all restore,**
> **with you we are becoming more.**

7. I accept that I have the capacity of mind to tune in to Saint Germain and to bring harmony between my spiritual and physical life.

> O Saint Germain, I'm karma-free,
> the past no longer burdens me,
> a brand new opportunity,
> I am in Christic unity.

> **O Saint Germain, what love you bring,**
> **it truly makes all matter sing,**
> **your violet flame does all restore,**
> **with you we are becoming more.**

8. I accept that fulfilling these goals is only a matter of making a shift inside my own mind, and no condition on earth or no dark force can interfere with this process.

> O Saint Germain, we are now one,
> I am for you a violet sun,
> as we transform this planet earth,
> your Golden Age is given birth.

> **O Saint Germain, what love you bring,**
> **it truly makes all matter sing,**
> **your violet flame does all restore,**
> **with you we are becoming more.**

9. I accept that when I do change the images and beliefs in my four lower bodies, by letting the internal spirits die, then my material conditions *must* and *will* change accordingly, for these conditions are simply projections of the images in my mind.

> O Saint Germain, the earth is free,
> from burden of duality,
> in oneness we bring what is best,
> your Golden Age is manifest.
>
> **O Saint Germain, what love you bring,**
> **it truly makes all matter sing,**
> **your violet flame does all restore,**
> **with you we are becoming more.**

Sealing:

In the name of the Divine Mother, I fully accept that the power of these calls is used to set free the River of Life, so it can outpicture the perfect vision of Christ for my own life, for all people and for the planet. In the name I AM THAT I AM, it is done! Amen.

8 | LOVING YOUR DIVINE PLAN MORE THAN A DAYDREAM

I AM the Ascended Master Saint Germain. This is the third level of initiation at my retreat, which corresponds to the Seventh Ray of Freedom and the Third Ray of Love. Freedom and love, of course, does not mean free love, as so many people interpreted it back in the 1960's and beyond. What it does mean is that we need to look at love, and the opposite of anti-love, when it comes to your relationship to the physical realm, the matter realm, the Mother realm. Now, I said in my last discourse that I wish to speak about how you can bring harmony between your spiritual life and your everyday, practical life. This is a topic that is very important for all spiritual people, especially as we move more and more into the Aquarian Age.

Separation between spiritual and everyday activities

My beloved, if you look back at the last 2,000 years in the western world, you will see that the Christian churches have created a relatively clear separation between what you might call spiritual (or at least religious) life and everyday, practical life. Now, in all fairness, this has to some degree been happening because people had to work so hard physically in order to make a living. You could not expect them to work ten hours a day and have much attention or energy left over for any kind of spiritual considerations. For the six days a week where people were working, they could not really focus on anything religious or spiritual so they had the one day where they could go to church.

However, the effect of all of this has been that in the collective consciousness of the West there has been created this very clear distinction between what you call normal, everyday life and a religious or spiritual life. You have many, many people who thought that if they go to church on Sunday, if they confess their sins, if they participate in the Mass and light a candle, then they can go out and live the way they want to live their normal lives for the other six days of the week. People did in many ways make some kind of bargain between God and themselves where they said: "God, I give you Sunday and then you give me the other six days to do what I want. Then, when Sunday comes around again, I go in and confess my sins and I am absolved from whatever I did during the week."

Now, many, many spiritual people have, especially since the 1960's, come to an inner realization that this clear separation of "church and state," so to speak, is no longer valid as we move into a new age. We need to find a different way to look at the spiritual aspect of life and the practical aspect of life. This is a big challenge for many spiritual people and it has, of course, required quite a bit of experimentation on people's part.

Hatred of the Mother realm

What we need to talk about first is that many spiritual people have built a sort of unrealistic daydream about what it means to live a spiritual life. There are, of course, many individual variations of this. There are also different groupings out there of spiritual and New Age movements where each of them have created their own vision of what it supposedly means to live a spiritual life. Common for many of these visions is that they are based on a certain attitude to the matter realm. This is, of course, also something that goes back, not only in the western Christian tradition but even in the East, in the Hindu and Buddhic traditions. There is a very, very strong beast in the collective consciousness that portrays matter as the enemy of your spiritual growth.

This, my beloved, is a complete illusion, created by the fallen beings. There is no other way to put it. It is a complete illusion, deliberately created by the fallen beings to prevent what they consider a big threat against their rule on earth. You see my beloved, what the fallen beings have done, is they have created this separation because they are in the consciousness of separation so they cannot help but create separation. They have created a separation between groupings of fallen beings. Some are focused on taking control of religion and religious life, others are focused on taking control of the secular life. That is why you have a certain division there. It is basically said that if you obey the fallen beings who control religion on Sunday, then you obey the fallen beings who control secular life on the other six days.

This is an attitude that is based on the fact that the fallen beings themselves hate matter, they hate the Mother realm (the matter realm). They hate it simply because it gives them consequences and they do not like consequences. Fallen beings hate consequences. Many of them believe that if you truly have free will, you should be able to make any choice you want without facing the consequences.

Of course, many spiritual people have, as we have talked about before, taken over some of this attitude, and it is not realistic. We have said it before: If you make a choice and there was no physical consequence, how would you know that you had made a choice? If you did not experience a consequence, how could you adjust your state of mind accordingly? If you cannot adjust your state of mind, how can you actually grow?

You see, for the fallen beings, growth is not the purpose of life because they long ago refused to grow, refused to transcend themselves. Their goal is to set themselves up in a powerful and privileged position and maintain that position indefinitely. What you see here is that the goal of the fallen beings is completely different from the goal of true spiritual seekers. Therefore, why does it make any sense to you, as a spiritual seeker, that you would have the same attitude to the matter realm as the fallen beings have?

Why spiritual people dislike matter

Now, we understand, of course, why so many spiritual people have this attitude. It is because you have also experienced consequences, or rather, you have experienced conditions in the physical that were very harsh and very unpleasant.

We have given you teachings about avatars who have come to earth and often been severely attacked by the fallen beings, maybe even tortured and killed brutally in their first embodiment. This is not a direct consequence of something you did, because you did not do anything to the fallen beings. It is a consequence of you making a choice to come to a planet as difficult as earth where the fallen beings have such influence. You see, it is not a *direct* consequence but it is an *indirect* consequence.

Naturally, on a planet like earth where there is so much violence, so much struggle, it is very, very understandable that people build this almost hatred or at least resentment towards the Mother realm, the matter realm. It is the matter realm that outpictures these very harsh, very unpleasant consequences. In many cases, it is your physical body that gives you this very intense pain and, naturally, the physical body is made of matter. Again, we have said this over and over and over again: There is no blame here from our side. It is perfectly understandable that so many spiritual people have this resentment of the matter realm, of the physical octave, of the Mother realm. You have now reached a point on your spiritual path, in this course, where it is time to just realize that while it is understandable that you have a certain reaction, it is no longer (or in fact it never was) constructive for you to have this attitude.

Resentment of matter blocks co-creation

My beloved, what have I said is part of my goal here? It is to help you precipitate a better situation for yourself. My goal for these seven levels of initiation is to help you precipitate a situation where you have more harmony between your spiritual outlook on life and your everyday practical situation. How can I do this, if you have resentment of matter? In order to have harmony between your spiritual and your practical life, something has to change in matter, does it not? If something has to change in matter, that means, my beloved, that you have to work *with* matter instead of resisting matter. You have to stop resisting matter. You have to stop resisting the mother realm! You have to stop looking at conditions on earth and (at least subconsciously) say to yourself: "Oh, if only conditions were different, *then* I could lead a more spiritual life, *then* I could feel at peace on earth, *then* I could be happy on this planet."

You see my beloved, so many of the spiritual people that you see on earth (in all kinds of traditional religions, spiritual, New Age movements, whatever you have, even people who are not in any movement) have this exact attitude: "If only matter would change, *then* my attitude could change." Has not the entire purpose of this course in self-mastery been to help you realize that matter can only outpicture what is projected upon it? If anything is to change here, the change has to begin in mind. As I said, all matter phenomena began in some kind of mind. If something has to change in mind relating to your situation, which mind is it that is going to have to change? Is it not *yours?* Do you have the power to change other minds, whether it be the mind of God or the mind of other people?

How to change matter

My beloved, look at people in traditional religions. They go into their church, they go up to the altar, they kneel before the altar and then they pray to God. They are essentially praying to God to change his mind: "God, please change *your* mind and give me a different consequence as a result of what *I* project with *my* mind." Well, even if it was possible to change God's mind, would it not be easier to change your own mind? What sense does it make, my beloved, that you, as a spiritual, ascended master student, still somewhere in the back of your mind have the idea that one day you will find the secret formula (and maybe Saint Germain will give it in this course on precipitation) so I can change matter without changing my mind? We have said it before. I know this, but did you *get it?* Did it click? My beloved, you need to come to a point where it clicks and you realize that you cannot work *with* matter and precipitate a better situation in matter if you are *resisting, resenting* matter—pushing it away from you.

Many of you have this idea that there should be some magical way to make matter change. Well, there *is,* my beloved. There *is* a magical way for you to change matter and that magical way is to use the powers of your mind. You cannot use those powers to change matter if you are resenting matter, if you are resisting. You need to come to a point where you accept that you are in matter, in the matter realm. You accept that you are here because you chose to be here, because you *want* to be here.

Now, I admit that coming to this point is not quite within the boundaries or the parameters we have set for this course. We have already given you other teachings in other books (starting with the "My Lives" and the workbooks that have come after it) that will help you make peace with being in matter. If you cannot make that shift right now, you need to use these books and make peace with being here. Some of you will be able to take what I am saying here and make that shift in the mind where, at least, you come to realize (even if you have not fully overcome your birth trauma, you can still come to realize) that you have this attitude in your mind where you are resisting matter. You have almost decided to refuse to work with matter or at least refused to use your mind to work with matter. You may be working with matter in physical ways but you are not using your mind to work with matter. This has in many cases something to do with the fact that there is this very old beast in the world that says that spiritual people should avoid being engaged in matter, in practical daily life, because it is against their spiritual growth.

Matter does not oppose spiritual growth

Now my beloved, look at the model that is out there, both in the East and in the West. What does it depict? In the East, you have this idea floating around that the really spiritual people withdraw to a cave in the Himalayas. There is a secret brotherhood of Indian adepts that nobody ever sees but they live in these remote places in the mountains and they are holding the spiritual balance for the planet. You also have this very old tradition in India of a guru setting up an ashram where students come and withdraw from the world to be in the guru's presence. You have Buddhist monasteries that have been set aside. Look at Tibet, for example, where they created these monasteries but they were only focused on what they saw as spiritual exercises, in many cases ignoring practical life. You see the same in the West where you have the monks and nuns of the Catholic tradition. It was seen that if you are really spiritual, you cannot be engaged in practical, everyday life. You have to withdraw from the world and so forth and so on.

Now again, there was a certain validity to this in past centuries because physical living conditions were much more demanding and difficult. They required more physical work, more attention. People were more tired after a day's work and so on. Today, you have (in large part because I have sponsored this) technology that allows you to live a life where you have more spare time—if you get off your phones and stop following everything that happens on Facebook. You have the option to have more spare time, more spare attention, if you choose to take it. What we see is that technology and the modern lifestyle has brought about a situation where it is fully possible to live a relatively active life in society and still make maximum spiritual growth.

Aquarian spirituality is not monastic

Now my beloved, we need to make a distinction here, perhaps. There are some spiritual people on earth who have no real connection to me or to the Golden Age that I desire to bring forth. What I am saying here does not apply to them but the vast majority of the people who are embodied at this time and who have some spiritual interest, they do have a certain tie to me. Therefore, they have as part of their Divine plans (that they themselves made up before they came into embodiment) a desire to support the manifestation of my Golden Age.

My beloved, if you are one of those who want to help bring about Saint Germain's Golden Age, then I tell you: You are not going to do it by withdrawing from the world and living in a monastery. I am not saying that you cannot do it for a short time, but you are not going to do it by living what many spiritual people call a spiritual lifestyle, the way they normally see it where they talk about withdrawing from the world. So many people have attempted to create these movements that create some kind of retreat. Then, they have people who live there and work there and they think this is a spiritual lifestyle, but this is not the Aquarian model of spirituality.

The Aquarian Age is the age of community, the age of the Holy Spirit. Community does not mean that you isolate yourself from the world and create a community of spiritual people with the same beliefs and interests. Community means that you live in the larger community. You are part of life out there in the world. You have, in many cases, a normal job where you work with other people. You are somewhat engaged in society. The age of the Holy Spirit means that the Holy Spirit can flow. Not just in what is traditionally seen as religious settings but in everyday life because you are out there. You never know when you can be the open door for saying something to another person that will help them take a leap forward on their spiritual path, even if they do not seem to be spiritual people.

Breaking the barrier between practical and spiritual

How are you going to bring harmony between your spiritual life and your practical life? You are going to do this only if you change your attitude to what it means to have a "spiritual life" and what it means to have a "practical life." You are going to have to break down the barriers in your own mind. Whom did I say had created these barriers: the fallen beings. How are you going to be a truly spiritual person if you are allowing the barriers created by the fallen beings to exist in your own mind? They have to go, my beloved.

You have to come to a point where you do not have this separation between church and state in your mind. You do not have a separation between what you consider a spiritual activity, what you consider a practical activity. This does not mean that you can somehow find a lifestyle where all of your activities are spiritual according to your spiritual model. No my beloved, it means that you have to do what very few people are willing to do (of those who call themselves spiritual). You have to change your attitude so you stop looking at "spiritual activities" as being spiritual. You break down this whole matrix that has been created in the collective consciousness of what a spiritual activity is.

It is not a matter of going to a church or a temple or a retreat center. It is not a matter of engaging in some activity, like chanting, decrees, prayer, meditation, contemplation, mindfulness or what have you. That is not what it means to be a spiritual activity in the Aquarian Age. In the Aquarian Age, *everything* is a spiritual activity—if you do it with the mindset that this is spiritual.

Overcoming resentment of matter

This begins, my beloved, with you taking a look and being honest and willing to admit that you have a certain resentment of matter in your mind. Again, it is very understandable you have it. I am not blaming you. I am not saying you should not have had this, you should never have built this. My beloved, I do not know how you can come as an avatar to a dense planet like earth and not build this resentment of matter. It is not that I am saying you should never have had it. I am just saying you need to recognize that you have it and that it is time to transcend it.

You do this by working with yourself and truly looking at the matter realm. I have said before that you need to look beyond these matter phenomena. You need to realize that matter is made from atoms, molecules, sub-atomic particles and energy waves. You need to realize here that all of these matter phenomena that you see are truly made of this basic substance.

My beloved, this basic substance, that we have called the Ma-ter Light, is not your enemy. It is not out to get you, it is not out to hurt you, it is not resisting you! When you go beyond all of these images and matrices that have been projected on the

Ma-ter Light, then you come in contact with the pure Ma-ter Light. That Ma-ter Light is not resisting you in any way. The Ma-ter Light itself is not separated from Spirit. When you go down and contact the pure Ma-ter Light, as the Conscious You is fully capable of doing (if you can set aside your normal attitude), then you see that the Ma-ter Light is not separated from Spirit. There is no separation here between the Divine Mother and the Divine Father.

In a sense, you could say that even this distinction that there is something we call the "father" aspect of God and the "mother" aspect of God can help create, or at least maintain, a certain duality, but they are not separate. The Ma-ter Light is an extension of the Father. The Ma-ter Light that is used to form planet earth is an extension of the Ma-ter Light in the spiritual realm, just with a slightly different vibration. Nevertheless my beloved, the important point here is that when you get down to the basic Ma-ter Light that forms planet earth, that Ma-ter Light can outpicture any form projected upon it within the matrix of possible forms that was set by the Elohim.

This means that the Ma-ter Light could as easily outpicture an Edenic state on earth as the current mess you see on earth. When you really ponder this, you realize that it is not the Ma-ter Light that is your enemy here. The Ma-ter Light is not resisting you, so why are *you* resisting *it*—because you *are* resisting it in your mind.

Again, it is perfectly understandable that you come to this planet, and you build this resentment of the Ma-ter Light (or even if you are one of the original inhabitants, once you encounter the fallen beings and what they have done with the Ma-ter Light in creating these very painful consequences, you build resentment). Again, there is no blame but it is time to take a look at this and realize that if you really want to change your situation in matter, what is the only way to change your situation in matter? It is to do it *through* matter. The only way to change matter is to accept and embrace matter and no longer resent it, resist it and push it away from you.

Cognitive dissonance of spiritual people

Do you see, my beloved, that many spiritual people have what they call "cognitive dissonance?" They have a contradiction between what they *believe* and what they *do*. On the one hand, you are believing that life has a spiritual side, there is a spiritual reality, but you still have adopted much of this religious stigma that there is a distinction or a separation between matter and Spirit. Matter is *here,* Spirit is *somewhere else,* therefore matter is not spiritual.

When you are awakening to the idea that life has a spiritual side, it is as if there is a part of you that finds it easy to accept Spirit. You are embracing, accepting that there is a Spirit. You may not have a clear concept of what Spirit is or a direct experience of it yet, but you find it easy to accept some spiritual teaching that tells you what Spirit is and what the spiritual realm is like. Many New Age people, for example, have this great faith and great interest in angels and how wonderful everything is in the angelic realm.

At the same time, you are still believing that the matter realm is separated from the spiritual realm. You are thinking that in order to change something in matter, you have to go through the spiritual realm. You have to somehow reach up to some spiritual being that has the power to change matter and they can then change matter for you. What is the title of this course, my beloved? It is a course in self-mastery—*self*-mastery! Self-mastery does not mean that you can find a spiritual being who is going to be like the wish-fulfilling god or Santa Claus.

Overcoming the spirit that resents matter

Self-mastery means that you yourself can change matter, but, again, you cannot change matter if you are resisting it. You have to come to see that resistance, see that it is an internal spirit or a separate self and you have to step back from this. You have to use these teachings I am giving you, use the invocation until the Conscious You suddenly steps outside of that spirit, sees that it is a spirit, sees that *that* spirit is created from this resentment of matter, this resisting matter. Then, you need to *not* go into any kind of argumentation with the spirit.

The spirit will try to defend its life. It will come up with all kinds of arguments (and the fallen beings might project all these arguments into your mind) of why matter is the way it is, why it is separated from Spirit and why all of these negative consequences you see in matter could not possibly come from Spirit, therefore matter must be separated from Spirit and lots of other arguments. You have to not go into arguing about this because you are not going to get rid of this spirit by proving it wrong. You are going to get rid of it only when you see it for what it is, see that it is a separate spirit in your being, realize that you are the Conscious You, you are not that spirit, you do not want it anymore in your life and you just let it die.

As long as you are arguing with it, trying to justify it or trying to prove it wrong, you are giving it energy. You need to stop giving it energy and just let it die. Who created it? *You* did. Who has sustained it? *You* have, through your attention, through your beliefs. When you stop feeding it your energy, it will die. You can, of course, make the calls for the masters to consume it but, nevertheless, when you stop feeding it, it will die. This is the goal at this level of my retreat. It is to come to that point where your spirit of resenting matter dies. It is no more.

Considering your daydreams

You have to come to accept that matter does not resist your effort to create a more spiritual life. However, matter is not going to conform to your current daydream about what it means to live a spiritual life. You have to make an effort to see that this idea of what a spiritual life should be is also an internal spirit. Of course, as the other one, it is tied to a collective spirit but it is an internal spirit and you have to let that die also.

As long as you are holding on to this internal spirit of what a spiritual life should be, you cannot see what you yourself put into your Divine plan of how you want to live your life. I can assure you, again, that most of you did not, in your Divine plan, create the desire to live in a retreat or monastic setting where you are withdrawn from the world. You designed your Divine plan so that you will live a fairly active life in society, interact with other people and, therefore, you can be the open door for, as I said previously, bringing forth some ideas from the ascended realm.

We are not here talking about all of you bringing forth major inventions. Everyday life is improved by everyday, normal people coming up with ideas of how to do something better. This happens in your work situations, in whatever situations you are in. There is room for improvement by new ideas but who is going to bring them forth? Well, somebody who has some attunement and some expertise or experience in the area.

You see here that there can be, and there *is* for most spiritual people, a vast difference between the daydream of what it means to have a spiritual life and what you actually put in your Divine plan. When you let go of the idea of what it means to have a spiritual life, when you let go of the resentment towards matter, you can begin to see what you actually put in your Divine plan. When you made your Divine plan, you were not in the same state of mind you are in now. You did not have that resentment of matter, you did not feel it. You did not have that far-flung idealistic idea of a spiritual lifestyle. You looked at it very realistically and said: "What is my potential for growth in this lifetime? How can I best implement this, given my history, given my karma, given the other people I am tied to? Which kind of society do I want to embody in so I can be an open door for the ascended masters and Saint Germain to bring forth new ideas?"

Progress is a practical matter

From a purely realistic viewpoint, what has created the progress in society you have seen over the last one thousand years? It is new ideas! Who brought forth those new ideas? Was it monks and nuns in a monastery? Was it spiritual people sitting in a cave in the Himalayas? Or was it people who were out there in practical life, therefore in many cases experiencing a problem and because of that, reaching up for a better way of doing things.

I am not saying there is no value to the people who are sitting in a cave in the Himalayas and having a high level of consciousness. I am only saying this is not what most of you put in your Divine plan because you saw very clearly that bringing civilization forward into Saint Germain's Golden Age is not an *idealistic* matter, it is a very *practical* matter.

So many ascended master students, who have heard about Saint Germain and who have heard about a golden age, have a completely unrealistic daydream about what this means. They think that I have some far-flung ideal, edenic, Utopian view of what society is supposed to become. They think that one day in the future there is going to be this breakthrough and then the Golden Age will be manifest. It is a lot like the hysteria you saw before 2012 where so many new age people believed that there would be a magical shift of the earth into a new dimension and everything would change.

My beloved, this is what we have talked about recently, namely that there is a gap between what spiritual people believe and then reality. The goal of the course of self-mastery is to help you overcome the gap so that you can manifest what you have in your mind. In order to overcome that gap, you have to adjust what is in your mind so you bring it down to a realistic, practical level. How is Saint Germain's Golden Age going to be manifest? Not in one big "poof." It is going to be manifest by many, many small seemingly insignificant steps. Many, many people will bring forth a small idea that in itself has very little impact on the global level, but taken together with all of these other small ideas, they will bring civilization forward.

There will not come a point, my beloved, where you say that on January 11, 2053 the Golden Age was manifest. Most people will not even notice that the Golden Age is becoming manifest. They will notice that there is a gradual improvement in living conditions. That is what the Golden Age is all about. It is not about these magical, idealistic shifts. It is about taking one step at a time and that is the same for you. So many of you have this idea in your mind that one day there will be a shift and suddenly you will have the spiritual lifestyle that you do not have now.

Closing the gap

You are seeing in your mind that, *here* is your practical situation right now, *there* is where your spiritual ideals say you should be and there is a huge gap between the two. If you step back and take a look at this gap, you will see that in your mind, there is no realistic way for you to close that gap. You cannot see how to close the gap. How am I going to get from my practical everyday situation (where I still have to make a living, I might have to take care of my children, I have a job, I have this, I have that obligation in the physical realm), how am I going to get from all these obligations to living this spiritual lifestyle that I envision? Well, you never will because the spiritual lifestyle that you envision is contrary to your own Divine plan.

I can assure you, my beloved, that if you are attempting to manifest something that is contrary to your Divine plan, there will be a part of your subconscious mind that will sabotage your efforts. Psychologists talk about the "self-sabotage syndrome" and in some cases it is because people have severe psychological problems. For many spiritual people the self-sabotage syndrome actually means that when their conscious minds have adopted a goal that is contrary to their Divine plans, then they will subconsciously sabotage themselves in order to avoid becoming trapped in an activity that takes them away from their Divine plan.

Ponder this very carefully, my beloved, and you might see certain things in your own life where you were tempted to move into a certain area but something came up. Somehow, you sabotaged this goal. You might look at this with resentment and regret and: "Why did I do this, and why was I so stupid?" The reality might be that it was because the conscious goal or desire you had was not in alignment with your Divine plan.

Paying attention to your attention

Therefore, you need to recognize that as long as you are fixating your mind on this unrealistic daydream, you will not be able to step back and have the stillness of mind where you can get a glimpse of your Divine plan. You need to realize that if you are to see something that you are not currently seeing with your conscious mind, you have to create a space in your mind where that vision can come through. You have to realize that your attention is extremely important.

There have been ascended master teachings where we talked about an energy veil. Evil means energy veil. There is an energy veil that prevents you from seeing. Many ascended master students have reasoned that this means that the dark forces have created this energy veil. Well, of course the dark forces have created an energy veil. The collective consciousness has created an energy veil, and of course you have to break through it. If you have followed this course up until this level of consciousness, then you have learned how to break through this with your decrees and invocations. You are not completely blinded by the energy veil of the dark forces and the collective consciousness.

What is blinding you? It is the energy veil that you have created and maintained in your own mind. That energy veil is created by your attention focusing on some of these unrealistic daydreams and images of what it means to be a spiritual person, what it means to live a spiritual lifestyle. My beloved, I would like – ideally – that you could come to see these idealistic ideas as a balloon and you could take a little needle and puncture the balloon and it would pop—and they would all be gone. Again, this is not quite realistic, at least for most of you. You are going to have to work a little bit with this.

You are going to have to be willing to realize a very, very simple truth. I have said it before in a previous dispensation that human beings are slaves of their attention. Where your attention goes, there goes your energy. When you put your attention on something, like a particular dream of what it means to live a spiritual lifestyle, your energies will go there. After you have put a certain amount of attention on it, this has created an energy veil. What does it prevent you from doing? It prevents you from seeing a vision that is in your Divine plan because you are so focused on the vision that you created in your outer mind that you cannot tune in to your higher mind.

What also happens is that the more energy you invest in something, the stronger this energy veil becomes and now it becomes not just an energy *veil* but an energy *magnet* and it pulls on your attention. You put your attention on a certain matrix, you allow energy to flow into it. When the energy reaches a critical mass, it starts pulling on your attention to focus more and more on this. This becomes a spiral that can eat up all of your energy, all of your attention, for the rest of this lifetime.

You can, theoretically, maintain your current vision of what it means to be a spiritual person. You can continue to pursue it for the rest of your lifetime, never getting there. This, of course, is not what I desire to see for you. I desire to see you pierce the energy veil, shatter the energy veil, shatter that unrealistic daydream and come to see what you put in your Divine plan that is realistic and practical for you in this lifetime. In order to do this, you have to be willing to create that opening,

The secret formula

Quite frankly, my beloved, here is a secret that you might say is one of those secret formulas that many people are dreaming about. It just will not be exactly what they have been dreaming about.

The secret is this: When your attention has been pulled into focusing on a certain area, you cannot see beyond it as long as you are still focused on it. You have to pull your attention away from the area—at least long enough that there is some kind of stillness, some kind of stillness in your mind, where the clouds part and a ray of sun can shine through from your I AM Presence. There has to be an opening. As long as you are focusing your attention on the dream, there is no attention left over for your I AM Presence. You are essentially saying: "Don't disturb me, I AM Presence, don't bother me here, I am focused on this outer vision!"

This is not how you make progress on the spiritual path. You have to start here by making a conscious decision: "Okay, I am taking a look at what is my dream about what it means to be a spiritual person and living a spiritual lifestyle. I am willing to question that vision. I am willing to see if it isn't the highest. I am especially willing to see if it doesn't correspond with my Divine plan. If it doesn't, then I want to know and I want to let the unrealistic daydream go and I want to see what is in my Divine plan."

The difficulty here, my beloved, is that your daydream about what it means to be a spiritual person may be a very complete, far-flung, detailed vision that you have in your outer mind. In many cases, once you have an opening where you receive something from your I AM Presence, it will not be the complete vision of your Divine plan for the rest of this lifetime. What you will get is the next step you need to take. It will not seem nearly as idealistic, nearly as romantic, nearly as wonderful as the outer daydream.

Again, you have to make the conscious decision that you are willing to let go of this, you are willing to follow the inner promptings you get and take them one step at a time. It may very well be that you get some impulse from your I AM Presence to do something very practical and you see no connection between that and your outer vision. That is why you have to, then, be willing to set aside the outer vision and say: "I will follow this intuitive, inner prompting no matter where it takes me." I can assure you that if you keep following these promptings from your I AM Presence, they will take you to the goal you defined in your Divine plan. It may not have very much to do with your outer vision but again, you then have to decide: "What do I want to follow—the realistic, practical vision I put into my Divine plan or this idealistic but unrealistic daydream that I have come to accept with my outer mind?"

Reconsidering your spiritual movement

There are people (and as these teachings spread further, there will be more people) who will find this book and who will be in a specific spiritual movement. They will have a vision of what it means to be a spiritual person based on the teachings of that movement. There will be people where that vision, that outer vision they have received, is in almost opposition to (or at least very far from) what they incorporated in their Divine plans. Now, you may say then: "Why did these people come to

8 | Loving your Divine plan more than a daydream

be in that spiritual movement?" They came because they had to learn a certain thing, they had to learn something.

In other words, it was in their Divine plan that they should go into that movement but it was not in their Divine plan that they should adopt the vision of that movement for what it means to be a spiritual person. They had to learn something and in some cases it is to learn how *not* to do certain things in a spiritual setting or how *not* to live a spiritual life. They have to learn something. Once you have learned it, it is time to move on, it is time to, then, let go of that vision of what it means to be a spiritual person.

There are also many spiritual people who are in embodiment today who in past lives were embodied in a monastic or retreat setting. For many lifetimes you have been a spiritual person, therefore you have gravitated towards what was at the time seemingly the most spiritual lifestyle. Many of you have these ideals that you have carried with you from lifetime to lifetime of: "How I should live as a spiritual person." You have this almost compulsion to live this spiritual lifestyle.

You see so many people out there, in the West for example, who are almost falling over themselves when they meet these lamas or gurus from the East. They think these eastern people are living such a wonderful spiritual lifestyle compared to what you can do in the West. They think everything in the West is anti-spiritual but these lamas, who walk around in these flowing robes of different colors, they are the real spiritual people. They think they should emulate this and live this way. My beloved, I am not saying you should *not*—if it is in your Divine plan. I submit to you that if it had been in your Divine plan to become a lama, you probably would not have embodied in the West.

Why did you embody in the West? Was it not because you saw that this was the best way to help further Saint Germain's

Golden Age? So, get on with this! Reach for the vision of how you can help manifest the Golden Age right here where you are instead of traveling to India, traveling to Tibet or going into some kind of retreat or monastery where you isolate yourself from the western world.

What do you love more?

I am not telling you to do something that you do not want to do with your *higher* mind. I may be telling you to do something that your *outer* mind does not want to do. That is why you are now facing the choice on the Third Ray of Love: "What do you love more?" Do you love the outer mind, the outer vision, or your I AM Presence and the vision that you put into your Divine plan? This is the vision that you yourself put into your Divine plan when you had a broader perspective than you have right now.

What I am telling you is that if you will use this lesson, you can actually shift your perspective. You can free yourself from this obsessive compulsion with these outer visions and goals, these daydreams. You can begin to get some clarity on what is your practical reality that you put into your Divine plan. My beloved, what do you love most? The far-flung ideals that may never be manifest or the practical reality that you can improve on step by step by step? We have talked about the gap. So many spiritual people see a gap and there continues to be a gap because they are waiting for the point where they see a clear, spiritual step to take. They overlook and refuse to take all the many small practical steps that they could have taken that would improve their lives.

There is an old saying that if you will lift your eyes towards the stars and reach for the stars, at least you will not come up with your hands full of mud. My beloved, if you are looking up towards the stars and overlook all of the pathways that lead you to a better life down here, what good does it do you? Would it not be better to get down, get your hands dirty but also discover those ways of how you can improve your life and come closer to what you put in your Divine plan?

The gap in the outer mind

When you made your Divine plan, you saw that you would start out life at a certain level. You also set a goal that was realistic for what you could reach in this lifetime, how much growth you could go through. In other words, to speak about the 144 levels, you might have said that you started out, say at the 56th level and you could go to the 120th level. There is a huge gap between the 56th level and the 120th level, is there not? Well, you might not even realize how big of a gap it is but it is quite a big gap. It is realistic for you to make it but how are you going to make it? Are you going to jump from the 56th level because you discover some secret formula in some old book? Or are you going to get to the 120th level by first getting to the 57th, then to the 58th, then to the 59th, then to the 60th and so on.

Do you see why there is a gap in the outer mind? It is because you are overlooking the small steps that take you to the goal. Or it is because you have a goal that is completely unrealistic and therefore you cannot set up a line of small steps that leads to the goal. Many, many spiritual people have a goal in their outer mind that is completely unrealistic. Nobody, including me, could take these people from where they are at right now to their goal and create a logical, practical progression of doable steps that would take them to the goal. There is simply no way to get there. This is why the fallen beings have set up these goals because they know that people cannot reach them. Therefore, they will always be chasing the pot of gold at the end of the rainbow and be dissatisfied and frustrated—and that is exactly what the fallen beings want. *I* do not want you to be dissatisfied and frustrated, I want you to be fulfilled in knowing you are following all of the small steps in your Divine plan. That is what I desire to see. That is what we all desire to see.

You do not seriously believe, do you, that we have created this entire course to have you come out at the other end and you still see a gap and you are still frustrated? We want you to close the gap. We want you to realize that the path is about taking one doable step at a time so that you are fulfilled in being at your present level. Nada made great efforts to help you get to that level. The other Chohans have mentioned it as well. I will mention it as well because it is the goal for us to help you come to the point where there is no longer a gap. You are fulfilled in doing what you *can* do and continuing to take those steps until you reach the highest level you can reach in your Divine plan, perhaps even go beyond it.

For some of you it will mean that you will reach the 144th level in this lifetime. That is our desire, my beloved. That is my desire. You can hear, can you not, that I am excited about it? I am hoping that you can also make a shift and be excited about being realistic, instead of being excited about some far-flung pipe dream that you can never manifest.

You see, my beloved, manifesting something is about having a realistic vision of what you *can* manifest, given your personal situation and given the planet you are on. There are avatars who have been misled by the fallen beings into adopting a vision of what they would like to manifest. That vision was realistic on a natural planet but it is not realistic on earth—again, chasing the pot of gold at the end of the rainbow. I want you to find the real gold, which is the vision in your Divine plan. It will come to you, one little speck at a time, not as a big pot of gold that is there all at once. Follow those little steps. Take every step and you will get where you wanted to go, and *that* is what I want for you.

9 | INVOKING LOVE FOR MY DIVINE PLAN

In the name I AM THAT I AM, Jesus Christ, I call to my I AM Presence to flow through the I Will Be Presence that I AM and give this invocation with full power. I call to Saint Germain to help me see the vision in my Divine plan for what it means to live as a spiritual person. Help me overcome all unrealistic daydreams that block the vision of my Divine plan, including …

[Make personal calls]

Part 1

1. I reject the division in the collective consciousness between normal everyday life and a religious or spiritual life.

O Saint Germain, you do inspire,
my vision raised forever higher,
with you I form a figure-eight,
your Golden Age I co-create.

**O Saint Germain, what love you bring,
it truly makes all matter sing,
your violet flame does all restore,
with you we are becoming more.**

2. This separation of "church and state" is no longer valid, and I see a different way to look at the spiritual aspect of life and the practical aspect of life.

O Saint Germain, what Freedom Flame,
released when we recite your name,
acceleration is your gift,
our planet it will surely lift.

**O Saint Germain, what love you bring,
it truly makes all matter sing,
your violet flame does all restore,
with you we are becoming more.**

3. I surrender my unrealistic daydream about what it means to live a spiritual life. I reject the beast in the collective consciousness that portrays matter as the enemy of my spiritual growth.

O Saint Germain, in love we claim,
our right to bring your violet flame,
from you Above, to us below,
it is an all-transforming flow.

**O Saint Germain, what love you bring,
it truly makes all matter sing,
your violet flame does all restore,
with you we are becoming more.**

4. I refuse to follow the fallen beings who control religion as well as the fallen beings who control secular life.

O Saint Germain, I love you so,
my aura filled with violet glow,
my chakras filled with violet fire,
I am your cosmic amplifier.

**O Saint Germain, what love you bring,
it truly makes all matter sing,
your violet flame does all restore,
with you we are becoming more.**

5. I surrender the hatred of the Mother realm that comes from the fallen beings and their belief that they should be able to make any choice they want without facing the consequences.

O Saint Germain, I am now free,
your violet flame is therapy,
transform all hang-ups in my mind,
as inner peace I surely find.

**O Saint Germain, what love you bring,
it truly makes all matter sing,
your violet flame does all restore,
with you we are becoming more.**

6. If I make a choice and there was no physical consequence, how would I know that I had made a choice? If I did not experience a consequence, how could I adjust my state of mind? If I cannot adjust my state of mind, how can I grow?

> O Saint Germain, my body pure,
> your violet flame for all is cure,
> consume the cause of all disease,
> and therefore I am all at ease.
>
> **O Saint Germain, what love you bring,
> it truly makes all matter sing,
> your violet flame does all restore,
> with you we are becoming more.**

7. I am a spiritual seeker, and I refuse to have the same attitude to the matter realm as the fallen beings have.

> O Saint Germain, I'm karma-free,
> the past no longer burdens me,
> a brand new opportunity,
> I am in Christic unity.
>
> **O Saint Germain, what love you bring,
> it truly makes all matter sing,
> your violet flame does all restore,
> with you we are becoming more.**

8. On a planet like earth where there is so much violence, so much struggle, it is understandable that I have built this almost hatred or at least resentment towards the Mother realm.

9 | Invoking Love for my Divine plan

O Saint Germain, we are now one,
I am for you a violet sun,
as we transform this planet earth,
your Golden Age is given birth.

**O Saint Germain, what love you bring,
it truly makes all matter sing,
your violet flame does all restore,
with you we are becoming more.**

9. While it is understandable that I have this reaction, it is no longer constructive for me to have this hatred of the Mother realm.

O Saint Germain, the earth is free,
from burden of duality,
in oneness we bring what is best,
your Golden Age is manifest.

**O Saint Germain, what love you bring,
it truly makes all matter sing,
your violet flame does all restore,
with you we are becoming more.**

Part 2

1. My goal is to precipitate a situation where I have harmony between my spiritual outlook on life and my everyday practical situation. How can I do this if I have resentment of matter?

> O Saint Germain, you do inspire,
> my vision raised forever higher,
> with you I form a figure-eight,
> your Golden Age I co-create.
>
> **O Saint Germain, what love you bring,**
> **it truly makes all matter sing,**
> **your violet flame does all restore,**
> **with you we are becoming more.**

2. In order to have harmony between my spiritual and my practical life, something has to change in matter. If something has to change in matter, I have to work *with* matter instead of resisting matter.

> O Saint Germain, what Freedom Flame,
> released when we recite your name,
> acceleration is your gift,
> our planet it will surely lift.
>
> **O Saint Germain, what love you bring,**
> **it truly makes all matter sing,**
> **your violet flame does all restore,**
> **with you we are becoming more.**

3. I stop resisting matter. I stop resisting the Mother realm! I stop thinking that if only conditions were different, then I could lead a more spiritual life, then I could feel at peace on earth, then I could be happy on this planet.

9 | Invoking Love for my Divine plan

O Saint Germain, in love we claim,
our right to bring your violet flame,
from you Above, to us below,
it is an all-transforming flow.

**O Saint Germain, what love you bring,
it truly makes all matter sing,
your violet flame does all restore,
with you we are becoming more.**

4. Matter can only outpicture what is projected upon it. If anything is to change, the change has to begin in mind. If something has to change in mind relating to *my* situation, it is *my* mind that has to change.

O Saint Germain, I love you so,
my aura filled with violet glow,
my chakras filled with violet fire,
I am your cosmic amplifier.

**O Saint Germain, what love you bring,
it truly makes all matter sing,
your violet flame does all restore,
with you we are becoming more.**

5. I surrender the idea that one day I will find the secret formula so I can change matter without changing my mind. It has clicked for me, and I realize that I cannot work with matter and precipitate a better situation in matter if I am resisting, resenting matter—pushing it away from me.

> O Saint Germain, I am now free,
> your violet flame is therapy,
> transform all hang-ups in my mind,
> as inner peace I surely find.
>
> **O Saint Germain, what love you bring,**
> **it truly makes all matter sing,**
> **your violet flame does all restore,**
> **with you we are becoming more.**

6. There *is* a magical way for me to change matter and that magical way is to use the powers of my mind. I cannot use those powers to change matter if I am resenting matter, if I am resisting.

> O Saint Germain, my body pure,
> your violet flame for all is cure,
> consume the cause of all disease,
> and therefore I am all at ease.
>
> **O Saint Germain, what love you bring,**
> **it truly makes all matter sing,**
> **your violet flame does all restore,**
> **with you we are becoming more.**

7. I accept that I am in matter, in the matter realm. I accept that I am here because I chose to be here, because I want to be here.

> O Saint Germain, I'm karma-free,
> the past no longer burdens me,
> a brand new opportunity,
> I am in Christic unity.

9 | Invoking Love for my Divine plan

> **O Saint Germain, what love you bring,**
> **it truly makes all matter sing,**
> **your violet flame does all restore,**
> **with you we are becoming more.**

8. I am making a shift in the mind where I realize that I have this attitude in my mind where I am resisting matter. I had decided to refuse to work with matter or at least refused to use my mind to work with matter.

> O Saint Germain, we are now one,
> I am for you a violet sun,
> as we transform this planet earth,
> your Golden Age is given birth.

> **O Saint Germain, what love you bring,**
> **it truly makes all matter sing,**
> **your violet flame does all restore,**
> **with you we are becoming more.**

9. I surrender this attitude and I reject the beast that says spiritual people should avoid being engaged in matter, in practical daily life because it is against our spiritual growth.

> O Saint Germain, the earth is free,
> from burden of duality,
> in oneness we bring what is best,
> your Golden Age is manifest.

> **O Saint Germain, what love you bring,**
> **it truly makes all matter sing,**
> **your violet flame does all restore,**
> **with you we are becoming more.**

Part 3

1. Technology and the modern lifestyle has brought about a situation where it is fully possible to live a relatively active life in society and still make maximum spiritual growth.

> O Saint Germain, you do inspire,
> my vision raised forever higher,
> with you I form a figure-eight,
> your Golden Age I co-create.
>
> **O Saint Germain, what love you bring,**
> **it truly makes all matter sing,**
> **your violet flame does all restore,**
> **with you we are becoming more.**

2. It is part of my Divine plan to support the manifestation of Saint Germain's Golden Age. I am not going to do this by withdrawing from the world and living in a monastery or living what many spiritual people call a spiritual lifestyle.

> O Saint Germain, what Freedom Flame,
> released when we recite your name,
> acceleration is your gift,
> our planet it will surely lift.
>
> **O Saint Germain, what love you bring,**
> **it truly makes all matter sing,**
> **your violet flame does all restore,**
> **with you we are becoming more.**

3. The Aquarian Age is the age of community. Community does not mean that I isolate myself from the world and create a community of spiritual people with the same beliefs and interests. Community means that I live in the larger community. I am part of life in the world.

> O Saint Germain, in love we claim,
> our right to bring your violet flame,
> from you Above, to us below,
> it is an all-transforming flow.
>
> **O Saint Germain, what love you bring,**
> **it truly makes all matter sing,**
> **your violet flame does all restore,**
> **with you we are becoming more.**

4. I am willing to work with other people, engage in society so that the Holy Spirit can flow through me in everyday life, saying something to another person that will help them take a leap forward on their spiritual path.

> O Saint Germain, I love you so,
> my aura filled with violet glow,
> my chakras filled with violet fire,
> I am your cosmic amplifier.
>
> **O Saint Germain, what love you bring,**
> **it truly makes all matter sing,**
> **your violet flame does all restore,**
> **with you we are becoming more.**

5. I can bring harmony between my spiritual life and my practical life only by changing my attitude to what it means to have a "spiritual life" and what it means to have a "practical life."

> O Saint Germain, I am now free,
> your violet flame is therapy,
> transform all hang-ups in my mind,
> as inner peace I surely find.

O Saint Germain, what love you bring,
it truly makes all matter sing,
your violet flame does all restore,
with you we are becoming more.

6. I am breaking down the barriers created by the fallen beings. How am I going to be a truly spiritual person if I am allowing the barriers created by the fallen beings to exist in my own mind? They have to go.

> O Saint Germain, my body pure,
> your violet flame for all is cure,
> consume the cause of all disease,
> and therefore I am all at ease.

O Saint Germain, what love you bring,
it truly makes all matter sing,
your violet flame does all restore,
with you we are becoming more.

7. I do not have this separation between church and state in my mind. I do not have a separation between what I consider a spiritual activity, what I consider a practical activity.

O Saint Germain, I'm karma-free,
the past no longer burdens me,
a brand new opportunity,
I am in Christic unity.

**O Saint Germain, what love you bring,
it truly makes all matter sing,
your violet flame does all restore,
with you we are becoming more.**

8. I change my attitude and I stop looking at "spiritual activities" as being spiritual. I break down the matrix that has been created in the collective consciousness of what a spiritual activity is.

O Saint Germain, we are now one,
I am for you a violet sun,
as we transform this planet earth,
your Golden Age is given birth.

**O Saint Germain, what love you bring,
it truly makes all matter sing,
your violet flame does all restore,
with you we are becoming more.**

9. In the Aquarian Age, everything is a spiritual activity—and I am doing it with the mindset that this *is* spiritual.

O Saint Germain, the earth is free,
from burden of duality,
in oneness we bring what is best,
your Golden Age is manifest.

> O Saint Germain, what love you bring,
> it truly makes all matter sing,
> your violet flame does all restore,
> with you we are becoming more.

Part 4

1. I am willing to admit that I have a certain resentment of matter in my mind. I recognize that I have it and that it is time to transcend it.

> O Saint Germain, you do inspire,
> my vision raised forever higher,
> with you I form a figure-eight,
> your Golden Age I co-create.

> O Saint Germain, what love you bring,
> it truly makes all matter sing,
> your violet flame does all restore,
> with you we are becoming more.

2. I am looking beyond all matter phenomena. I realize that matter is made from atoms, molecules, sub-atomic particles and energy waves. I realize that all matter phenomena are truly made of this basic substance.

> O Saint Germain, what Freedom Flame,
> released when we recite your name,
> acceleration is your gift,
> our planet it will surely lift.

**O Saint Germain, what love you bring,
it truly makes all matter sing,
your violet flame does all restore,
with you we are becoming more.**

3. The Ma-ter Light is not my enemy. It is not out to get me, it is not out to hurt me, it is not resisting me!

O Saint Germain, in love we claim,
our right to bring your violet flame,
from you Above, to us below,
it is an all-transforming flow.

**O Saint Germain, what love you bring,
it truly makes all matter sing,
your violet flame does all restore,
with you we are becoming more.**

4. I go beyond all of the images and matrices that have been projected on the Ma-ter Light, and I am in contact with the pure Ma-ter Light. That Ma-ter Light is not resisting me in any way.

O Saint Germain, I love you so,
my aura filled with violet glow,
my chakras filled with violet fire,
I am your cosmic amplifier.

**O Saint Germain, what love you bring,
it truly makes all matter sing,
your violet flame does all restore,
with you we are becoming more.**

5. The Ma-ter Light itself is not separated from Spirit. As the Conscious You, I contact the pure Ma-ter Light and I see that the Ma-ter Light is not separated from Spirit. There is no separation between the Divine Mother and the Divine Father.

> O Saint Germain, I am now free,
> your violet flame is therapy,
> transform all hang-ups in my mind,
> as inner peace I surely find.
>
> **O Saint Germain, what love you bring,**
> **it truly makes all matter sing,**
> **your violet flame does all restore,**
> **with you we are becoming more.**

6. The Ma-ter Light is an extension of the Father. The Ma-ter Light that is used to form planet earth is an extension of the Ma-ter Light in the spiritual realm, just with a slightly different vibration.

> O Saint Germain, my body pure,
> your violet flame for all is cure,
> consume the cause of all disease,
> and therefore I am all at ease.
>
> **O Saint Germain, what love you bring,**
> **it truly makes all matter sing,**
> **your violet flame does all restore,**
> **with you we are becoming more.**

7. The basic Ma-ter Light that forms planet earth, can outpicture any form projected upon it. This Ma-ter Light could as

easily outpicture an Edenic state on earth as the current mess on earth.

> O Saint Germain, I'm karma-free,
> the past no longer burdens me,
> a brand new opportunity,
> I am in Christic unity.

> **O Saint Germain, what love you bring,**
> **it truly makes all matter sing,**
> **your violet flame does all restore,**
> **with you we are becoming more.**

8. It is not the Ma-ter Light that is my enemy. The Ma-ter Light is not resisting *me,* so why am I resisting *it?*

> O Saint Germain, we are now one,
> I am for you a violet sun,
> as we transform this planet earth,
> your Golden Age is given birth.

> **O Saint Germain, what love you bring,**
> **it truly makes all matter sing,**
> **your violet flame does all restore,**
> **with you we are becoming more.**

9. I really want to change my situation in matter, and the only way to change my situation in matter is to do it *through* matter. The only way to change matter is to accept and embrace matter and no longer resent it, resist it and push it away from me.

> O Saint Germain, the earth is free,
> from burden of duality,
> in oneness we bring what is best,
> your Golden Age is manifest.
>
> **O Saint Germain, what love you bring,
> it truly makes all matter sing,
> your violet flame does all restore,
> with you we are becoming more.**

Part 5

1. I rise above all "cognitive dissonance," the contradiction between what I *believe* and what I *do*. I reject the religious stigma that there is a separation between matter and Spirit, therefore matter is not spiritual.

> O Saint Germain, you do inspire,
> my vision raised forever higher,
> with you I form a figure-eight,
> your Golden Age I co-create.
>
> **O Saint Germain, what love you bring,
> it truly makes all matter sing,
> your violet flame does all restore,
> with you we are becoming more.**

2. I reject the belief that in order to change something in matter, I have to go through the spiritual realm and find a spiritual being that has the power to change matter for me.

9 | Invoking Love for my Divine plan

O Saint Germain, what Freedom Flame,
released when we recite your name,
acceleration is your gift,
our planet it will surely lift.

**O Saint Germain, what love you bring,
it truly makes all matter sing,
your violet flame does all restore,
with you we are becoming more.**

3. Self-mastery does not mean that I can find a spiritual being who is going to be like the wish-fulfilling god or Santa Claus. Self-mastery means that I myself can change matter, but I cannot change matter if I am resisting it.

O Saint Germain, in love we claim,
our right to bring your violet flame,
from you Above, to us below,
it is an all-transforming flow.

**O Saint Germain, what love you bring,
it truly makes all matter sing,
your violet flame does all restore,
with you we are becoming more.**

4. I see that resistance, see that it is an internal spirit, a separate self. I am stepping back from this. My Conscious You steps outside of that spirit, sees that it is a spirit, sees that the spirit is created from resentment of matter.

O Saint Germain, I love you so,
my aura filled with violet glow,
my chakras filled with violet fire,
I am your cosmic amplifier.

**O Saint Germain, what love you bring,
it truly makes all matter sing,
your violet flame does all restore,
with you we are becoming more.**

5. I refuse to go into any kind of argumentation with the spirit because I am not going to get rid of this spirit by proving it wrong. I see it for what it is, see that it is a separate spirit in my being. I realize that I am the Conscious You, I am not that spirit. I do not want it anymore in my life and I just let it die.

O Saint Germain, I am now free,
your violet flame is therapy,
transform all hang-ups in my mind,
as inner peace I surely find.

**O Saint Germain, what love you bring,
it truly makes all matter sing,
your violet flame does all restore,
with you we are becoming more.**

6. As long as I am arguing with it, trying to justify it or trying to prove it wrong, I am giving it energy. I stop giving it energy and just let it die. I created it, I have sustained it through my attention and beliefs. When I stop feeding it my energy, it *will* die.

> O Saint Germain, my body pure,
> your violet flame for all is cure,
> consume the cause of all disease,
> and therefore I am all at ease.
>
> **O Saint Germain, what love you bring,**
> **it truly makes all matter sing,**
> **your violet flame does all restore,**
> **with you we are becoming more.**

7. I call for Archangel Michael and Astrea to consume the spirit that resents matter, and I accept that it is no more. Therefore, I am no longer feeding it my energy.

> O Saint Germain, I'm karma-free,
> the past no longer burdens me,
> a brand new opportunity,
> I am in Christic unity.
>
> **O Saint Germain, what love you bring,**
> **it truly makes all matter sing,**
> **your violet flame does all restore,**
> **with you we are becoming more.**

8. I accept that matter does not resist my effort to create a more spiritual life. I accept that matter is not going to conform to my current daydream about what it means to live a spiritual life.

> O Saint Germain, we are now one,
> I am for you a violet sun,
> as we transform this planet earth,
> your Golden Age is given birth.

**O Saint Germain, what love you bring,
it truly makes all matter sing,
your violet flame does all restore,
with you we are becoming more.**

9. I see that this idea of what a spiritual life should be is also an internal spirit, and I am letting it die.

O Saint Germain, the earth is free,
from burden of duality,
in oneness we bring what is best,
your Golden Age is manifest.

**O Saint Germain, what love you bring,
it truly makes all matter sing,
your violet flame does all restore,
with you we are becoming more.**

Part 6

1. As long as I am holding on to this internal spirit of what a spiritual life should be, I cannot see what I myself put into my Divine plan of how I want to live my life.

O Saint Germain, you do inspire,
my vision raised forever higher,
with you I form a figure-eight,
your Golden Age I co-create.

9 | Invoking Love for my Divine plan

> **O Saint Germain, what love you bring,**
> **it truly makes all matter sing,**
> **your violet flame does all restore,**
> **with you we are becoming more.**

2. I designed my Divine plan so that I will live a fairly active life in society, interact with other people and be the open door for bringing forth some ideas from the ascended realm.

> O Saint Germain, what Freedom Flame,
> released when we recite your name,
> acceleration is your gift,
> our planet it will surely lift.

> **O Saint Germain, what love you bring,**
> **it truly makes all matter sing,**
> **your violet flame does all restore,**
> **with you we are becoming more.**

3. Everyday life is improved by everyday, normal people coming up with ideas of how to do something better. New ideas are brought forth by people who have some attunement and some expertise or experience in the area.

> O Saint Germain, in love we claim,
> our right to bring your violet flame,
> from you Above, to us below,
> it is an all-transforming flow.

> **O Saint Germain, what love you bring,**
> **it truly makes all matter sing,**
> **your violet flame does all restore,**
> **with you we are becoming more.**

4. There is a vast difference between the daydream of what it means to have a spiritual life and what I actually put in my Divine plan. I let go of the idea of what it means to have a spiritual life, I let go of the resentment towards matter, and I see what I put in my Divine plan.

> O Saint Germain, I love you so,
> my aura filled with violet glow,
> my chakras filled with violet fire,
> I am your cosmic amplifier.

> **O Saint Germain, what love you bring,**
> **it truly makes all matter sing,**
> **your violet flame does all restore,**
> **with you we are becoming more.**

5. When I made my Divine plan, I looked at it very realistically and said: "What is my potential for growth in this lifetime? How can I best implement this, given my history, given my karma, given the other people I am tied to? Which kind of society do I want to embody in, so I can be an open door for the ascended masters and Saint Germain to bring forth new ideas?"

> O Saint Germain, I am now free,
> your violet flame is therapy,
> transform all hang-ups in my mind,
> as inner peace I surely find.

> **O Saint Germain, what love you bring,**
> **it truly makes all matter sing,**
> **your violet flame does all restore,**
> **with you we are becoming more.**

6. What has created the progress in society is new ideas, brought forth by people in practical life. Bringing civilization forward into Saint Germain's Golden Age is not an *idealistic* matter, it is a very *practical* matter.

> O Saint Germain, my body pure,
> your violet flame for all is cure,
> consume the cause of all disease,
> and therefore I am all at ease.
>
> **O Saint Germain, what love you bring,**
> **it truly makes all matter sing,**
> **your violet flame does all restore,**
> **with you we are becoming more.**

7. There is a gap between what spiritual people believe and reality. I want to overcome the gap so that I can manifest what I have in my Divine plan.

> O Saint Germain, I'm karma-free,
> the past no longer burdens me,
> a brand new opportunity,
> I am in Christic unity.
>
> **O Saint Germain, what love you bring,**
> **it truly makes all matter sing,**
> **your violet flame does all restore,**
> **with you we are becoming more.**

8. In order to overcome that gap, I adjust what is in my mind so I bring it down to a realistic, practical level. Saint Germain's Golden Age will be manifest by many people bringing forth a small idea.

> O Saint Germain, we are now one,
> I am for you a violet sun,
> as we transform this planet earth,
> your Golden Age is given birth.
>
> **O Saint Germain, what love you bring,
> it truly makes all matter sing,
> your violet flame does all restore,
> with you we are becoming more.**

9. The Golden Age is not about these magical, idealistic shifts. It is about taking one step at a time and that is the same for me. I surrender the idea that one day there will be a shift and suddenly I will have the spiritual lifestyle that I do not have now.

> O Saint Germain, the earth is free,
> from burden of duality,
> in oneness we bring what is best,
> your Golden Age is manifest.
>
> **O Saint Germain, what love you bring,
> it truly makes all matter sing,
> your violet flame does all restore,
> with you we are becoming more.**

Part 7

1. In my mind there is a gap between my practical situation and where my spiritual ideals say I should be. I see that in my mind, there is no realistic way to close that gap.

9 | Invoking Love for my Divine plan

> O Saint Germain, you do inspire,
> my vision raised forever higher,
> with you I form a figure-eight,
> your Golden Age I co-create.
>
> **O Saint Germain, what love you bring,**
> **it truly makes all matter sing,**
> **your violet flame does all restore,**
> **with you we are becoming more.**

2. How am I going to get from my practical everyday situation to living this spiritual lifestyle that I envision? I never will because the spiritual lifestyle that I envision is contrary to my Divine plan.

> O Saint Germain, what Freedom Flame,
> released when we recite your name,
> acceleration is your gift,
> our planet it will surely lift.
>
> **O Saint Germain, what love you bring,**
> **it truly makes all matter sing,**
> **your violet flame does all restore,**
> **with you we are becoming more.**

3. If I am attempting to manifest something that is contrary to my Divine plan, there will be a part of my subconscious mind that will sabotage my efforts.

> O Saint Germain, in love we claim,
> our right to bring your violet flame,
> from you Above, to us below,
> it is an all-transforming flow.

> **O Saint Germain, what love you bring,**
> **it truly makes all matter sing,**
> **your violet flame does all restore,**
> **with you we are becoming more.**

4. For a spiritual person, the self-sabotage syndrome means that when my conscious mind has adopted a goal that is contrary to my Divine plan, then I will subconsciously sabotage myself in order to avoid becoming trapped in an activity that takes me away from my Divine plan.

> O Saint Germain, I love you so,
> my aura filled with violet glow,
> my chakras filled with violet fire,
> I am your cosmic amplifier.

> **O Saint Germain, what love you bring,**
> **it truly makes all matter sing,**
> **your violet flame does all restore,**
> **with you we are becoming more.**

5. I see in my own life where I was tempted to move into a certain area but I sabotaged this goal. I make peace with the fact that it was because the conscious goal or desire I had was not in alignment with my Divine plan.

> O Saint Germain, I am now free,
> your violet flame is therapy,
> transform all hang-ups in my mind,
> as inner peace I surely find.

**O Saint Germain, what love you bring,
it truly makes all matter sing,
your violet flame does all restore,
with you we are becoming more.**

6. As long as I am fixating my mind on this unrealistic daydream, I will not be able to step back and have the stillness of mind where I can get a glimpse of my Divine plan.

O Saint Germain, my body pure,
your violet flame for all is cure,
consume the cause of all disease,
and therefore I am all at ease.

**O Saint Germain, what love you bring,
it truly makes all matter sing,
your violet flame does all restore,
with you we are becoming more.**

7. If I am to see something that I am not currently seeing with my conscious mind, I have to create a space in my mind where that vision can come through.

O Saint Germain, I'm karma-free,
the past no longer burdens me,
a brand new opportunity,
I am in Christic unity.

**O Saint Germain, what love you bring,
it truly makes all matter sing,
your violet flame does all restore,
with you we are becoming more.**

8. There is an energy veil that prevents me from seeing. What is blinding me is the energy veil that I have created and maintained in my own mind. That energy veil is created by my attention focusing on some of these unrealistic daydreams of what it means to be a spiritual person, what it means to live a spiritual lifestyle.

> O Saint Germain, we are now one,
> I am for you a violet sun,
> as we transform this planet earth,
> your Golden Age is given birth.
>
> **O Saint Germain, what love you bring,**
> **it truly makes all matter sing,**
> **your violet flame does all restore,**
> **with you we are becoming more.**

9. I see these idealistic ideas as a balloon and I am puncturing the balloon so it pops and they are all gone.

> O Saint Germain, the earth is free,
> from burden of duality,
> in oneness we bring what is best,
> your Golden Age is manifest.
>
> **O Saint Germain, what love you bring,**
> **it truly makes all matter sing,**
> **your violet flame does all restore,**
> **with you we are becoming more.**

Part 8

1. I realize that I am a slave of my attention. Where my attention goes, there goes my energy.

> O Saint Germain, you do inspire,
> my vision raised forever higher,
> with you I form a figure-eight,
> your Golden Age I co-create.
>
> **O Saint Germain, what love you bring,**
> **it truly makes all matter sing,**
> **your violet flame does all restore,**
> **with you we are becoming more.**

2. When I put my attention on a particular dream, my energies will go there. After I have put a certain amount of attention on this, it has created an energy veil that prevents me from seeing the vision in my Divine plan. I am so focused on the vision that I created in my outer mind that I cannot tune in to my higher mind.

> O Saint Germain, what Freedom Flame,
> released when we recite your name,
> acceleration is your gift,
> our planet it will surely lift.
>
> **O Saint Germain, what love you bring,**
> **it truly makes all matter sing,**
> **your violet flame does all restore,**
> **with you we are becoming more.**

3. The more energy I invest in something, the stronger this energy veil becomes and now it becomes an energy magnet that pulls on my attention.

> O Saint Germain, in love we claim,
> our right to bring your violet flame,
> from you Above, to us below,
> it is an all-transforming flow.

> **O Saint Germain, what love you bring,**
> **it truly makes all matter sing,**
> **your violet flame does all restore,**
> **with you we are becoming more.**

4. I put my attention on a certain matrix, I allow energy to flow into it. When the energy reaches a critical mass, it starts pulling on my attention to focus more and more on this. This becomes a spiral that can eat up all of my energy and attention.

> O Saint Germain, I love you so,
> my aura filled with violet glow,
> my chakras filled with violet fire,
> I am your cosmic amplifier.

> **O Saint Germain, what love you bring,**
> **it truly makes all matter sing,**
> **your violet flame does all restore,**
> **with you we are becoming more.**

5. I pierce the energy veil, shatter the energy veil, shatter that unrealistic daydream and see what I put in my Divine plan that is realistic and practical for me in this lifetime. I create that

opening, that stillness in my mind where I can suddenly see
through the energy veil.

> O Saint Germain, I am now free,
> your violet flame is therapy,
> transform all hang-ups in my mind,
> as inner peace I surely find.

> **O Saint Germain, what love you bring,**
> **it truly makes all matter sing,**
> **your violet flame does all restore,**
> **with you we are becoming more.**

6. When my attention has been pulled into focusing on a certain area, I cannot see beyond it as long as I am still focused on it. I pull my attention away from the area and create stillness in my mind, where the clouds part and a ray of sun can shine through from my I AM Presence.

> O Saint Germain, my body pure,
> your violet flame for all is cure,
> consume the cause of all disease,
> and therefore I am all at ease.

> **O Saint Germain, what love you bring,**
> **it truly makes all matter sing,**
> **your violet flame does all restore,**
> **with you we are becoming more.**

7. As long as I am focusing my attention on the dream, there is no attention left over for my I AM Presence. I am making a conscious decision to take a look at my dream about what it means to be a spiritual person. I am willing to question that

vision. I am willing to see if it isn't the highest. I am especially willing to see if it doesn't correspond with my Divine plan. If it does not, then I want to know and I want to let the unrealistic daydream go and I want to see what is in my Divine plan.

> O Saint Germain, I'm karma-free,
> the past no longer burdens me,
> a brand new opportunity,
> I am in Christic unity.

> **O Saint Germain, what love you bring,**
> **it truly makes all matter sing,**
> **your violet flame does all restore,**
> **with you we are becoming more.**

8. I realize that my daydream may be very detailed and what I receive from my I AM Presence is the next step I need to take. I am making the conscious decision that I am willing to let go of the dream and follow the inner promptings I get and take one step at a time.

> O Saint Germain, we are now one,
> I am for you a violet sun,
> as we transform this planet earth,
> your Golden Age is given birth.

> **O Saint Germain, what love you bring,**
> **it truly makes all matter sing,**
> **your violet flame does all restore,**
> **with you we are becoming more.**

9. If I get an impulse from my I AM Presence to do something very practical, I will follow this intuitive, inner prompting no matter where it takes me.

> O Saint Germain, the earth is free,
> from burden of duality,
> in oneness we bring what is best,
> your Golden Age is manifest.

> **O Saint Germain, what love you bring,**
> **it truly makes all matter sing,**
> **your violet flame does all restore,**
> **with you we are becoming more.**

Part 9

1. When I keep following the promptings from my I AM Presence, they *will* take me to the goal I defined in my Divine plan. I want to follow the realistic, practical vision I put into my Divine plan and *not* the idealistic but unrealistic daydream that I have come to accept with my outer mind.

> O Saint Germain, you do inspire,
> my vision raised forever higher,
> with you I form a figure-eight,
> your Golden Age I co-create.

> **O Saint Germain, what love you bring,**
> **it truly makes all matter sing,**
> **your violet flame does all restore,**
> **with you we are becoming more.**

2. I am willing to consider any spiritual movement I am into and consider what my Divine plan says I have to learn from that movement.

> O Saint Germain, what Freedom Flame,
> released when we recite your name,
> acceleration is your gift,
> our planet it will surely lift.

> **O Saint Germain, what love you bring,**
> **it truly makes all matter sing,**
> **your violet flame does all restore,**
> **with you we are becoming more.**

3. I want to know if it was in my Divine plan that I should go into that movement but it was not in my Divine plan that I should adopt the vision of that movement for what it means to be a spiritual person.

> O Saint Germain, in love we claim,
> our right to bring your violet flame,
> from you Above, to us below,
> it is an all-transforming flow.

> **O Saint Germain, what love you bring,**
> **it truly makes all matter sing,**
> **your violet flame does all restore,**
> **with you we are becoming more.**

4. I embodied where I embodied because I saw that this was the best way to help further Saint Germain's Golden Age. I reach for the vision of how I can help manifest the Golden

Age right here where I am instead of traveling somewhere that seems more spiritual.

> O Saint Germain, I love you so,
> my aura filled with violet glow,
> my chakras filled with violet fire,
> I am your cosmic amplifier.

> **O Saint Germain, what love you bring,**
> **it truly makes all matter sing,**
> **your violet flame does all restore,**
> **with you we are becoming more.**

5. I love first of all my I AM Presence and the vision that I put into my Divine plan. This is the vision that I myself put into my Divine plan when I had a broader perspective than I have right now.

> O Saint Germain, I am now free,
> your violet flame is therapy,
> transform all hang-ups in my mind,
> as inner peace I surely find.

> **O Saint Germain, what love you bring,**
> **it truly makes all matter sing,**
> **your violet flame does all restore,**
> **with you we are becoming more.**

6. I am shifting my perspective and I am free from this obsessive compulsion with these outer visions and goals, these daydreams. I have clarity on what is my practical reality that I put into my Divine plan.

> O Saint Germain, my body pure,
> your violet flame for all is cure,
> consume the cause of all disease,
> and therefore I am all at ease.
>
> **O Saint Germain, what love you bring,**
> **it truly makes all matter sing,**
> **your violet flame does all restore,**
> **with you we are becoming more.**

7. I breach the gap because I am no longer waiting to see a clear, spiritual step to take. I take all the many small practical steps that are improving my life and bringing me closer to what I put in my Divine plan.

> O Saint Germain, I'm karma-free,
> the past no longer burdens me,
> a brand new opportunity,
> I am in Christic unity.
>
> **O Saint Germain, what love you bring,**
> **it truly makes all matter sing,**
> **your violet flame does all restore,**
> **with you we are becoming more.**

8. I am fulfilled in knowing I am following all of the small steps in my Divine plan. The path is about taking one doable step at a time so that I am fulfilled in being at my present level.

> O Saint Germain, we are now one,
> I am for you a violet sun,
> as we transform this planet earth,
> your Golden Age is given birth.

**O Saint Germain, what love you bring,
it truly makes all matter sing,
your violet flame does all restore,
with you we are becoming more.**

9. Manifesting something is about having a realistic vision of what I *can* manifest, given my personal situation and given the planet I am on. I find the real gold, which is the vision in my Divine plan. I take every step and I will get where I wanted to go.

O Saint Germain, the earth is free,
from burden of duality,
in oneness we bring what is best,
your Golden Age is manifest.

**O Saint Germain, what love you bring,
it truly makes all matter sing,
your violet flame does all restore,
with you we are becoming more.**

Sealing:

In the name of the Divine Mother, I fully accept that the power of these calls is used to set free the River of Life, so it can outpicture the perfect vision of Christ for my own life, for all people and for the planet. In the name I AM THAT I AM, it is done! Amen.

10 | WELCOME TO REALITY SIMULATOR EARTH

I AM the Ascended Master Saint Germain, and for this fourth lesson at my retreat, we are dealing with the Fourth Ray of Purity or Acceleration. What is it I intend to purify? It is your view of the material realm, the physical octave, the physical universe.

My beloved, I have talked about how everything is made out of matter, which is really made of smaller particles, going all the way to energy. Truly, what is energy? Well, energy can be compared to what you have in the computer world where you deal with these on-off signals. Something is either on or off, only, of course, the energy that makes up the material universe is more complex than what you have in the computer world. So far, the level of computing that you have is very primitive because it is binary. It is based on only two possible signals, on or off.

The on-of screen of the matter universe

In reality, you are dealing with a system that has not just an on or off state. It has an on state and it has an off state but the on state is not simply that something is on. When something is on, it can take on seven different shadings or colorings, depending on the seven rays. In other words, you can imagine that the physical universe is made up (and this is the way it is most easy for you to see it) of a screen. The Ma-ter Light forms a screen. The screen is normally blank (or rather it is not normally blank but before anything was created, before the earth was created, the screen was blank) and then the Elohim imposed certain matrices on the screen that then caused these tiny little dots to turn on—and to turn on with the colorings of each one of the seven rays. You now have this screen that turns on, and it has a very complex pattern of these tiny dots that are colored according to the seven rays.

Understand, of course, that what I am giving you here is a symbolic representation that is not entirely linearly accurate. It is adapted to your current level of consciousness so it is something you can grasp with the images, with the understanding, you have of the universe. As you grow towards the 144th level, I do not want you to think that this is going to be the final understanding of how the universe works because you can, of course, attain deeper and deeper levels of understanding.

Nevertheless, for this, we will imagine that you are inside a room and the room is like a half a sphere. The sphere is like a dome above you and on the inside of this sphere is almost like a television screen where you have all of these dots that can turn on or off, which means that they can display absolutely any image that could possibly be imagined. Realize that this is how the universe works on planet earth. This is how planet earth was created. It was created by the Elohim by turning on all of these small signals and giving them a certain coloring according to each of the seven rays. This does not mean that everything you see on earth, including the unbalanced manifestations, is made up of the pure coloring of one the seven rays or a combination of the seven rays. There are also perversions of the seven rays and these are, of course, the ones that are used to create the unbalanced manifestations that you see today.

The earth is a reality simulator

The purpose for which I am giving you this illustration is to help you see that planet earth is simply a screen that can display various images. I am not saying that the earth could display *any* image because the Elohim chose a certain matrix for the earth, but within that matrix, the earth can display a wide variety of images. This means that the earth is capable of displaying the current imbalances that you see, but it is equally capable of displaying the harmonious state you had before humankind went into duality and before the fallen beings came here. It could also display an even higher state than you had back then, a higher state than was there when the Elohim created the earth. It was, of course, the intention that co-creators should raise the earth up from the original creation, and the first three waves of lifestreams did indeed do this.

What does this actually mean? It means that we could question: "Is the earth a real world?" I know we touched upon this in my first lesson but I am returning to it because you have now had time to process this idea. The reality that you come to is that the earth is *not* a real world. What, then, is the earth? We can compare it to what you today call a reality simulator. You know that you have these flight simulators. You may even have had one of these on your computer at one point. The computer screen displays what you would see from the cockpit of an airplane when you are taking off, flying and landing. You have many others of these simulators. You have virtual reality goggles today that you can put on and it seems like you are in an entirely different world.

What I want you to ponder with your conscious mind (because you are already seeing, experiencing, this at my retreat) is that the material universe is simply a reality simulator. What does it actually mean? First of all, it means that whatever you see on earth is not a real world, it is simulated but it is not simulated in order to seem like a simulation. It is simulated in order to seem *real*. You can go into a movie theatre and you know that the movie screen can display any movie. You also know that whatever movie you are watching in the movie theatre, it is not the real world you are watching. It is all made up, it is make-believe. You know this because you walked into the theatre and you know that when you go outside the theatre, you are seeing your hometown and not some little village in the Old West.

Now, imagine that you were born in the movie theatre, you grew up in the movie theatre you have never been outside. You have no idea that there is anything outside the movie theatre and *that* is your situation as being in embodiment on earth. You were born inside the reality simulator, for that matter you have lived inside it for many lifetimes. When you are born, you have no frame of reference that there is anything outside the simulator. You do not know that this is a simulation so how can you question it? You have nothing to compare it to. All you have ever seen and experienced is the simulation.

You may have some inner intuitive sensations based on a past life, maybe going back to when you came as an avatar, or going back as an original inhabitant of the earth when you experienced the earth in a purer state. You may have this inner sense that there must be something that is not right here, there must be something different, there must be another way for a world to be. You may even have a sense that you do not really belong here, that this is not your real environment, maybe even a sense that you are not meant to be here and many other sensations like this that spiritual people have. It is probably because you had those sensations that you ended up being a spiritual person who is studying spiritual teachings. Deep within you, you know that there is something beyond the material universe, you sense that there must be a spiritual world, there must be beings in that spiritual world and it must be possible to interact with those beings, which is exactly what you are doing right now. You can have these sensations and what I am asking you to do is to take these sensations and use them as your frame of reference to look at the earth and now recognize with your conscious mind: "This is simply a reality simulator."

Why the simulation seems real

Once you begin to ponder this idea, and get some intuitive validation that it really is a correct idea, then we can take the next step. Now, we can ask ourselves: "Why is it that the simulation of earth seems real?" We have given you an explanation of this. We have said that there are 144 levels of consciousness. We have said that when you first descend to earth, first take embodiment on earth, you start at the 48th level. We have also said that when you descend into embodiment, you take on an illusion for each of the levels from the 144th level to the 48th level. In other words, for each level of the 144, there is a certain illusion that you need to resolve, a certain enigma, a certain riddle, that you need to resolve before you are free of that level.

In order to descend to the 48th level, you take on an illusion for each of the levels from the 144th to 48th level and it is those illusions that make the earth seem like a real world. Of course, if you descend even below the 48th level (to the lowest level of consciousness), you take on more and more illusions and they make it seem even more real that the earth is an actual world, a world that is what it seems to be to your senses and to your outer mind.

Now, you have risen quite close to the 96th level and we are now dealing with a whole different level of consciousness where you have already shed many of these illusions. That is why you need to, at the conscious level, take this step of recognizing that the earth is a reality simulator. You also need to recognize a deeper understanding of how the earth simulates reality and here we already need to deal with words. What did I just say? "How the earth simulates reality." You see, my beloved, the earth does *not* simulate reality. This is an idea that you need to truly ponder so that it is locked into your conscious mind.

The earth is not a living thing that does anything or has any intention. Regardless of what some cultures may project (that nature is a living thing and that it has consciousness, which I am not denying), for the purpose of this initiation, what I want you to focus on is that the earth is a screen, the Ma-ter Light is a screen. It displays whatever image is projected upon it. It has no intention, it has no opinion about what should or should not be projected. It has no opinion about how you should experience what is projected. In other words, the earth does not do anything to you. It is not manipulating your mind, there is nothing here in the reality simulator that is manipulating your mind.

10 | Welcome to reality simulator earth

How does the earth simulate reality? It does not! Then, *what* simulates reality? Your mind, your four lower bodies simulate reality. The sense of reality that you have had about the world here on earth is entirely a product of your mind. This is the crucial idea that you need to get, not only at this level, but you need to keep that idea with you all the way to the 144th level because it is the one idea that will carry you to the 144th level.

What is it that you are dealing with when you go above the 96th level? Well, you are dealing with a different level of initiation than below. Below the 96th level, you are primarily focused on yourself, you see everything from a certain perspective, very centered around yourself. There are many questions you are not even able to ask or consider below that level. When you get to the 96th level, as I already said, the crucial initiation is: Will you continue to focus on yourself or will you focus on the whole?

In order to overcome these illusions (that pull you into focusing on yourself), you need to keep this idea in your mind that the earth does not simulate reality, but that any sense or view of reality that you have concerning the earth is a product of an illusion in your mind. This is a crucial idea, absolutely crucial as far as anything can be absolute inside a reality simulator. Nevertheless, there *is* something absolute about the reality simulator and that is that absolutely nothing is real. This means that there is absolutely nothing that can stop your spiritual growth, prevent your spiritual growth, hold you back in an illusion—except what is going on in your own mind. There is nothing absolute inside the reality simulator except the belief, the illusion, that you are not willing to question.

The prison is in your mind

If there is an illusion in your mind that you are not willing to question (because you think it does not need to be questioned, you are not allowed to question it or you think it is real), then that is the absolute that will hold you at that level almost indefinitely, at least until something happens that breaks down that illusion. I need you to recognize that an illusion, of course, is never absolute. It is an illusion. It is not real. It has no enduring quality whatsoever. It has no longevity, no existence except in the mind. It is *your* mind that assigns reality to what you see on earth. I need you to ponder this and I would like you to take a notebook and sit down with the invocation. Study this lesson first, then do the invocation associated with this lesson and then, after you have done the invocation, you spontaneously write down whatever comes to you that seems real on earth. I want you to do that for each of the nine days that you are doing this exercise, at least nine days (or even more if you do it more, and I actually recommend you do it more).

You will see that as you do this, there will be a certain progression. First of all, you will discover more and more things that you think are real. You will also realize that, as you do the exercise, some of the things you think are real will fade away. Not all of them will fade away because you will not jump to the 144th level (and I am not asking you to, I am not expecting you to). What I am asking you to realize is that, now that you are at this particular level, you have overcome a certain number of illusions from when you started this course. It is possible to overcome a certain illusion about yourself that helps you rise to the next level of consciousness, but you have not actually transferred that to how you look at the world. In other words, you can actually rise in consciousness by changing your own mind but there can be a certain overall view of life that you have not actually questioned. You are able to question it when you rise in consciousness, but it does not mean that you have consciously questioned it. What I am asking you to do during this lesson is to begin to consciously question your view of the world and what you think is real inside the reality simulator.

The ego makes everything seem real

My beloved, we have talked to you and given you very profound teachings on the human ego. You might say that the "real" reality simulator is your ego because it is your ego that makes everything seem real. Also, my beloved, it makes everything seem to matter: It is important, it has some significance.

This ties in with the teachings we have given about the duality consciousness. All of the illusions I am talking about up to 144th level are based on the duality consciousness and the sense of separation. You will not fully overcome the illusion that you are a separate being until you crack that last enigma at the 144th level, but you can certainly come much closer to seeing yourself as a being who is one with the All.

The other thing that comes out (and that we have talked extensively about) of the duality consciousness and the ego is the epic mindset, the mindset that there is something that has an ultimate and epic importance. This mindset is something that many spiritual students have taken and they have transferred it to the teaching that helped them discover the spiritual path. Many ascended master students have done this with the ascended master teachings, and this especially happened during the Piscean Age and the organizations we could sponsor there. These people who had not passed the initiations of Pisces, they needed, still, to feel that what they were doing was epically important and that they were, so to speak, saving the world for

Saint Germain and bringing the world into the Golden Age, the Aquarian Age.

Many other New Age and spiritual people have done the same, and you see many of these New Age groups out there who give their students this sense that it is epically important what they are doing. I am not belittling that what they are doing is important but what I am asking you to do, at this level of initiation, is to begin to truly, at the conscious level, question that epic mindset. Why am I doing this? For the very simple reason that my purpose is to teach you how to precipitate better circumstances for yourself and for the planet—in matter. This requires us to change matter. My beloved, how will you ever get better material circumstances if you cannot change matter? How will you ever be able to change matter with the mind if you think matter is unchangeable and if you think what happens in matter is so important that it can influence you as a spiritual being?

The epic trap that eats your attention

Do you not see, my beloved, that there are two aspects, two sides, of every coin? In duality, there are always two sides. What does the epic consciousness do for you? It gives you a sense that everything you do is important, that *you* are important. What is the other side of the coin, what is the price you pay for this sense that something is important? It is that you also think that there are certain conditions in the matter world that you cannot change. You may sit there (and there are many spiritual students who are in precisely this situation, including many ascended master students) and feel very important but it is a gilded cage.

10 | Welcome to reality simulator earth

You feel you are important but you are trapped in a cage and the fallen beings have you exactly where they want you. You are not where *I* want you because I want you to be free. I want you to get out of the cage and that is what I am aiming to teach you during this course. In this lesson we begin by questioning your sense of reality.

You think conditions in matter are real. For example, you think (to give you a primitive example) that there are these other people "over there" (if we go back a few decades) in the Soviet Union who are opposing your freedom in the West. You think they are a threat to the entire world and the freedom of the entire world. You feel that even though you are born in the West, you cannot just enjoy the freedom you have in the West because it could be gone tomorrow. You have to engage in an epic fight against the Soviet Union and this eats up all your time and all your attention. Doing this makes you feel very, very important but what if you instead had used the freedom you have to not fight somebody else but to work on yourself and overcome your illusions? Many, many people get trapped in this epic struggle where there is something they have to change.

Now, you take this to an ascended master student, and we have seen this over and over again. Ascended master students have reasoned: "It is epically important to overcome certain conditions in matter so we can move into the Golden Age." The way they can help do this is to give several hours of decrees a day. Again, it is not that it was not important and that it did not have an effect for people to give all these decrees and invocations, but the thing is, for many students it became an excuse. They were so focused on doing this very important thing that they simply did not have attention left over to focus on resolving the issues in their psychology.

Rising to the path to Christhood

Well, my beloved, it has never been our intention to have a student find the ascended master teachings at, say the 60th level of consciousness, and then the person rises to the 65th level of consciousness by studying the teachings. Then, it decides that: "Now, I have to focus on giving all these decrees to save the world for Saint Germain," and the person does not rise. For twenty years, the person gives lots of decrees but it does not rise in consciousness because it is not looking at itself and overcoming its illusions. This is not our intention. This does not actually do what the teachings have the potential to do because it does not help people rise closer to fulfilling their Divine plans. It may very well be that giving decrees and invocations is part of their Divine plan, but not to the point where it should eat up all other aspects of their Divine plan.

You see my beloved, we are at the point right now where we need you to step back from all of this and realize that (of course most of you have already realized that during the course) the key to progress is to work on yourself, look at yourself, overcome these illusions. What you need to look at right now is: "Why do I think certain things are real?" In a certain sense, we can say: Well, of course, there are fallen beings on the planet in the four levels of the material universe. There are many people who are at a lower level of consciousness who are promoting, expanding, intensifying, the struggle between themselves and other people. Yes, there is an entire planetary beast of this struggle that is constantly seeking to pull the planet into more and more conflict.

However, the question for you is: What does this mean for you? Not what it meant for you at ten or fifteen or twenty levels of consciousness below where you are at, but what does it mean for you right now? Is it of epic importance that you continue to fight this epic fight? Or is it of greater importance that you overcome the illusions that I am seeking to help you overcome so you can rise to the 96th level and go beyond the 96th level, and stop being focused on yourself and instead put yourself on the path to Christhood and Buddhahood that leads to the 144th level? That is what, in *my* mind, is important.

Questioning your view of the spiritual path

My hope is that during these initiations at my retreat, this will also be the most important thing for you in your conscious mind. This means you need to start questioning everything, including your view of the spiritual path. What is it that has brought you to the point where you are at, what has helped you? How have you looked at the path? Have you focused on outer things? Have these things seemed important to you? Have they seemed to have some epic importance?

You see, my beloved, it is true that there are fallen beings on the planet but what is the effect of them being here in terms of a spiritual student who is walking the path? What is it the fallen beings want to do? They want to take you away from the path to Christhood. As we have said many times over, engaging in the dualistic struggle against the fallen beings is not the path to Christhood and it will take you away from that path.

Whether you engage in a dualistic struggle against the fallen beings by fighting them with physical weapons or by fighting them with decrees and invocations, you are still engaged in the struggle. In order to get beyond the initiation at the 96th level, you need to get yourself disentangled from the struggle. What I am saying is this: "Is the epic struggle real?" Well, that depends on how you define reality. It is real in the sense that there *are* fallen beings on the planet. There is a certain collective consciousness. There *are* many people at lower levels of consciousness. That is real enough in the sense that it is a temporary condition that exists. It is not real in the sense that it has any eternality. It will not exist forever. It is a temporary condition but it is there right now.

The question is: "Do the fallen beings have any real reality? Do the conditions on earth have any real reality?" They are here but they are temporary. If they are only temporary, what does that mean for you? Well, who are you, *what* are you? Are you a human being walking the spiritual path? Or are you a spiritual being walking the path of initiation offered in the reality simulator called earth? You are, of course, a spiritual being. What does that mean? It means, my beloved, that the conditions that temporarily exist on earth right now do not have any power to alter your Spirit.

We have said it so many times! The Conscious You is pure awareness, which means it cannot be permanently changed by anything on earth. In fact, it cannot even be temporarily changed by anything on earth but it can, of course, take on these illusions that color the way it looks at the world. What have you done? You have taken on certain illusions. Again, no blame here, nothing wrong with it, it is part of the experience of being in the reality simulator. First, you immerse yourself, then you are awakened. You are in the process of awakening and it is time, at this level of initiation, that you awaken from this illusion that matter has an influence on you as a spiritual being.

Matter cannot change a spiritual being

My voice is intense, my beloved. It is not angry. I am not angry with you. I am not blaming you. I am simply accelerating your

10 | Welcome to reality simulator earth

consciousness to make it easier for you to have that click, that Aha experience at the conscious level that you have already had at the higher levels of my retreat, so that you experience the reality of what I am saying. The step you need to take now is to recognize consciously that there is no condition in matter that can alter you as a spiritual being. Why is this so important? Well, because how can you change matter if you think matter changes *you?*

What is it the fallen beings want you to think? They want you to think that (even if you think you are a spiritual being), you have come into this world and you have made a mistake that you can never undo. You are trapped forever by this mistake. You are a sinner, you have done this, you have done that and you can never overcome it. You may have come in here as a spiritual being but now that you are here, you have done something that has altered who you are as a spiritual being and therefore you can never get out of here. You can never get out of the struggle with the fallen beings as long as you believe in this illusion. What is your frame of reference in terms of the ultimate reality of earth? Well, your frame of reference is the fallen beings and the lies they have perpetrated on humankind for thousands and millions of years.

What I want, what we all want as the Chohans, is to have your frame of reference be the ascended masters so that you know that our teachings and the experience we can give you directly in your heart is the ultimate reality. The experience we all want to give you is that you are a Conscious You. You are pure awareness, which means that when you experience yourself as pure awareness, nothing on earth matters, nothing in matter matters. Matter does not matter. It has not altered who you are.

No matter how things are in matter, they cannot change you and therefore they ultimately do not matter to you. You see my beloved, why do you have a sense of reality about anything on earth? Yes, it is because you have taken on an illusion but what is the illusion? The illusion is that there is a certain condition in matter that matters to you but why would anything matter to you? Because you think it defines you. It defines who you are, what you *can* do and what you *cannot* do. It limits you. It traps you. Otherwise it does not matter.

Changing your perspective

Right now, you are sitting in a comfortable position somewhere that is probably a fairly warm room you are sitting in. Now, you can mentally project yourself to the South Pole where there may be a howling wind and the temperature is far below the freezing point. You would freeze in a matter of minutes if you were there. Now, these conditions are, you would say, quite real. They are there but do they matter to you? Well, no, because even though they may be real, they are not real where you are.

What I am asking you to do here is look at the earth, look at where you have grown up, the society, the situation you have grown up in. Look at the people around you and see how they are trapped in certain conditions and then look at those and say: "Do those conditions really matter to me anymore? Of course, they mattered to me when I was growing up. I grew up in this environment, I had a certain loyalty and affinity with my parents and the people around me and that was natural. But now I can step back, I can look at this and I can say: 'Does it really matter to me anymore,' given who I am now? Do these conditions matter? So will I let them continue to define me, define what I think I *can* or *cannot* do?"

10 | Welcome to reality simulator earth

Making a list

I know I am giving you a lot to ponder in this lesson but it is the Fourth Ray of Acceleration so what else can I do? I want to give you one more thing. I need you to step back, and again it might help you to do the invocation and then write down what comes to you afterwards. I need you to step back and consider which physical conditions, in the situation you grew up in, that you think you cannot change with the mind. It would be helpful for you to make a list and the list could consist of several items:

- You have a list of the conditions you think absolutely cannot be changed, no matter what. There is no power on earth, as they say, which can change the conditions on this list.

- You have a list of conditions that can be changed but it can only be changed by physical means. In other words, you may say that you have an empty plot of land and there is a potential to build a house on it. In order to build that house, you have to do the physical steps of digging the foundation, pouring the concrete, putting on the bricks, or building the wood structure, putting the roof on and so forth and so on. In other words, it requires physical labor, physical technology and then you can change certain things.

- The third list is things that you think could potentially be changed by the mind.

I need you to make these three lists and then see what conditions you have on the third list that you think could be changed with the mind. Then, when you look at those conditions that you think could be changed with the mind, I need you to make a fourth list, which is somewhat similar to the first list but nevertheless it is a specific list of things that you think could *not* be changed with the mind.

I need you to make these lists and then I will give you further instructions in my next lesson on how to use these lists, what to do with them and how to go through some shifts in your mind that question your sense of reality. You realize, I am sure, that the things you think cannot be changed with the mind, they are things to which your mind has ascribed this sense of absolute reality. My beloved, it is this sense of absolute reality that is imprisoning you in a gilded cage.

Even spiritual teachings, even ascended master teachings, can imprison you in a gilded cage where you feel you are one of the most advanced spiritual students on the planet. You are doing important work for Saint Germain so you feel that you are epically important. Nevertheless, you are still trapped because when you really consider how you look at the world and your relationship to the matter world, you think that matter defines you even though you also think you are a spiritual being.

The question here is: "What is real to you?" The reason this question is important is that what you think is real and what you think cannot be changed, *that* is what defines you. It defines how you see yourself as a being in physical embodiment on earth. It defines how you see yourself. You may see yourself as a spiritual being but you still see yourself as a spiritual being in the matter universe. You have a certain sense of how you can relate to the matter universe, what you *can* do and what you *cannot* do and this is what defines you.

I need you to start questioning what it is that defines you because in order to come up higher, you need to stop letting these matter conditions define you. Instead, you find a new way to define yourself as a being in the material realm.

11 | INVOKING A NEW SENSE OF REALITY

In the name I AM THAT I AM, Jesus Christ, I call to my I AM Presence to flow through the I Will Be Presence that I AM and give this invocation with full power. I call to Saint Germain to help me attain a new sense of what is *real* and what is *unreal* on earth. Help me overcome the illusion that matter can change me as a spiritual being, including ...

[Make personal calls]

Part 1

1. Everything is made out of matter, which is really made of smaller particles, going all the way to energy. Energy is a form of on-off signals.

> O Saint Germain, you do inspire,
> my vision raised forever higher,
> with you I form a figure-eight,
> your Golden Age I co-create.
>
> **O Saint Germain, what love you bring,**
> **it truly makes all matter sing,**
> **your violet flame does all restore,**
> **with you we are becoming more.**

2. When these signals are on, they can take on seven different shadings or colorings depending on the seven rays.

> O Saint Germain, what Freedom Flame,
> released when we recite your name,
> acceleration is your gift,
> our planet it will surely lift.
>
> **O Saint Germain, what love you bring,**
> **it truly makes all matter sing,**
> **your violet flame does all restore,**
> **with you we are becoming more.**

3. The physical universe is made up of a screen. The Ma-ter Light forms a screen. The Elohim imposed certain matrices on the screen that then caused these tiny little dots to turn on—and to turn on with the colorings of the seven rays.

> O Saint Germain, in love we claim,
> our right to bring your violet flame,
> from you Above, to us below,
> it is an all-transforming flow.

11 | Invoking a new sense of reality

**O Saint Germain, what love you bring,
it truly makes all matter sing,
your violet flame does all restore,
with you we are becoming more.**

4. The Ma-ter light is a screen with all of these dots that can turn on or off, which means they can display absolutely any image that could possibly be imagined. This is how the universe works and how planet earth was created.

O Saint Germain, I love you so,
my aura filled with violet glow,
my chakras filled with violet fire,
I am your cosmic amplifier.

**O Saint Germain, what love you bring,
it truly makes all matter sing,
your violet flame does all restore,
with you we are becoming more.**

5. Planet earth is simply a screen that can display various images within the range chosen by the Elohim. The earth is capable of displaying the current imbalances, but it is equally capable of displaying a harmonious state.

O Saint Germain, I am now free,
your violet flame is therapy,
transform all hang-ups in my mind,
as inner peace I surely find.

**O Saint Germain, what love you bring,
it truly makes all matter sing,
your violet flame does all restore,
with you we are becoming more.**

6. The earth is not a real world but a reality simulator. The material universe is a reality simulator. Whatever I see on earth is not a real world, it is simulated but it is not simulated in order to seem like a simulation. It is simulated in order to seem real.

O Saint Germain, my body pure,
your violet flame for all is cure,
consume the cause of all disease,
and therefore I am all at ease.

**O Saint Germain, what love you bring,
it truly makes all matter sing,
your violet flame does all restore,
with you we are becoming more.**

7. I was born inside the reality simulator, and I have lived inside it for many lifetimes. I have no frame of reference that there is anything outside the simulator. I do not know that this is a simulation so how can I question it? I have nothing to compare it to. All I have ever seen and experienced is the simulation.

O Saint Germain, I'm karma-free,
the past no longer burdens me,
a brand new opportunity,
I am in Christic unity.

11 | Invoking a new sense of reality

**O Saint Germain, what love you bring,
it truly makes all matter sing,
your violet flame does all restore,
with you we are becoming more.**

8. I do have some inner intuitive sensations that there must be another way for a world to be, that I do not really belong here, that this is not my real environment.

O Saint Germain, we are now one,
I am for you a violet sun,
as we transform this planet earth,
your Golden Age is given birth.

**O Saint Germain, what love you bring,
it truly makes all matter sing,
your violet flame does all restore,
with you we are becoming more.**

9. Deep within me, I know that there is something beyond the material universe. I sense that there is a spiritual world, there are beings in that spiritual world and it is possible to interact with those beings, which is exactly what I am doing right now.

O Saint Germain, the earth is free,
from burden of duality,
in oneness we bring what is best,
your Golden Age is manifest.

**O Saint Germain, what love you bring,
it truly makes all matter sing,
your violet flame does all restore,
with you we are becoming more.**

Part 2

1. I now take these sensations and use them as my frame of reference for looking at the earth. I now recognize with my conscious mind: "This is simply a reality simulator."

> O Saint Germain, you do inspire,
> my vision raised forever higher,
> with you I form a figure-eight,
> your Golden Age I co-create.
>
> **O Saint Germain, what love you bring,**
> **it truly makes all matter sing,**
> **your violet flame does all restore,**
> **with you we are becoming more.**

2. Why is it that the simulation of earth seems real? It is because I took on the illusions that brought me down to the 48th level of consciousness. It is those illusions that make the earth seem like a real world.

> O Saint Germain, what Freedom Flame,
> released when we recite your name,
> acceleration is your gift,
> our planet it will surely lift.
>
> **O Saint Germain, what love you bring,**
> **it truly makes all matter sing,**
> **your violet flame does all restore,**
> **with you we are becoming more.**

11 | Invoking a new sense of reality

3. I have already shed many of these illusions. At the conscious level, I take the step of recognizing that the earth is a reality simulator.

> O Saint Germain, in love we claim,
> our right to bring your violet flame,
> from you Above, to us below,
> it is an all-transforming flow.

> **O Saint Germain, what love you bring,**
> **it truly makes all matter sing,**
> **your violet flame does all restore,**
> **with you we are becoming more.**

4. Yet, the earth does not actually simulate reality. What simulates reality is my mind, my four lower bodies. The sense of reality that I have had about the world here on earth is entirely a product of my mind.

> O Saint Germain, I love you so,
> my aura filled with violet glow,
> my chakras filled with violet fire,
> I am your cosmic amplifier.

> **O Saint Germain, what love you bring,**
> **it truly makes all matter sing,**
> **your violet flame does all restore,**
> **with you we are becoming more.**

5. In order to overcome the illusions that pull me into focusing on myself, I will keep the idea in my mind that the earth does not simulate reality but that any sense or view of reality that

I have concerning the earth is a product of an illusion in my mind.

> O Saint Germain, I am now free,
> your violet flame is therapy,
> transform all hang-ups in my mind,
> as inner peace I surely find.
>
> **O Saint Germain, what love you bring,**
> **it truly makes all matter sing,**
> **your violet flame does all restore,**
> **with you we are becoming more.**

6. There is something absolute about the reality simulator and that is that absolutely nothing is real. There is absolutely nothing that can stop my spiritual growth—except what is going on in my own mind. There is nothing absolute inside the reality simulator—except the belief that I am not willing to question.

> O Saint Germain, my body pure,
> your violet flame for all is cure,
> consume the cause of all disease,
> and therefore I am all at ease.
>
> **O Saint Germain, what love you bring,**
> **it truly makes all matter sing,**
> **your violet flame does all restore,**
> **with you we are becoming more.**

7. If there is an illusion in my mind that I am not willing to question, then that is the absolute that will hold me at that level until something happens that breaks down the illusion.

O Saint Germain, I'm karma-free,
the past no longer burdens me,
a brand new opportunity,
I am in Christic unity.

**O Saint Germain, what love you bring,
it truly makes all matter sing,
your violet flame does all restore,
with you we are becoming more.**

8. An illusion is never absolute. It is an illusion. It is not real. It has no enduring quality whatsoever; it has no longevity, no existence except in the mind.

O Saint Germain, we are now one,
I am for you a violet sun,
as we transform this planet earth,
your Golden Age is given birth.

**O Saint Germain, what love you bring,
it truly makes all matter sing,
your violet flame does all restore,
with you we are becoming more.**

9. It is my mind that assigns reality to what I see on earth.

O Saint Germain, the earth is free,
from burden of duality,
in oneness we bring what is best,
your Golden Age is manifest.

**O Saint Germain, what love you bring,
it truly makes all matter sing,
your violet flame does all restore,
with you we are becoming more.**

Part 3

1. I have overcome a certain number of illusions from when I started this course, but it is possible to overcome a certain illusion without transferring that to how I look at the world.

> O Saint Germain, you do inspire,
> my vision raised forever higher,
> with you I form a figure-eight,
> your Golden Age I co-create.

> **O Saint Germain, what love you bring,
> it truly makes all matter sing,
> your violet flame does all restore,
> with you we are becoming more.**

2. I can rise in consciousness but there can be a certain overall view of life that I have not questioned. I will consciously question my view of the world and what I think is real inside the reality simulator.

> O Saint Germain, what Freedom Flame,
> released when we recite your name,
> acceleration is your gift,
> our planet it will surely lift.

11 | Invoking a new sense of reality

**O Saint Germain, what love you bring,
it truly makes all matter sing,
your violet flame does all restore,
with you we are becoming more.**

3. The "real" reality simulator is my ego because it is my ego that makes everything seem real. It also makes everything seem to matter, to be important and have significance.

O Saint Germain, in love we claim,
our right to bring your violet flame,
from you Above, to us below,
it is an all-transforming flow.

**O Saint Germain, what love you bring,
it truly makes all matter sing,
your violet flame does all restore,
with you we are becoming more.**

4. The ego is trapped in the epic mindset, the mindset that there is something that has an ultimate and epic importance.

O Saint Germain, I love you so,
my aura filled with violet glow,
my chakras filled with violet fire,
I am your cosmic amplifier.

**O Saint Germain, what love you bring,
it truly makes all matter sing,
your violet flame does all restore,
with you we are becoming more.**

5. I refuse to transfer the epic mindset to the teachings of the ascended masters or any other spiritual teachings or organizations.

> O Saint Germain, I am now free,
> your violet flame is therapy,
> transform all hang-ups in my mind,
> as inner peace I surely find.

> **O Saint Germain, what love you bring,**
> **it truly makes all matter sing,**
> **your violet flame does all restore,**
> **with you we are becoming more.**

6. I surrender the need to feel that what I am doing is epically important and that I am "saving the world for Saint Germain." I am consciously questioning the epic mindset.

> O Saint Germain, my body pure,
> your violet flame for all is cure,
> consume the cause of all disease,
> and therefore I am all at ease.

> **O Saint Germain, what love you bring,**
> **it truly makes all matter sing,**
> **your violet flame does all restore,**
> **with you we are becoming more.**

7. I want to learn how to precipitate better circumstances for myself and for the planet—in matter. This requires me to change matter.

11 | Invoking a new sense of reality

O Saint Germain, I'm karma-free,
the past no longer burdens me,
a brand new opportunity,
I am in Christic unity.

**O Saint Germain, what love you bring,
it truly makes all matter sing,
your violet flame does all restore,
with you we are becoming more.**

8. How will I ever get better material circumstances if I cannot change matter? How will I ever be able to change matter with the mind if I think matter is unchangeable, and if I think what happens in matter is so important that it can influence me as a spiritual being?

O Saint Germain, we are now one,
I am for you a violet sun,
as we transform this planet earth,
your Golden Age is given birth.

**O Saint Germain, what love you bring,
it truly makes all matter sing,
your violet flame does all restore,
with you we are becoming more.**

9. The epic consciousness gives me a sense that everything I do is important, that *I* am important. The price I pay is that I also think that there are certain conditions in the matter world that I cannot change.

O Saint Germain, the earth is free,
from burden of duality,
in oneness we bring what is best,
your Golden Age is manifest.

**O Saint Germain, what love you bring,
it truly makes all matter sing,
your violet flame does all restore,
with you we are becoming more.**

Part 4

1. I want to be free, and I am willing to question my sense of reality and why I think conditions in matter are real.

O Saint Germain, you do inspire,
my vision raised forever higher,
with you I form a figure-eight,
your Golden Age I co-create.

**O Saint Germain, what love you bring,
it truly makes all matter sing,
your violet flame does all restore,
with you we are becoming more.**

2. I will not use decrees and invocations as an excuse. I will focus my attention on resolving the issues in my psychology.

11 | Invoking a new sense of reality

O Saint Germain, what Freedom Flame,
released when we recite your name,
acceleration is your gift,
our planet it will surely lift.

**O Saint Germain, what love you bring,
it truly makes all matter sing,
your violet flame does all restore,
with you we are becoming more.**

3. The key to progress is to work on myself, look at myself, overcome my illusions. I am willing to look at why I think certain things are real.

O Saint Germain, in love we claim,
our right to bring your violet flame,
from you Above, to us below,
it is an all-transforming flow.

**O Saint Germain, what love you bring,
it truly makes all matter sing,
your violet flame does all restore,
with you we are becoming more.**

4. It is no longer of epic importance that I continue to fight some epic fight. It is of greater importance that I overcome the illusions so I can rise to the 96th level and go beyond to the path to Christhood.

O Saint Germain, I love you so,
my aura filled with violet glow,
my chakras filled with violet fire,
I am your cosmic amplifier.

**O Saint Germain, what love you bring,
it truly makes all matter sing,
your violet flame does all restore,
with you we are becoming more.**

5. I am questioning everything, including my view of the spiritual path and any sense that the epic struggle is real. The fallen beings have no real reality. The conditions on earth have no real reality. They are here but they are temporary.

O Saint Germain, I am now free,
your violet flame is therapy,
transform all hang-ups in my mind,
as inner peace I surely find.

**O Saint Germain, what love you bring,
it truly makes all matter sing,
your violet flame does all restore,
with you we are becoming more.**

6. If conditions are only temporary, what does that mean for me? Who am I, *what* am I? I am not a human being walking the spiritual path. I am a spiritual being walking the path of initiation offered in the reality simulator called earth.

O Saint Germain, my body pure,
your violet flame for all is cure,
consume the cause of all disease,
and therefore I am all at ease.

> **O Saint Germain, what love you bring,**
> **it truly makes all matter sing,**
> **your violet flame does all restore,**
> **with you we are becoming more.**

7. The conditions that temporarily exist on earth do not have any power to alter my spirit. The Conscious You is pure awareness, and it cannot be permanently changed by anything on earth.

> O Saint Germain, I'm karma-free,
> the past no longer burdens me,
> a brand new opportunity,
> I am in Christic unity.

> **O Saint Germain, what love you bring,**
> **it truly makes all matter sing,**
> **your violet flame does all restore,**
> **with you we are becoming more.**

8. I have taken on certain illusions, yet I am in the process of awakening. It is time that I awaken from the illusion that matter has an influence on me as a spiritual being.

> O Saint Germain, we are now one,
> I am for you a violet sun,
> as we transform this planet earth,
> your Golden Age is given birth.

> **O Saint Germain, what love you bring,**
> **it truly makes all matter sing,**
> **your violet flame does all restore,**
> **with you we are becoming more.**

9. I am allowing Saint Germain to accelerate my consciousness to have that Aha experience at the conscious level that I have already had in his retreat.

> O Saint Germain, the earth is free,
> from burden of duality,
> in oneness we bring what is best,
> your Golden Age is manifest.
>
> **O Saint Germain, what love you bring,**
> **it truly makes all matter sing,**
> **your violet flame does all restore,**
> **with you we are becoming more.**

Part 5

1. I recognize consciously that there is no condition in matter that can alter me as a spiritual being. This is important because how can I change matter if I think matter changes *me?*

> O Saint Germain, you do inspire,
> my vision raised forever higher,
> with you I form a figure-eight,
> your Golden Age I co-create.
>
> **O Saint Germain, what love you bring,**
> **it truly makes all matter sing,**
> **your violet flame does all restore,**
> **with you we are becoming more.**

2. The fallen beings want me to think I have made a mistake that I can never undo and that I am trapped forever by this mistake. I can never get out of the struggle with the fallen beings as long as I believe in this illusion.

> O Saint Germain, what Freedom Flame,
> released when we recite your name,
> acceleration is your gift,
> our planet it will surely lift.

> **O Saint Germain, what love you bring,**
> **it truly makes all matter sing,**
> **your violet flame does all restore,**
> **with you we are becoming more.**

3. I will no longer allow the fallen beings to be my frame of reference in terms of the ultimate reality of earth. I reject the lies they have perpetrated on humankind for millions of years.

> O Saint Germain, in love we claim,
> our right to bring your violet flame,
> from you Above, to us below,
> it is an all-transforming flow.

> **O Saint Germain, what love you bring,**
> **it truly makes all matter sing,**
> **your violet flame does all restore,**
> **with you we are becoming more.**

4. My frame of reference is the ascended masters and I know their teachings and the experience they give me directly in my heart is the ultimate reality.

> O Saint Germain, I love you so,
> my aura filled with violet glow,
> my chakras filled with violet fire,
> I am your cosmic amplifier.
>
> **O Saint Germain, what love you bring,
> it truly makes all matter sing,
> your violet flame does all restore,
> with you we are becoming more.**

5. I have the experience that I am a Conscious You. I am pure awareness. When I experience myself as pure awareness, nothing on earth matters, nothing in matter matters. Matter does not matter. It has not altered who I am.

> O Saint Germain, I am now free,
> your violet flame is therapy,
> transform all hang-ups in my mind,
> as inner peace I surely find.
>
> **O Saint Germain, what love you bring,
> it truly makes all matter sing,
> your violet flame does all restore,
> with you we are becoming more.**

6. No matter how things are in matter, they cannot change me and therefore they ultimately do not matter to me. I have a sense of reality about anything on earth because I have taken on an illusion.

11 | Invoking a new sense of reality

> O Saint Germain, my body pure,
> your violet flame for all is cure,
> consume the cause of all disease,
> and therefore I am all at ease.

> **O Saint Germain, what love you bring,**
> **it truly makes all matter sing,**
> **your violet flame does all restore,**
> **with you we are becoming more.**

7. The illusion is that there is a certain condition in matter that matters to me but why would anything matter to me? Because I think it defines me. It defines who I am, what I *can* do and what I *cannot* do. It limits me. It traps me. Otherwise it does not matter. I now see through this illusion.

> O Saint Germain, I'm karma-free,
> the past no longer burdens me,
> a brand new opportunity,
> I am in Christic unity.

> **O Saint Germain, what love you bring,**
> **it truly makes all matter sing,**
> **your violet flame does all restore,**
> **with you we are becoming more.**

8. I look at the people around me and see how they are trapped in certain conditions. Do those conditions really matter to me anymore? They mattered to me when I was growing up. I grew up in this environment, I had a certain loyalty and affinity with my parents and the people around me and that was natural.

O Saint Germain, we are now one,
I am for you a violet sun,
as we transform this planet earth,
your Golden Age is given birth.

**O Saint Germain, what love you bring,
it truly makes all matter sing,
your violet flame does all restore,
with you we are becoming more.**

9. I step back, I look at this and I say: "Does it really matter to me anymore, given who I am now? Do these conditions matter? Will I let them continue to define me, define what I think I can or cannot do?"

O Saint Germain, the earth is free,
from burden of duality,
in oneness we bring what is best,
your Golden Age is manifest.

**O Saint Germain, what love you bring,
it truly makes all matter sing,
your violet flame does all restore,
with you we are becoming more.**

Part 6

1. The things I think cannot be changed with the mind, they are things to which my mind has ascribed this sense of absolute reality. It is this sense of absolute reality that is imprisoning me in a gilded cage.

11 | *Invoking a new sense of reality*

O Saint Germain, you do inspire,
my vision raised forever higher,
with you I form a figure-eight,
your Golden Age I co-create.

**O Saint Germain, what love you bring,
it truly makes all matter sing,
your violet flame does all restore,
with you we are becoming more.**

2. I will not let ascended master teachings imprison me in a gilded cage where I feel I am one of the most advanced spiritual students on the planet, but I am still trapped.

O Saint Germain, what Freedom Flame,
released when we recite your name,
acceleration is your gift,
our planet it will surely lift.

**O Saint Germain, what love you bring,
it truly makes all matter sing,
your violet flame does all restore,
with you we are becoming more.**

3. I consider how I look at the world and my relationship to the matter world. I dismiss any belief that matter defines me because I fully accept that I am a spiritual being.

O Saint Germain, in love we claim,
our right to bring your violet flame,
from you Above, to us below,
it is an all-transforming flow.

> **O Saint Germain, what love you bring,**
> **it truly makes all matter sing,**
> **your violet flame does all restore,**
> **with you we are becoming more.**

4. What is real to me, what I think is real and what I think cannot be changed, *that* is what defines me.

> O Saint Germain, I love you so,
> my aura filled with violet glow,
> my chakras filled with violet fire,
> I am your cosmic amplifier.

> **O Saint Germain, what love you bring,**
> **it truly makes all matter sing,**
> **your violet flame does all restore,**
> **with you we are becoming more.**

5. It defines how I see myself as a being in physical embodiment on earth. It defines how I see myself.

> O Saint Germain, I am now free,
> your violet flame is therapy,
> transform all hang-ups in my mind,
> as inner peace I surely find.

> **O Saint Germain, what love you bring,**
> **it truly makes all matter sing,**
> **your violet flame does all restore,**
> **with you we are becoming more.**

6. So far, I have seen myself as a spiritual being but a spiritual being in the matter universe.

O Saint Germain, my body pure,
your violet flame for all is cure,
consume the cause of all disease,
and therefore I am all at ease.

**O Saint Germain, what love you bring,
it truly makes all matter sing,
your violet flame does all restore,
with you we are becoming more.**

7. I have had a certain sense of how I can relate to the matter universe, what I *can* do and what I *cannot* do—and this is what has defined me.

O Saint Germain, I'm karma-free,
the past no longer burdens me,
a brand new opportunity,
I am in Christic unity.

**O Saint Germain, what love you bring,
it truly makes all matter sing,
your violet flame does all restore,
with you we are becoming more.**

8. I am willing to question what it is that defines me because I want to come up higher, and I will no longer let these matter conditions define me.

O Saint Germain, we are now one,
I am for you a violet sun,
as we transform this planet earth,
your Golden Age is given birth.

> **O Saint Germain, what love you bring,
> it truly makes all matter sing,
> your violet flame does all restore,
> with you we are becoming more.**

9. With Saint Germain's help, I am finding a new way to define myself as a being in the material realm.

> O Saint Germain, the earth is free,
> from burden of duality,
> in oneness we bring what is best,
> your Golden Age is manifest.

> **O Saint Germain, what love you bring,
> it truly makes all matter sing,
> your violet flame does all restore,
> with you we are becoming more.**

Sealing:

In the name of the Divine Mother, I fully accept that the power of these calls is used to set free the River of Life, so it can outpicture the perfect vision of Christ for my own life, for all people and for the planet. In the name I AM THAT I AM, it is done! Amen.

12 | THE WAY YOU SEE THINGS CO-CREATES THOSE THINGS

I AM the Ascended Master Saint Germain, and for this fifth lesson we are dealing with the Fifth Ray of Vision. Vision, my beloved, is not what it has been made out to be, what you have come to see it as, as you grew up in the modern world. The image you have been given since you were a child is that vision is a passive thing. There is some objective thing out there, there is something called light that hits that thing, bounces back from the thing and then enters the retina of your eye where it is transformed into an image that your brain can see and process.

Vision changes over time

We have talked about this before of how this is an illusion because vision is not passive. The fallen beings want you to think it is passive and that is why they have managed to make all societies on earth bring up their children with this illusion of the passivity of vision.

Vision is, as we have mentioned before, an active thing. We need to talk more about why it is active and how this works. This, then, ties in with the lists I asked you to make in my last discourse. I had you make a list of things that absolutely cannot be changed. If we think about the wording here, I was playing a little bit of a trick on you by saying that I wanted you to make a list of "things" that absolutely could not be changed, or at least that no power on earth could change. I have said before that there is a certain matrix for the earth that was set and defined by the Elohim and there is no power on earth, not even the entire collective consciousness, that could change this. So there *are* things that absolutely cannot be changed.

Technology changes vision

Then, of course, you have been brought up in a world where there is a lot of technology. This brings us to the second list of things that *could* be changed but only by physical, technological means or by physical labor. Of course, modern technology (inspired primarily by me but also other ascended masters) has actually, within the last decades, made discoveries that in a way challenge many of the previous views of life. There were things a hundred years ago that people would say absolutely could not be changed but now you know that they *can* be changed.

The atom can be split, the very building block of matter, as it was seen at one point, can be split. There was a time when people would absolutely have denied that this was a possibility. You see that there has been some movement because of technology where things have now become possible that were not possible even decades ago. People in general have, of course, not adjusted their view of life based on this. I need you to start adjusting your view of life. I need you to recognize here

12 | The way you see things co-creates those things

what technology actually is. Why do you have, again to use this example, technology today that can split the atom? Why do you have technology that can even split subatomic particles into smaller components? It is because you have knowledge today that was not there in previous times.

Before Albert Einstein's theory of relativity came out in 1905, there was no knowledge of even the theoretical possibility of splitting the atom. That was because, at the time, scientists had a completely dualistic view of the world where they saw an absolute barrier between matter and energy. The world was made of two separate components and one could not be transformed into the other. Einstein, then, discovers the theory of relativity and realizes that all matter is actually a form of energy. This is completely in line with what I have told you previously. You need to start seeing that behind all of the visible forms that you see, there is pure energy. There is a complex pattern of energy waves, of on-and-off signals, of interference patterns between energies. This is the deeper reality.

Seeing everything as fluid

The reason this is important is that when you see that there is an energetic reality below the level of matter (or the macroscopic level), you realize that this level of energy is fluid. You have certain physical phenomena, such as Mount Everest or any other mountain that you have personally seen. You look at this massive rock and you see that it is beyond any power to change. It is solid, it is massive. When you look beyond the physical level, the macroscopic level, you see that the deeper reality is that even this solid mountain is made out of vibrating energy and the energy is much more fluid than matter. There is at least a theoretical possibility that the energy that makes up the mountain could change. Of course, if the energy changes, matter *must* change with it. What Einstein actually did was that he changed the traditional view, the classical physical view, of cause and effect.

This, unfortunately, is something that scientists in general have not been willing to acknowledge. They have not been willing to acknowledge it at the surface level because they do not want to give up materialism, they do not want to see a link between matter and mind. At the deeper level, it is truly because they are blinded by the fallen beings who have managed to infiltrate the scientific establishment as they had influenced the Catholic church during the Middle Ages. (But that is beside the point, as I do not really want to go into a political discussion here.)

Seeing energy as cause and matter as effect

What I want to point out is that in the classical physical view of reality, it was seen that there was cause and there was effect. In other words, if a billiard ball is moving across a billiard table, this is a physical action. The ball is a physical thing that is moving in a physical space and there has to be a physical cause, namely a cue that hit the ball and set it in motion. This was how, in classical physics, people thought about cause and effect, a *physical* cause must have a *physical* effect.

Einstein shattered this view—if people had been willing to shatter it in their minds. He did this because he essentially said that matter, all matter phenomena, are effects. They are effects of an unseen cause called energy, in Einstein's view. We can go beyond this, but nevertheless in the Einsteinian view, the deeper cause of all matter phenomena is energy, the energy world. You may still say that there is a physical thing called a

12 | The way you see things co-creates those things

billiard ball and there is a physical cue that is hitting it, but the reason these physical things can exist is that there is an underlying cause of vibrating, fluid energy.

All solid physical things exist as an effect of an underlying cause of fluid energy. This is important to keep in mind. We will go even further. The reason scientists (or at least the materialistic variety of them) do not want to acknowledge Einstein's theories or the consequences of quantum physics, is that they do not want to give up their dream of objectivity. Due to the influence of the fallen beings, they have defined the dream of objectivity as making observations that are not influenced by the mind of the scientist.

This goes back to the attempt to distance science from the Catholic church and portray all religion as subjective. In other words, all experience in the mind is subjective and therefore the mind should be eliminated from science. What scientists or materialists do not acknowledge is that this is, of course, impossible to do because everything you do is done with the mind. It is far more constructive (if you want to be objective) to investigate how the mind influences your observations. Or, even influences what observations you choose to make, how you choose to make them and how you choose to interpret those observations afterwards. Then, it would have become obvious that there is no such thing as an objective scientific observation.

An observation means nothing unless it is interpreted, meaning put in a larger context. The context that materialists have created, of wanting to look only at the material universe for explanations, is highly subjective. It is not an objective worldview that materialists have created. It is as subjective as the medieval worldview created by the Catholic church. This is what they will not acknowledge.

Accepting that you have a subjective view

What we need to do here is to recognize something very simple. You are a spiritual student. You are at a certain level of consciousness. As we have explained to you, you are looking at life through the filter of certain illusions. Therefore, regardless of what scientists believe, you can make the determination with your conscious mind to accept that the way you look at life is entirely subjective. It is a product of the illusions that you still have, that you have not yet shed.

There is no need for you, as a spiritual student, as an individual, to seek some kind of objectivity. Now, I know there is a self in you that has a desire to spread your spiritual beliefs and knowledge to other people and to get other people to accept them. We are going to set that aside for now. We are simply going to set that aside and say that you, as an individual, can admit that the way you look at life is a product of your current state of consciousness, the illusions you have taken on to descend below the 144th level and that you have not yet shed. You do not need to seek an objective view of reality, as scientists are doing.

The question for you, therefore, is not what is the absolute truth, what is some objective reality. The question is simply this: How can you improve your current material conditions? How can you improve upon the conditions you have right now? It is not a matter of reaching some ultimate level. It is a matter of, as we have given you throughout this course, realizing that life improves one small step at a time. How can you come from the level you are at right now to the next level up and then continue to go up and thereby gradually improve your physical, material conditions so that they become in alignment with what I have said before: What is in your own Divine plan

12 | The way you see things co-creates those things

and what allows you to receive ideas that will help manifest my Golden Age. How can you do this?

Saint Germain's retreat is not made of things

What you can do is admit that you have been brought up with a distorted view of reality, a distorted view of cause and effect, a distorted view of matter and energy. This has led you, due to no fault of your own, to have certain beliefs about what *can* be changed and what *cannot* be changed. When you admit this, then you can see that the next logical step for you is to question how you look at reality, what you think *can* be changed and *cannot* be changed.

This is where we go into the other aspects of my lists, the lists I asked you to make. I asked you to make a list of things that you think can potentially be changed by the mind and then things that you think cannot be changed by the mind. These are, of course, the more important things for you to consider during this lesson, the fifth lesson at my retreat. What I show you at my retreat is something that I wish I could show all people in the physical but the technology is not there yet. I show you that what you see as matter is not at all the way it appears through your physical senses. When you are in your identity body at my retreat, you are not experiencing my retreat through your physical senses. This is actually an important thing to ponder. I have talked about the fact that in previous ascended master dispensations, certain images of the Cave of Symbols were given. If you read those books, you will see that those images were very much based on people's sensory view.

In other words, due to the collective consciousness at the time, there could only be given a certain view of the Cave of

Symbols. It was based on the sensory view, extending that a little bit and then seeing something that you normally do not see with the senses but that you could *potentially* see with the senses. Of course, when you are in your identity body, you are not limited by the sensory perception. You have a whole different perception and, therefore, my retreat is not actually as physical, linear, as you would believe from your waking consciousness.

There really is no easy way to bridge that gap. There is no easy way to describe in words what my retreat is like because your perception is so different. When you come back down into your physical body and wake up, then you are, of course, again seeing life through the physical senses. This is something you can begin to change. I am not saying that I expect you to fully change this as a result of this lesson or even as a result of this course. It takes that you move closer to the 144th level before you can truly free your vision from the physical senses. But you can begin. You can begin by realizing in your conscious mind (as I have said) that vision is an active faculty.

How vision is programmed

You see my beloved, you have all learned to ride a bicycle. What you will recall, if you think back to this, is that in the beginning it was very difficult to keep your balance. Then, there came a point where this became automatic. This is because there are many, many things in the physical octave (there are many things you do with the physical body) that would require a lot of attention—unless your four lower bodies had the ability to act like a computer and create these programs that can, so to speak, "run in the background." Today, when you get on a bicycle, you do not have to put your attention on keeping

12 | The way you see things co-creates those things

the balance. You just get on there and there is a program in your subconscious mind that takes over and it is completely automatic. You have your attention left over to look at the surroundings or even to pull out your phone and look at the latest text message, as you constantly see people doing when they bicycle in the cities around the world.

What you need to realize here is that there are many of these programs. It is not that I am telling you that there is anything wrong with this or that these programs are malicious. I am just telling you that it is time to be aware that when it comes to seeing something – to actually using your physical eyes – there is a program in your four lower bodies that is meant to make your vision automatic. This is actually something that there is a field of science that has studied to some degree. It is called "pattern recognition."

What this program does, is it looks at patterns. What have I told you? I have told you that the entire world is made up of this very complex image. I have said it is like a screen with many, many small dots and these dots form these very intricate patterns. What your mind program does is it imposes certain images on this pattern. Now, if you can remember when you were a child, perhaps you took a newspaper photograph and looked at it through a magnifying glass. You could see that this black-and-white newspaper photograph was made up of smaller dots, black dots. It was the density of the dots that created the shade of gray that you saw in the photograph and this is, in a sense, how reality is.

When you looked at one of these old newspaper photographs, you did not see the individual dots. This was not actually because your eyes could not see them but because the subconscious program superimposed an image on the dots. You were looking for a pattern. The program was looking for a pattern.

People tend to name things

This, then, requires us to go back to one of these old religious scriptures, called *Genesis*. There is the story of how God created Adam as the first man. Now, of course, this is not an entirely accurate teaching. It is, in fact, influenced by the fallen beings, as you will see by the presence of the serpent in the Garden of Eden. Nevertheless, it is said in here that first God created all of the animals, and then God created Adam and then God gave Adam the power to name all the animals and plants and things in the earth. Whatever name Adam gave to them, that was the name. This, of course, is deeply influenced by the fallen beings—in a profound and fundamental way influenced by the fallen beings. They are in the consciousness of separation and it is only in the consciousness of separation that you need to name something.

Now, you think about this. Imagine you are on the African savanna and you see a complex pattern of colors and shapes. You could potentially look at this image as just an interaction of light rays, of smaller dots or even of certain shapes. You might even identify that there are certain shapes that are moving across the savanna while they are supposedly doing something to the grass. Others are different shapes and are reaching up to do something to the trees. Now, if you think back to primitive man who lived on this African savanna, the question was: How would he survive on the savanna? One of the big challenges was, of course, how to avoid being eaten by what you today call a lion.

What did this primitive man have to do? He had to create a pattern in the subconscious mind that could recognize the shape of a lion, recognize it as dangerous and therefore take immediate evasive action before the person could even consciously think through what was happening. You see here that

12 | The way you see things co-creates those things

out of this came a need to name something. "Lion! Dangerous! Move." This had to happen very quickly, so quickly that the conscious mind really did not have time to do this.

You see here that in the original Edenic state of the earth, there was not the same need to name things, to see them as separate things. After the fall into duality, there was a need to name something and to see it as an absolute thing. What has happened here is that you have been brought up, even in the modern world, to use your power of vision in such a way that you are not seeing energy, you are not seeing complex patterns of energy waves or dots or shapes. You are seeing "things" and you are naming those things. Your power of vision has been very much correlated with the language, the language of naming something with words.

This is not necessarily such a big problem. It becomes a problem when you reach the higher levels of the path. You need to start recognizing here that what at a certain level is a helpful feature (that, for example, helps you ride a bicycle) becomes a hindrance at the higher levels. Once you have named something as a thing, you think not only that it has an objective reality but you also think it is something separate. What does that mean?

How things become separate

It means that on the immediate level, it is separate from you. I am *here,* *there* is a thing that is my bicycle. It is separate from me. I can leave it in the garage when I walk into the house. I cannot leave my body in the garage when I walk into the house but I can leave my bicycle. It is a separate thing, it is separate from me. On a more subtle level, the bicycle has now become separated from the fabric of reality. It is a separate thing that is floating in space, or rather sitting on the ground, but nevertheless you get my meaning. It is a separate thing now. It is not connected to anything. What has happened here is that through this descent into duality, using your power of vision to look for these shapes and naming them as things that have some objective, separate existence, you have completely obscured the underlying reality that everything is connected and that everything is part of one whole.

Imagine you go to the ocean on a day where the wind is very strong and the waves are very high. Now, you imagine that you are seeing this ocean and you are seeing that the waves are a part of the ocean, obviously. They can be big, they can be turbulent, they can be very tall waves, there are troughs in between the waves. Nevertheless, you see that a wave is formed out of the ocean and it is not separated from it. Now, imagine that you could create a fog and the fog was just at a level where you could see the tops of the waves but not the ocean underneath. In that case, you would see all of these separate piles of water, shapes of water, and you would see them as being separate. You might even wonder: Where did that particular pile of water come from. Why did it suddenly appear right there? Is it at all connected to that other wave over there?

This is essentially what has happened to humankind as a result of this process I have described. You have come to see a world of separate things. You do not see that they are all connected because they are all expressions of the one underlying reality. What is the effect of this? Well, it is that you think that: "Here is a separate thing, it is separated from me, it is separated from my mind and therefore I have no way to influence it or change it with my mind. How could I possibly change this with my mind when there is no connection between my mind and the thing?"

12 | *The way you see things co-creates those things*

Finding a different way of seeing

In order to overcome this illusion (that there are so many things you cannot change and cannot change with the mind), you need to start questioning this view. You need to start very gradually realizing that there is a different way of seeing.

You might go and find some of these optical illusions that have been created that trick your eyes. You see something at first and then you take a closer look and now you see something different. You might take some of these popular pictures that show just a pattern of dots, but when you look closely, suddenly the shape of a dolphin emerges, or whatever it may be. You might use this to realize that you cannot totally rely on your senses. It is not really your senses but it is actually the program in the subconscious mind that takes your sensory input and superimposes this image based on pattern recognition, defining certain things and looking for those things.

You realize that when you are looking at something, you are not actually looking at what is there. The subconscious program looks at the scene, looks for patterns that it already recognizes, that are already stored in this database. Once it finds this, it simply superimposes this upon what you are seeing. You are actually, in many cases, seeing one thing with your eyes but your brain is displaying a different image inside your head. The brain displays the image created by this subconscious program that looks for patterns. Here is a lion. Here is a giraffe. Here is a zebra and so forth and so on. You are not looking at what is there because what is there is a complex pattern of energy waves, of dots, of on-and-off signals. What is there is fluid but in your mind it is turned into something absolute, something objective. You are thinking, you have been programmed to think, that what you are seeing is an objective reality that is outside of your mind and separated from the mind.

What I need you to start pondering here is that this is an illusion. It is time for you to begin to question it, for the simple reason that you will never be able to change anything with the mind if you see it as separated from the mind. For you, for your mind, to be able to change something, there must be a connection between your mind and the thing. Therefore, as long as you are looking at the world through this subconscious program that portrays everything as being separate things, then you will never be able to change your material, physical situation with the mind. It cannot be done.

Manifesting what seems possible

You look, again, at all of these books and courses that are out there about precipitating gold out of thin air. People are not successful for the simple reason that they are trying to do exactly this. They are trying to manifest things that they see as being separate from themselves. That is why what I desire for this course, is that you do not try to do some of these things that are already impossible from the outset—that you instead adjust your view here. That is why I said: "Adjust your expectation" so that you can do something, you can precipitate something that is more easy for you to accept as being possible. In other words, we want you to start with something that is clearly possible—that is possible for you to change by changing your mind.

Again, you may look at your physical situation and you may see that there are certain changes you would like to have happen. At this point, we may consider: How could these changes happen? I have already said that you do not want to force the

12 | The way you see things co-creates those things

free will of other people. If the changes require other people to change, that is not what I am asking you to focus on. I am asking you to pick a certain aspect of your life that does not require you to force other people in order to bring about a change. Then, I am asking you to take that situation and realize that even at the physical level, there are certain things that could happen, that are not necessarily miraculous changes. They just require you to make a shift so that you see something you do not currently see.

You may look (and you may have gone through it yourself in your life or you have seen other people go through it) at people who are going through a depression. They have gone into a downward spiral, they have adopted a very negative, limiting view of life or of themselves. They think they are no good: "I couldn't possibly get a good job, I am not good enough, I don't have the skills, I don't have the education, I don't have this, I don't have that." If you look at this situation, you will see that there are other people who have been in a similar situation at the physical, material level but, suddenly, something happened and they found a good job.

Why was it that the one person did not find a job but the other person did? It was because the second person was open to possibilities that the first person was not open to and therefore could not see. The first shift you can make here is that you can begin to look at your situation and realize that there are certain aspects of your situation that you have so far seen as being either impossible to change or difficult to change. Or you have, perhaps, not even thought about them as being changeable because you were brought up to think that this is just the way it is.

Seeing new possibilities

This messenger, for example, grew up in a relatively small town in Denmark and his entire family had been born and raised in that town. They all still live there and they are all going to be buried there. The possibility of moving to another town to get a better job did not occur to them. You could only conceive of getting the kind of jobs that were available in your hometown. Moving or getting an education or doing something else was simply not the way they were brought up to look at life. You see, of course, other people who are not afraid of moving, who are not afraid of seeking an education at some level and therefore manage to get better jobs. You can see here that it should be relatively believable for you at this level to look at your situation and ask yourself: "Are there actually opportunities that I'm not currently seeing because something in my attitude is blocking them out? I am not thinking that I could do this."

Again, you can look back at this messenger and you can see that from the time he was a child, he dreamed of being a writer. He was told as he was growing up that: "You can't make a living as a writer in Denmark because there are too few people who can read Danish." Not necessarily a completely unrealistic statement, although some writers in Denmark have managed to make a living from writing. Nevertheless, what did this messenger do? Well, as a child he always had a strong sense that he needed to learn English. Now, that he is writing in English, he has been able to make a living as a writer for some time.

I am not saying you need to do exactly the same thing, but you need to recognize that as you are brought up, you take on certain things from your family, from your surroundings, from your society. There are certain things where it is not that you deliberately consider them *impossible,* you just do not consider them *possible.* You do not even think about them as being possible and the people around you do not think about this as being a possibility.

This is something you can begin to look at right away and realize that there may actually be opportunities out there in the physical, already manifest in the physical. You just need to tune in to them and then you need to be willing to move and change accordingly. This may apply to many things in your life, such as relationships, where you live, how you live, your education, your career. Many, many people today have more than one career during a lifetime. They are not locked in to doing just one thing for the next 40 years once they have gotten a certain education or a certain job. Actually, society has become much more fluid. People, especially the younger generation, are much more fluid in their minds than the older generation.

All I am asking you, as a spiritual student at this level of initiation, is to, again, look at what are the things you have in your mind where your mind is not fluid, is not flexible. You think there are certain borders, certain limitations that you cannot go beyond. Then, you need to question those limitations and start going beyond them. This is at a very practical, doable level. Beyond that, I, of course, want you to go further. I want you to start questioning the very way you look at physical reality. I have already told you how to do this by looking beyond the level of things that you name.

The deeper level of reality

You need to see that beyond these things there is this deeper level of reality—the energy waves, the interference patterns, the on-off signals, the dots. You can actually train yourself to come to a point where, at least in glimpses, you can either see (not necessarily physically) or sense that all of the things you see around you are not solid, are not unchangeable. They are just expressions of this underlying level of fluid energy. Then, you can take this one step further and recognize: "What is it that at the macroscopic level makes everything seem as separate things? If they really are not separate (and scientists have proven over and over again that nothing is separate, that everything is interconnected), then why do they *seem* separate?"

They seem separate for one reason only. Your mind is superimposing that image upon them. It is your mind that makes them seem separate. You have been programmed to think that they are objective realities, that they are separate things but they are not. There is not any separate thing anywhere in the universe. Everything is part of the fabric of life. Once you begin to tune in to this, you realize that (as I have already told you) everything is a creation of the mind.

The Elohim created the planet, humankind has collectively created many of the current conditions but they are all creations of the mind. This means that from a certain perspective, there are no things that cannot be changed by mind. The question is: "Which mind?" There are certain things that can only be changed by a mind at the Elohimic level. There are certain things that cannot be changed at the level of mind of a human being. Nevertheless, there are many, many more things that can be changed at the level of the human mind than most people can accept.

That is what I am asking you to begin to question because there are two things that are involved with changing your outer situation. There is the alpha, the omega. The omega is that you attract conditions to you that are already in the physical. You attract that job, you attract that partner in a relationship. You are attracting, you become a magnet.

How do you become a magnet? Again, you need to overcome the sense of separation. In a sense, you could say that

12 | *The way you see things co-creates those things*

even the concept of a magnet reinforces the sense of separation because you see the magnet as an objective thing that is attracting some other objective thing. Nevertheless, I am using the image of magnetism here to show you that there are certain conditions that are already manifest in the physical. You just need to discover them, to magnetize them to you, to magnetize yourself to them, to attract them to you, to attract yourself to the circumstance.

It is not a matter of creating something that is not already in the physical. It is a matter of discovering it and realizing that right now it is the mindset you have that prevents you from discovering what is already there. This is the omega aspect of improving your situation, the omega aspect of manifestation.

Now, the alpha aspect is that you are actually materializing something that is not currently there in the physical world. This may sound mysterious, even magical, but it is not quite that magical. What have I said is one of the goals I would like you to set for yourself? It is that you become able to receive an idea from me that can help manifest the Golden Age. Look at this messenger again. All of the books he has written have been inspired from the ascended realm. He has manifested something that was not there in the physical before. This is, of course, not the only way of manifesting something but I am just giving you an example.

There is nothing mystical or magical about it. It is simply a matter of receiving an idea from the ascended realm that you bring through the three higher levels of your mind until it manifests at the physical level. This is not beyond what any of you can do. I am not setting a goal for you that is beyond what you can do and what you can begin to do at your present level of consciousness. Of course, I am not giving you the goal of manifesting gold out of thin air because you cannot do that at the present level of consciousness. In fact, most of the people who are at a level of consciousness where they can do it, choose not to do it for a variety of reasons. I am giving you a realistic goal here of what can be done, what you can do by beginning to shift your vision, shift the way you look at life.

Your situation is co-created

My beloved, I have talked about a reality simulator, and that the material universe is a reality simulator. Up until the level that you are at now, it has not been necessary for you to question the basic workings of the reality simulator. Now, you need to make this simple little shift of realizing that I have told you that the earth does not actually simulate reality—what simulates reality is your mind. It is your mind that gives this sense of reality so that you look at a thing: "This is a lion, this is a giraffe" and you think it has an objective reality. You are just naming something that is there.

You need to realize that you are not just naming something that is already there, you are co-creating something. Now, I know you are going to say (and it is a logical question): "Well, aren't there some things that are there, that I don't create with my mind?" Yes, of course. I have already told you the Elohim created the earth and humankind has collectively created many of the things you see on earth. There are things that are already there. You could say that if you died right now and were no longer in embodiment, lions and giraffes in Africa would not disappear. Of course they would not. The point I am making here is that the objective things, the things that are there in your mind, are not what matter to you.

I would say that the lions and the giraffes are not objective realities in the sense that science uses that word. They are still created by a mind, they are still creations of the mind, just not *your* mind. What I am saying here is: Fine, there are certain things out there that are not created by your mind. But your personal situation, even your physical situation, is co-created by your mind. It is not entirely created by your mind because, again, there are outer situations created by other people and so forth and so on. You are living inside of this reality simulator that is affected by other people, but there are certainly aspects of your personal situation that are co-created by *your* mind.

It is not, my beloved – ponder this very carefully – a matter of you seeing something that is there before you see it. There are certain aspects of your personal situation that are co-created by the act of you looking at them. It is by looking at them that you actually create these circumstances. You may not create all aspects of the circumstances but you create certain aspects of them that are affecting you personally. Your experience of life is co-created in your four lower bodies.

As we have said many times, what is the one thing you do have power to change? It is your own mind, the four levels of your mind. This you have the power to change, regardless of other people's choices, regardless of outer conditions. When you do change the way you look at life, certain aspects of your outer situation *will* change. Why is this so? How can I make this statement when it contradicts everything you have been brought up to believe? It is because I am an ascended master, my beloved, and I ascended by overcoming this illusion that I am seeking to help you overcome, namely the separation between mind and matter.

Changing your life experience

You see my beloved, as I said in a previous discourse, the weather at the South Pole does not matter to you when you are sitting here in your warm room. What matters to you is your experience of your surroundings, your experience of your own life. *That* is what matters to you. It is not necessary for you to change physical circumstances on earth in order to qualify for your ascension. The only thing that is necessary to change for you to qualify for your ascension is the conditions inside your four lower bodies.

The only thing that is necessary for you to change in order to have a more positive life experience than you are having right now, is the conditions inside your four lower bodies. There is a popular saying that has been going around in the New Age community. It is that: "When you change the way you look at things, the things you look at change." There is not necessarily an absolute reality to it (in the sense that you can change anything), but as I said, in your personal situation, there are things that you *can* change by changing the way you look at them.

You are at the level of initiation now where this is your next step. You need to recognize this, to acknowledge this, and therefore begin to look at how you look at things, how you look at your life, how you look at conditions.

Recognize that regardless of outer conditions, regardless of other people, regardless of the weather in Antarctica, there is *something* you can begin to change right now and it is the way you look at life. You can start to shift away from looking at all of these separate things. You can start to look beyond this image of solidity. You can start to see that everything is connected, that everything is fluid and why is it fluid?

How does the reality simulator of earth produce all of these phenomena that your senses tell you are separate, solid things? The reality simulator on earth has four levels, the identity, mental, emotional and physical. What is the physical? It is a screen. There is an image projected on the screen. How is that image projected on the screen of the physical world? It is projected by there being an image formed in the identity realm that sets certain overall parameters. Then, it is projected into the mental and there it becomes more concrete, more detailed. Then, it is projected into the emotional where it receives the impetus, the urge, the energy impulse that makes it physical.

I need you to begin to consciously shift your mind to where you realize that whatever you are seeing is not an objective world that exists out there. Whatever you are seeing is a projection on a screen of images that exist at the emotional, mental and identity level. Your situation right now—there are certain aspects of it that are not created by your four lower bodies, as I have said now many times. There are other aspects of it that are nothing but a projection on the screen of the physical world of the images you have in your emotional, mental and identity bodies. Those images you have the power to begin changing. You cannot snap your fingers and change them all at once but you can begin changing them. When you do, certain aspects of your outer situation will change. They *will* change, my beloved!

Go to a movie theatre if you need to and look at the screen. You will see that when there is no movie playing, it is just white, there is no image on it. You will see that whatever film you put into the projector, that image will be displayed on the screen. If you change the images, the filmstrips in your three higher bodies, you *will* change the image that is projected on the screen because it has no longevity in and of itself, it has no objective reality. It is an image that is projected on the screen of the physical world and it is projected many, many times every second. The light simply shines through those filmstrips in your three higher minds. Change the filmstrip, and you *will* change what is projected on the screen. It can be no other way, my beloved.

I know this contradicts everything you were brought up to believe. Of course, it does. That is the whole point of our course: to change so that you are not trapped by what you were brought up to believe. Because in that case, you definitely cannot make your ascension after this lifetime, as the fallen beings have done everything to program the collective consciousness, with the impossibility of ascending.

This is, in essence, what we have been doing from the very first lesson given by Master MORE in this course. It is time to step up and really begin to question the way you look at reality and realize that certain aspects of your situation are projections of the images you hold for what you think is possible, what you think *can* be changed, what you think *cannot* be changed.

Things are maintained by the mind

Do you see, my beloved, what I am saying here? You have been programmed to believe that there are certain aspects of your situation that have an objective reality outside your mind. They are outer conditions that are defining what you *can* and *cannot* do. I told you: "You are a spiritual being. You are not defined by physical conditions." What are you defined by? By the images in your own mind, *that* is what defines you. Can you change certain external conditions? No, because they are created by a different mind than yours. You *can* change those aspects of your situation that are created by *your* mind.

Why are there certain conditions that are maintained over time? Because there is still a filmstrip in your three higher bodies through which the light is shining. The light takes on that form and that is what is projected onto the screen. As long as you do not go to the three higher bodies and change what you believe is possible, you will continue to project that image, and

12 | The way you see things co-creates those things

it will take on what you think is an external circumstance that limits you.

The limitation is (not in all cases in your life but in many cases, many aspects of your life) only in your mind. You are not seeing that there is a different way to look at this. There is actually a whole different opportunity and there is a whole different possibility of precipitating something that you currently think is impossible. There are things that are impossible for you to change as a human being.

There are things that are impossible for you to change at your current level of consciousness. It is possible to raise your level of consciousness and change those things. There are things that you *can* change at your current level of consciousness. The only thing that prevents you from changing them is that you have a subconscious belief or program that makes you think it is impossible to change them. *That* is what you need to question at this fifth level of initiation at my retreat.

Is it an easy switch to make? No, my beloved! It is not. Now, if you monitor yourself, you will see that there will be a reaction in you, of a certain sense of relief by hearing me say this. There is an internal spirit, there is a separate self in you that does not want you to break free of this barrier, this limitation—because then it will die. It is not an *easy* switch to make but it is a *possible* switch to make at your present level of initiation.

That is why Master MORE did not confront you with this at the very first level of this course, but now it is possible for you to make this shift. When you do, you will find that it becomes a little bit easier to believe that certain aspects of your physical situation can actually be changed.

You will find it easier to believe that you can receive a new understanding, a new insight, a new vision, a new idea of how you can change something in your personal life (or even do something that can help manifest my Golden Age) by changing something in the outer world as you may see it.

This is what I wanted to give you for this lesson. As always, a big mouthful, but as we get closer and closer to the 96th level, of course, the initiations will in a sense be more subtle, more tricky, therefore require a little more explanation. I thank you for your attention, and I look forward to giving you the next lesson.

13 | INVOKING THE VISION OF HOW I CO-CREATE

In the name I AM THAT I AM, Jesus Christ, I call to my I AM Presence to flow through the I Will Be Presence that I AM and give this invocation with full power. I call to Saint Germain to help me overcome the program that causes me to see separate things. Help me see how I co-create my own circumstances through my four lower bodies, including ...

[Make personal calls]

Part 1

1. Vision is an active faculty. My eyes see energy waves, but my mind imposes patterns on these waves and calls them things. It then attaches an evaluation to these things and their potential for being changed.

> O Saint Germain, you do inspire,
> my vision raised forever higher,
> with you I form a figure-eight,
> your Golden Age I co-create.
>
> **O Saint Germain, what love you bring,**
> **it truly makes all matter sing,**
> **your violet flame does all restore,**
> **with you we are becoming more.**

2. There is an energetic reality below the level of things, and this level of energy is fluid. Even a seemingly solid mountain is made out of vibrating energy and the energy is much more fluid than matter.

> O Saint Germain, what Freedom Flame,
> released when we recite your name,
> acceleration is your gift,
> our planet it will surely lift.
>
> **O Saint Germain, what love you bring,**
> **it truly makes all matter sing,**
> **your violet flame does all restore,**
> **with you we are becoming more.**

3. There is a possibility that the energy that makes up the mountain could change, and if the energy changes, matter must change with it. Energy is cause, and matter is only effect.

> O Saint Germain, in love we claim,
> our right to bring your violet flame,
> from you Above, to us below,
> it is an all-transforming flow.

**O Saint Germain, what love you bring,
it truly makes all matter sing,
your violet flame does all restore,
with you we are becoming more.**

4. Matter, all matter phenomena, are effects. They are effects of an unseen cause, namely energy, the energy world. Physical things can exist because there is an underlying cause of vibrating, fluid energy.

O Saint Germain, I love you so,
my aura filled with violet glow,
my chakras filled with violet fire,
I am your cosmic amplifier.

**O Saint Germain, what love you bring,
it truly makes all matter sing,
your violet flame does all restore,
with you we are becoming more.**

5. I reject the materialist goal of objectivity by eliminating the influence of the mind. I accept that everything I do is done with the mind, and therefore everything I do is subjective.

O Saint Germain, I am now free,
your violet flame is therapy,
transform all hang-ups in my mind,
as inner peace I surely find.

**O Saint Germain, what love you bring,
it truly makes all matter sing,
your violet flame does all restore,
with you we are becoming more.**

6. I am a spiritual student. I am at a certain level of consciousness. I am looking at life through the filter of certain illusions. I accept that the way I look at life is entirely subjective. It is a product of the illusions that I still have, that I have not yet shed.

> O Saint Germain, my body pure,
> your violet flame for all is cure,
> consume the cause of all disease,
> and therefore I am all at ease.
>
> **O Saint Germain, what love you bring,**
> **it truly makes all matter sing,**
> **your violet flame does all restore,**
> **with you we are becoming more.**

7. There is no need for me as a spiritual student to seek some kind of objectivity. I admit that the way I look at life is a product of my current state of consciousness, the illusions I have taken on to descend below the 144th level.

> O Saint Germain, I'm karma-free,
> the past no longer burdens me,
> a brand new opportunity,
> I am in Christic unity.
>
> **O Saint Germain, what love you bring,**
> **it truly makes all matter sing,**
> **your violet flame does all restore,**
> **with you we are becoming more.**

8. I do not seek ultimate truth but knowledge of how to improve my current material conditions. I want to know what

is in my own Divine plan and what allows me to receive ideas that will help manifest Saint Germain's Golden Age.

> O Saint Germain, we are now one,
> I am for you a violet sun,
> as we transform this planet earth,
> your Golden Age is given birth.

> **O Saint Germain, what love you bring,**
> **it truly makes all matter sing,**
> **your violet flame does all restore,**
> **with you we are becoming more.**

9. I admit that I have been brought up with a distorted view of reality, a distorted view of cause and effect, a distorted view of matter and energy. I have certain beliefs about what *can* be changed and what *cannot* be changed. I am willing to question this view of reality.

> O Saint Germain, the earth is free,
> from burden of duality,
> in oneness we bring what is best,
> your Golden Age is manifest.

> **O Saint Germain, what love you bring,**
> **it truly makes all matter sing,**
> **your violet flame does all restore,**
> **with you we are becoming more.**

Part 2

1. What I see as matter is not at all the way it appears through my physical senses. I am beginning to free my vision from the physical senses. I am beginning to realize in my conscious mind that vision is an active faculty.

> O Saint Germain, you do inspire,
> my vision raised forever higher,
> with you I form a figure-eight,
> your Golden Age I co-create.

> **O Saint Germain, what love you bring,**
> **it truly makes all matter sing,**
> **your violet flame does all restore,**
> **with you we are becoming more.**

2. There is a program in my four lower bodies that is meant to make my vision automatic. This program looks for patterns in the complex image on the screen of the matter universe.

> O Saint Germain, what Freedom Flame,
> released when we recite your name,
> acceleration is your gift,
> our planet it will surely lift.

> **O Saint Germain, what love you bring,**
> **it truly makes all matter sing,**
> **your violet flame does all restore,**
> **with you we are becoming more.**

13 | *Invoking the vision of how I co-create*

3. The world is like a screen with many small dots that form these very intricate images. My mind program imposes certain patterns on what my eyes see.

> O Saint Germain, in love we claim,
> our right to bring your violet flame,
> from you Above, to us below,
> it is an all-transforming flow.
>
> **O Saint Germain, what love you bring,**
> **it truly makes all matter sing,**
> **your violet flame does all restore,**
> **with you we are becoming more.**

4. After humankind descended into the consciousness of separation, we started naming these patterns and we started seeing them as things that are separate from ourselves.

> O Saint Germain, I love you so,
> my aura filled with violet glow,
> my chakras filled with violet fire,
> I am your cosmic amplifier.
>
> **O Saint Germain, what love you bring,**
> **it truly makes all matter sing,**
> **your violet flame does all restore,**
> **with you we are becoming more.**

5. I have been brought up, even in the modern world, to use my power of vision in such a way that I am not seeing energy, I am not seeing complex patterns of energy waves or dots or shapes.

O Saint Germain, I am now free,
your violet flame is therapy,
transform all hang-ups in my mind,
as inner peace I surely find.

**O Saint Germain, what love you bring,
it truly makes all matter sing,
your violet flame does all restore,
with you we are becoming more.**

6. I am seeing "things" and I am naming those things. My power of vision has been correlated with the language of naming something with words.

O Saint Germain, my body pure,
your violet flame for all is cure,
consume the cause of all disease,
and therefore I am all at ease.

**O Saint Germain, what love you bring,
it truly makes all matter sing,
your violet flame does all restore,
with you we are becoming more.**

7. I am recognizing that what at a certain level is a helpful feature becomes a hindrance at the higher levels of the path. Once I have named something as a thing, I think not only that it has an objective reality but that it is something separate.

O Saint Germain, I'm karma-free,
the past no longer burdens me,
a brand new opportunity,
I am in Christic unity.

> **O Saint Germain, what love you bring,**
> **it truly makes all matter sing,**
> **your violet flame does all restore,**
> **with you we are becoming more.**

8. The thing my mind sees has become separated from the fabric of reality. It is a separate thing that is floating in space. It is not connected to anything.

> O Saint Germain, we are now one,
> I am for you a violet sun,
> as we transform this planet earth,
> your Golden Age is given birth.

> **O Saint Germain, what love you bring,**
> **it truly makes all matter sing,**
> **your violet flame does all restore,**
> **with you we are becoming more.**

9. Through the descent into duality, using my power of vision to look for these shapes and naming them as things that have some objective, separate existence, I have completely obscured the underlying reality that everything is connected and that everything is part of one whole.

> O Saint Germain, the earth is free,
> from burden of duality,
> in oneness we bring what is best,
> your Golden Age is manifest.

**O Saint Germain, what love you bring,
it truly makes all matter sing,
your violet flame does all restore,
with you we are becoming more.**

Part 3

1. I have come to see a world of separate things. I do not see that they are all connected because they are all expressions of the one underlying reality.

> O Saint Germain, you do inspire,
> my vision raised forever higher,
> with you I form a figure-eight,
> your Golden Age I co-create.

> **O Saint Germain, what love you bring,
> it truly makes all matter sing,
> your violet flame does all restore,
> with you we are becoming more.**

2. When I think that a thing is separated from me, is separated from my mind, I also think I have no way to change it with my mind. How could I possibly change this with my mind when there is no connection between my mind and the thing?

> O Saint Germain, what Freedom Flame,
> released when we recite your name,
> acceleration is your gift,
> our planet it will surely lift.

> **O Saint Germain, what love you bring,**
> **it truly makes all matter sing,**
> **your violet flame does all restore,**
> **with you we are becoming more.**

3. I want to overcome the illusion that there are so many things I cannot change with the mind. I am questioning this view and realizing that there is a different way of seeing.

> O Saint Germain, in love we claim,
> our right to bring your violet flame,
> from you Above, to us below,
> it is an all-transforming flow.

> **O Saint Germain, what love you bring,**
> **it truly makes all matter sing,**
> **your violet flame does all restore,**
> **with you we are becoming more.**

4. I realize that I cannot rely on my senses, or rather the program in the subconscious mind that takes my sensory input and superimposes this image based on pattern recognition, defining certain things and looking for those things.

> O Saint Germain, I love you so,
> my aura filled with violet glow,
> my chakras filled with violet fire,
> I am your cosmic amplifier.

> **O Saint Germain, what love you bring,**
> **it truly makes all matter sing,**
> **your violet flame does all restore,**
> **with you we are becoming more.**

5. When I am looking at something, I am not actually looking at what is there. The subconscious program looks at the scene, looks for patterns that it already recognizes, that are already stored in this database. Once it finds this, it simply superimposes this upon what I am seeing.

> O Saint Germain, I am now free,
> your violet flame is therapy,
> transform all hang-ups in my mind,
> as inner peace I surely find.
>
> **O Saint Germain, what love you bring,**
> **it truly makes all matter sing,**
> **your violet flame does all restore,**
> **with you we are becoming more.**

6. In many cases, I am seeing one thing with my eyes but my brain is displaying a different image inside my head because the brain displays the image created by this subconscious program that looks for patterns.

> O Saint Germain, my body pure,
> your violet flame for all is cure,
> consume the cause of all disease,
> and therefore I am all at ease.
>
> **O Saint Germain, what love you bring,**
> **it truly makes all matter sing,**
> **your violet flame does all restore,**
> **with you we are becoming more.**

7. I am not looking at what is there because what is there is a complex pattern of energy waves, dots, or on-and-off signals.

O Saint Germain, I'm karma-free,
the past no longer burdens me,
a brand new opportunity,
I am in Christic unity.

**O Saint Germain, what love you bring,
it truly makes all matter sing,
your violet flame does all restore,
with you we are becoming more.**

8. What is there is fluid but in my mind it is turned into something absolute, something objective. I have been programmed to think, that what I am seeing is an objective reality that is outside of my mind and separated from the mind.

O Saint Germain, we are now one,
I am for you a violet sun,
as we transform this planet earth,
your Golden Age is given birth.

**O Saint Germain, what love you bring,
it truly makes all matter sing,
your violet flame does all restore,
with you we are becoming more.**

9. I am questioning this illusion. I will never be able to change anything with the mind if I see it as separated from the mind. For me to be able to change something, there must be a connection between my mind and the thing.

> O Saint Germain, the earth is free,
> from burden of duality,
> in oneness we bring what is best,
> your Golden Age is manifest.
>
> **O Saint Germain, what love you bring,
> it truly makes all matter sing,
> your violet flame does all restore,
> with you we are becoming more.**

Part 4

1. As long as I am looking at the world through the subconscious program that portrays everything as being separate things, then I will never be able to change my material, physical situation with the mind.

> O Saint Germain, you do inspire,
> my vision raised forever higher,
> with you I form a figure-eight,
> your Golden Age I co-create.
>
> **O Saint Germain, what love you bring,
> it truly makes all matter sing,
> your violet flame does all restore,
> with you we are becoming more.**

2. Trying to precipitate gold out of thin air is impossible for the simple reason that we cannot manifest things that we see as being separate from ourselves.

O Saint Germain, what Freedom Flame,
released when we recite your name,
acceleration is your gift,
our planet it will surely lift.

**O Saint Germain, what love you bring,
it truly makes all matter sing,
your violet flame does all restore,
with you we are becoming more.**

3. I adjust my view, my expectation so I seek to precipitate something that I can accept as being possible for me to change by changing my mind.

O Saint Germain, in love we claim,
our right to bring your violet flame,
from you Above, to us below,
it is an all-transforming flow.

**O Saint Germain, what love you bring,
it truly makes all matter sing,
your violet flame does all restore,
with you we are becoming more.**

4. I realize that at the physical level, there are certain things that could happen that require me to make a shift so that I see something I do not currently see.

O Saint Germain, I love you so,
my aura filled with violet glow,
my chakras filled with violet fire,
I am your cosmic amplifier.

**O Saint Germain, what love you bring,
it truly makes all matter sing,
your violet flame does all restore,
with you we are becoming more.**

5. I look at my situation and realize that there are certain aspects of my situation that I have so far seen as being either impossible to change or difficult to change. Or I have not even thought about them as being changeable because I was brought up to think that this is just the way it is.

O Saint Germain, I am now free,
your violet flame is therapy,
transform all hang-ups in my mind,
as inner peace I surely find.

**O Saint Germain, what love you bring,
it truly makes all matter sing,
your violet flame does all restore,
with you we are becoming more.**

6. Are there actually opportunities that I am not currently seeing because something in my attitude is blocking them, and I am not thinking that I could do this?

O Saint Germain, my body pure,
your violet flame for all is cure,
consume the cause of all disease,
and therefore I am all at ease.

13 | Invoking the vision of how I co-create

> **O Saint Germain, what love you bring,
> it truly makes all matter sing,
> your violet flame does all restore,
> with you we are becoming more.**

7. I was brought up to take on certain things from my family, from my surroundings, from my society. There are certain things where it is not that I deliberately consider them impossible, I just do not consider them *possible*. I do not even think about them as being possible and the people around me do not think about this as being a possibility.

> O Saint Germain, I'm karma-free,
> the past no longer burdens me,
> a brand new opportunity,
> I am in Christic unity.

> **O Saint Germain, what love you bring,
> it truly makes all matter sing,
> your violet flame does all restore,
> with you we are becoming more.**

8. There are opportunities that are already manifest in the physical. I just need to tune in to them and then I need to be willing to move and change accordingly.

> O Saint Germain, we are now one,
> I am for you a violet sun,
> as we transform this planet earth,
> your Golden Age is given birth.

**O Saint Germain, what love you bring,
it truly makes all matter sing,
your violet flame does all restore,
with you we are becoming more.**

9. I look at what are the things in my mind where my mind is not fluid, is not flexible. I think there are certain borders, certain limitations that I cannot go beyond. I question those limitations and start going beyond them.

O Saint Germain, the earth is free,
from burden of duality,
in oneness we bring what is best,
your Golden Age is manifest.

**O Saint Germain, what love you bring,
it truly makes all matter sing,
your violet flame does all restore,
with you we are becoming more.**

Part 5

1. I start questioning the way I look at physical reality by looking beyond the level of things that I name.

O Saint Germain, you do inspire,
my vision raised forever higher,
with you I form a figure-eight,
your Golden Age I co-create.

> O Saint Germain, what love you bring,
> it truly makes all matter sing,
> your violet flame does all restore,
> with you we are becoming more.

2. Beyond these things there is this deeper level of reality—the energy waves, the interference patterns, the on-off signals, the dots.

> O Saint Germain, what Freedom Flame,
> released when we recite your name,
> acceleration is your gift,
> our planet it will surely lift.

> O Saint Germain, what love you bring,
> it truly makes all matter sing,
> your violet flame does all restore,
> with you we are becoming more.

3. I train myself to sense that all of the things I see around me are not solid, are not unchangeable. They are expressions of this underlying level of fluid energy.

> O Saint Germain, in love we claim,
> our right to bring your violet flame,
> from you Above, to us below,
> it is an all-transforming flow.

> O Saint Germain, what love you bring,
> it truly makes all matter sing,
> your violet flame does all restore,
> with you we are becoming more.

4. At the macroscopic level, everything seems to be separate things. They seem separate for one reason only. My mind is superimposing that image upon them. It is my mind that makes them seem separate.

> O Saint Germain, I love you so,
> my aura filled with violet glow,
> my chakras filled with violet fire,
> I am your cosmic amplifier.
>
> **O Saint Germain, what love you bring,**
> **it truly makes all matter sing,**
> **your violet flame does all restore,**
> **with you we are becoming more.**

5. I have been programmed to think that they are objective realities, that they are separate things but they are not. There is not any separate thing anywhere in the universe. Everything is part of the fabric of life. Everything is a creation of the mind.

> O Saint Germain, I am now free,
> your violet flame is therapy,
> transform all hang-ups in my mind,
> as inner peace I surely find.
>
> **O Saint Germain, what love you bring,**
> **it truly makes all matter sing,**
> **your violet flame does all restore,**
> **with you we are becoming more.**

6. There are many more things that can be changed at the level of the human mind than most people can accept.

O Saint Germain, my body pure,
your violet flame for all is cure,
consume the cause of all disease,
and therefore I am all at ease.

**O Saint Germain, what love you bring,
it truly makes all matter sing,
your violet flame does all restore,
with you we are becoming more.**

7. The omega aspect of changing my outer situation is that I attract conditions to me that are already in the physical. I am attracting. I become a magnet.

O Saint Germain, I'm karma-free,
the past no longer burdens me,
a brand new opportunity,
I am in Christic unity.

**O Saint Germain, what love you bring,
it truly makes all matter sing,
your violet flame does all restore,
with you we are becoming more.**

8. I become a magnet by overcoming the sense of separation. There are certain conditions that are already manifest in the physical. I just need to discover them, to magnetize them to me, to attract myself to the circumstances.

O Saint Germain, we are now one,
I am for you a violet sun,
as we transform this planet earth,
your Golden Age is given birth.

**O Saint Germain, what love you bring,
it truly makes all matter sing,
your violet flame does all restore,
with you we are becoming more.**

9. It is not a matter of creating something that is not already in the physical. It is a matter of discovering it and realizing that, right now, it is the mindset I have that prevents me from discovering what is already there.

O Saint Germain, the earth is free,
from burden of duality,
in oneness we bring what is best,
your Golden Age is manifest.

**O Saint Germain, what love you bring,
it truly makes all matter sing,
your violet flame does all restore,
with you we are becoming more.**

Part 6

1. The alpha aspect is that I materialize something that is not currently there in the physical world. This means I become able to receive an idea from Saint Germain that can help manifest the Golden Age.

O Saint Germain, you do inspire,
my vision raised forever higher,
with you I form a figure-eight,
your Golden Age I co-create.

13 | *Invoking the vision of how I co-create*

**O Saint Germain, what love you bring,
it truly makes all matter sing,
your violet flame does all restore,
with you we are becoming more.**

2. It is a matter of receiving an idea from the ascended realm that I bring through the three higher levels of my mind until it manifests at the physical level. This is not beyond what I can do. This goal is something I can do, and I can begin to do it at my present level of consciousness.

O Saint Germain, what Freedom Flame,
released when we recite your name,
acceleration is your gift,
our planet it will surely lift.

**O Saint Germain, what love you bring,
it truly makes all matter sing,
your violet flame does all restore,
with you we are becoming more.**

3. The material universe is a reality simulator and I am ready to question the basic workings of the reality simulator. The earth does not actually simulate reality—what simulates reality is my mind.

O Saint Germain, in love we claim,
our right to bring your violet flame,
from you Above, to us below,
it is an all-transforming flow.

**O Saint Germain, what love you bring,
it truly makes all matter sing,
your violet flame does all restore,
with you we are becoming more.**

4. My mind is not just naming something that is already there, it is co-creating something. There are certain things out there that are not created by my mind. But my personal situation, even my physical situation, is co-created by my mind.

O Saint Germain, I love you so,
my aura filled with violet glow,
my chakras filled with violet fire,
I am your cosmic amplifier.

**O Saint Germain, what love you bring,
it truly makes all matter sing,
your violet flame does all restore,
with you we are becoming more.**

5. It is not a matter of me seeing something that is there before I see it. There are certain aspects of my personal situation that are co-created by the act of me looking at them. It is by looking at them that I actually create these circumstances.

O Saint Germain, I am now free,
your violet flame is therapy,
transform all hang-ups in my mind,
as inner peace I surely find.

**O Saint Germain, what love you bring,
it truly makes all matter sing,
your violet flame does all restore,
with you we are becoming more.**

6. My experience of life is co-created in my four lower bodies. The one thing I do have power to change is my own mind, the four levels of my mind. This I have the power to change, regardless of other people's choices, regardless of outer conditions.

O Saint Germain, my body pure,
your violet flame for all is cure,
consume the cause of all disease,
and therefore I am all at ease.

**O Saint Germain, what love you bring,
it truly makes all matter sing,
your violet flame does all restore,
with you we are becoming more.**

7. When I do change the way I look at life, certain aspects of my outer situation *will* change. Even though this contradicts everything I have been brought up to believe, I am willing to overcome the illusion of the separation between mind and matter.

O Saint Germain, I'm karma-free,
the past no longer burdens me,
a brand new opportunity,
I am in Christic unity.

> O Saint Germain, what love you bring,
> it truly makes all matter sing,
> your violet flame does all restore,
> with you we are becoming more.

8. What matters to me is my experience of my surroundings, my experience of my own life. It is not necessary for me to change physical circumstances on earth in order to qualify for my ascension. The only thing that is necessary to change is the conditions inside my four lower bodies.

> O Saint Germain, we are now one,
> I am for you a violet sun,
> as we transform this planet earth,
> your Golden Age is given birth.

> O Saint Germain, what love you bring,
> it truly makes all matter sing,
> your violet flame does all restore,
> with you we are becoming more.

9. The only thing that is necessary for me to change in order to have a more positive life experience than I am having right now is the conditions inside my four lower bodies. In my personal situation, there are things that I *can* change by changing the way I look at them.

> O Saint Germain, the earth is free,
> from burden of duality,
> in oneness we bring what is best,
> your Golden Age is manifest.

13 | Invoking the vision of how I co-create

**O Saint Germain, what love you bring,
it truly makes all matter sing,
your violet flame does all restore,
with you we are becoming more.**

Part 7

1. I am at the level of initiation now, where this is my next step. I recognize this, I acknowledge this, and therefore I begin to look at how I look at things, how I look at my life, how I look at conditions.

> O Saint Germain, you do inspire,
> my vision raised forever higher,
> with you I form a figure-eight,
> your Golden Age I co-create.

> **O Saint Germain, what love you bring,
> it truly makes all matter sing,
> your violet flame does all restore,
> with you we are becoming more.**

2. I recognize that regardless of outer conditions, regardless of other people, regardless of the weather in Antarctica, there is *something* I can begin to change right now and it is the way I look at life.

> O Saint Germain, what Freedom Flame,
> released when we recite your name,
> acceleration is your gift,
> our planet it will surely lift.

> **O Saint Germain, what love you bring,**
> **it truly makes all matter sing,**
> **your violet flame does all restore,**
> **with you we are becoming more.**

3. I start to shift away from looking at all of these separate things. I start to look beyond this image of solidity. I start to see that everything is connected, that everything is fluid.

> O Saint Germain, in love we claim,
> our right to bring your violet flame,
> from you Above, to us below,
> it is an all-transforming flow.

> **O Saint Germain, what love you bring,**
> **it truly makes all matter sing,**
> **your violet flame does all restore,**
> **with you we are becoming more.**

4. The reality simulator of earth produces all of these phenomena that my senses tell me are separate, solid things. It does so because it has four levels, the identity, mental, emotional and physical. The physical is a screen. There is an image projected on the screen.

> O Saint Germain, I love you so,
> my aura filled with violet glow,
> my chakras filled with violet fire,
> I am your cosmic amplifier.

**O Saint Germain, what love you bring,
it truly makes all matter sing,
your violet flame does all restore,
with you we are becoming more.**

5. The image is projected on the screen of the physical world by there being an image formed in the identity realm that sets certain overall parameters. Then, it is projected into the mental and there it becomes more concrete, more detailed. Then, it is projected into the emotional where it receives the impetus, the urge, the energy impulse that makes it physical.

O Saint Germain, I am now free,
your violet flame is therapy,
transform all hang-ups in my mind,
as inner peace I surely find.

**O Saint Germain, what love you bring,
it truly makes all matter sing,
your violet flame does all restore,
with you we are becoming more.**

6. I consciously shift my mind and realize that whatever I am seeing is not an objective world that exists out there. Whatever I am seeing is a projection on a screen of images that exist at the emotional, mental and identity level.

O Saint Germain, my body pure,
your violet flame for all is cure,
consume the cause of all disease,
and therefore I am all at ease.

**O Saint Germain, what love you bring,
it truly makes all matter sing,
your violet flame does all restore,
with you we are becoming more.**

7. In my situation, there are certain aspects of it that are not created by my four lower bodies. There are other aspects of it that are nothing but a projection on the screen of the physical world of the images I have in my emotional, mental and identity bodies.

O Saint Germain, I'm karma-free,
the past no longer burdens me,
a brand new opportunity,
I am in Christic unity.

**O Saint Germain, what love you bring,
it truly makes all matter sing,
your violet flame does all restore,
with you we are becoming more.**

8. Those images, I have the power to begin changing. When I do, certain aspects of my outer situation will change. They *will* change!

O Saint Germain, we are now one,
I am for you a violet sun,
as we transform this planet earth,
your Golden Age is given birth.

> O Saint Germain, what love you bring,
> it truly makes all matter sing,
> your violet flame does all restore,
> with you we are becoming more.

9. This contradicts everything I was brought up to believe, but the whole point of this course is to change so that I am not trapped by what I was brought up to believe.

> O Saint Germain, the earth is free,
> from burden of duality,
> in oneness we bring what is best,
> your Golden Age is manifest.

> O Saint Germain, what love you bring,
> it truly makes all matter sing,
> your violet flame does all restore,
> with you we are becoming more.

Part 8

1. I question the way I look at reality and I realize that certain aspects of my situation are projections of the images I hold for what I think is possible, what I think *can* be changed, what I think *cannot* be changed.

> O Saint Germain, you do inspire,
> my vision raised forever higher,
> with you I form a figure-eight,
> your Golden Age I co-create.

**O Saint Germain, what love you bring,
it truly makes all matter sing,
your violet flame does all restore,
with you we are becoming more.**

2. I have been programmed to believe that there are certain aspects of my situation that have an objective reality outside my mind. They are outer conditions that are defining what I *can* and *cannot* do.

O Saint Germain, what Freedom Flame,
released when we recite your name,
acceleration is your gift,
our planet it will surely lift.

**O Saint Germain, what love you bring,
it truly makes all matter sing,
your violet flame does all restore,
with you we are becoming more.**

3. I am a spiritual being. I am not defined by physical conditions. I am defined by the images in my own mind, *that* is what defines me. I can change those aspects of my situation that are created by my mind.

O Saint Germain, in love we claim,
our right to bring your violet flame,
from you Above, to us below,
it is an all-transforming flow.

13 | Invoking the vision of how I co-create

> **O Saint Germain, what love you bring,**
> **it truly makes all matter sing,**
> **your violet flame does all restore,**
> **with you we are becoming more.**

4. Certain conditions are maintained over time because there is still a filmstrip in my three higher bodies through which the light is shining. The light takes on that form and that is what is projected onto the screen.

> O Saint Germain, I love you so,
> my aura filled with violet glow,
> my chakras filled with violet fire,
> I am your cosmic amplifier.

> **O Saint Germain, what love you bring,**
> **it truly makes all matter sing,**
> **your violet flame does all restore,**
> **with you we are becoming more.**

5. As long as I do not go to the three higher bodies and change what I believe is possible, I will continue to project that image, and it will take on what I think is an external circumstance that limits me.

> O Saint Germain, I am now free,
> your violet flame is therapy,
> transform all hang-ups in my mind,
> as inner peace I surely find.

> **O Saint Germain, what love you bring,**
> **it truly makes all matter sing,**
> **your violet flame does all restore,**
> **with you we are becoming more.**

6. The limitation is in many cases only in my mind. I am now seeing that there is a different way to look at this. There is a whole different opportunity and there is a whole different possibility of precipitating something that I currently think is impossible.

> O Saint Germain, my body pure,
> your violet flame for all is cure,
> consume the cause of all disease,
> and therefore I am all at ease.

> **O Saint Germain, what love you bring,**
> **it truly makes all matter sing,**
> **your violet flame does all restore,**
> **with you we are becoming more.**

7. There are things that I can change at my current level of consciousness. The only thing that prevents me from changing them is that I have a subconscious belief or program that makes me think it is impossible to change them. I question this program.

> O Saint Germain, I'm karma-free,
> the past no longer burdens me,
> a brand new opportunity,
> I am in Christic unity.

> **O Saint Germain, what love you bring,**
> **it truly makes all matter sing,**
> **your violet flame does all restore,**
> **with you we are becoming more.**

8. There is an internal spirit, there is a separate self in me that does not want me to break free of this barrier, this limitation—because then it will die. I am letting it die.

> O Saint Germain, we are now one,
> I am for you a violet sun,
> as we transform this planet earth,
> your Golden Age is given birth.

> **O Saint Germain, what love you bring,**
> **it truly makes all matter sing,**
> **your violet flame does all restore,**
> **with you we are becoming more.**

9. This is a big switch, but it is a *possible* switch to make at my present level of initiation. I make this switch, and I *know* that certain aspects of my physical situation *will* actually change.

> O Saint Germain, the earth is free,
> from burden of duality,
> in oneness we bring what is best,
> your Golden Age is manifest.

> **O Saint Germain, what love you bring,**
> **it truly makes all matter sing,**
> **your violet flame does all restore,**
> **with you we are becoming more.**

Sealing:

In the name of the Divine Mother, I fully accept that the power of these calls is used to set free the River of Life, so it can outpicture the perfect vision of Christ for my own life, for all people and for the planet. In the name I AM THAT I AM, it is done! Amen.

14 | OVERCOMING THE THINGS THAT TAKE YOUR PEACE

I AM the Ascended Master Saint Germain, and for this sixth level of initiation at my retreat, we are, of course, dealing primarily with the Sixth Ray of Peace. What does it take to be at peace at your level of consciousness on a planet like earth? Well, the question should really be reformulated: "What is the 'you' that has the potential to be at peace on earth?"

Making peace with having an outer self

We have, throughout this course, made it clear to you that you have an outer self and you have what we have called the Conscious You, which we could also call the inner self or the pure self. We have made it clear that when you start this course at the 48th level, you are fairly identified with the outer self, the Conscious You is fairly identified with the outer self. You are not *completely* identified with it or you would not be able to start the course. We have also made it clear that the major purpose of this course is to gradually decrease the Conscious You's sense of identification with the outer self. This now comes full circle where, at this level, you are ready to make a certain shift in your attitude, the way you look at yourself, and take a major step forward in this process of dis-identification.

We have made it clear that as you descend into embodiment on earth, you take on all of these illusions that correspond to the 144 levels of consciousness. Even though the goal of this course is to bring you to the 96th level, you still have quite a few illusions that you have not shed at that level and that you are not meant to have shed. This means that you will have elements of an outer self with you as long as you are in embodiment on earth. As you go higher towards the 144th level, it is actually these elements of the outer self that keep you in embodiment. They keep you tied to the physical body, otherwise you would simply not be able to stay in the physical body but would go out of it, even to the point where you might actually withdraw the life force. It can even happen that you could withdraw this prematurely, before you are actually quite ready to ascend. That would mean you would have to take another embodiment. Therefore, above a certain level, the outer self that you have left is a safety mechanism.

You realize, of course, that below the 48th level (where people are totally identified with the outer self) the outer self does not in any way assist your spiritual growth. What you do between the 48th and the 96th level is that you start dis-identifying yourself from that outer self, which means that you are not pulled back down by the collective consciousness. You are not pulled into following the currents in the mass consciousness. You are, so to speak, building an individuality that helps you separate yourself from the mass consciousness. You are not doing the things that all of these other people are doing. When you go above the 48th level, there comes a point where the outer self you have left is not actually a hindrance to your spiritual growth. This happens when you come to the point where you make peace with what I have just told you. You make peace with the fact that as long as you are remaining in embodiment, you will have elements of the outer self.

Giving up the dream of reaching an ultimate level

This means that you will have to give up a dream that many spiritual people have. It is even a dream that is very much in the collective consciousness and you see it outplayed in different ways. For example, you see some children's games where there is a certain zone that is defined as the home base or the home zone. If the children run into that zone, they cannot be taken by the other team. They are "home free," so to speak.

You also have the dream that many people have of winning the lottery so that one day, you just have more money than you could even spend for the rest of this lifetime. Or you have other dreams that people have of attaining immortality or perfect health, or some other state where now they can feel completely safe on earth. There are many spiritual people, including ascended master students, who when they find a spiritual teaching that talks about rising to higher levels of consciousness, they then formulate this dream that one day they will reach a level of consciousness where now they will be "home free." They will be enlightened. They will reach cosmic consciousness. They will be un-ascended ascended masters. They will be ego-free. They will be whatever people can dream of, but it is, in a sense, a dream of being on earth without being affected by anything on earth.

Now, it is important to look at this dream and recognize that you have it. All people have it. I had it when I was in my earlier embodiments and was not close to my ascension. We all have had this dream because it is part of the collective and we all live inside the collective. We only get free of the collective by looking at what is in the collective and overcoming it.

What you need to do here, at this level of my retreat, is to simply shift your mind a little bit. You need to recognize that you will have an element of the outer self with you as long as you are in embodiment. Then, you need to accept this and make peace with it. Of course, you will not be identified with that outer self, as you are not fully identified with it now. This means that the outer self does not really matter anymore. Once you come to the point where you are not identified with it and it is not running your life, then it does not really matter.

The outer self and your Divine plan

You realize that there can come a point where the outer self you have left is not really preventing you from fulfilling the goals you have set in your Divine plan. Therefore, you can outplay some outer self to a certain degree and it does not detract from your Divine plan. One of the ways this can manifest is that you can have certain legitimate desires of what you want to experience on earth. It is obvious that when you are above the 96th level, you do not have an outer self that wants to manipulate and control other people or make them feel bad or whatever it may be. You do not have an outer self that makes you want to do something illegal in order to get money, for example. You have risen above the more egotistical aspects of the outer self.

You might very well have had a long history on this planet where there are certain things, certain desires you have, certain experiences you would like to have and you might not feel that you have had quite enough of those experiences. Well, in that case, it is perfectly possible to continue to walk the path above the 96th level, still have certain desires that you have and you are still seeking to fulfill those desires but doing so in a balanced manner that does not disturb the progression of your Divine plan.

Just as one example, many, many people on earth still do not feel that they have quite fulfilled their desire for sex. Again, we have never said that when you reach the 96th level, you need to be celibate for the rest of your life. This has never been a goal that we have defined for you. If you exercise sexual activity in a balanced and responsible manner, you can perfectly well have sex and it does not detract from your Divine plan. This may go for other desires as well, such as the desire to have a certain materialistic lifestyle, to have a nice house, to travel and to see different places of the earth, whatever desires you may have that are not destructive desires.

You need to make peace with the fact that you have an outer self, that you will have an outer self, that it may affect the way you look at life and that it may pull you into seeking to fulfill certain desires. You need to be aware that this is okay as long as it does not disturb the progression of your Divine plan. This means that you go into a state where you are accepting that you have an outer self. You are not accepting that this will never change.

You are constantly monitoring yourself and your reactions. You realize that for each level of consciousness that you rise above the 96th level, you are going to have to see a particular illusion of the outer self and let it go. There is an inner spirit, there is a certain self that you need to let die. You are monitoring this constantly—not that you are in any way imbalanced about it, you are just being aware. You are monitoring your own reactions but you are not disturbed by it. You are not feeling that you are imperfect or not good enough because you have this outer self. You actually come to the point where, as other Chohans have talked about, you accept yourself for who you are right now. You accept that you are at a certain level of the path and that it is simply natural, inevitable for you to have a certain outer self.

Avoiding denial

The reason this is so important is that, as I have said from the beginning, the 96th level does present you with a very important initiation. You will see that if you monitor spiritual people, including ascended master students, there are some people that simply do not get, at the conscious level, the basic dynamic of the spiritual path. They simply do not make this shift in their minds where they realize that the outer self has to die—and that requires you to see it. Instead, they continue to believe in the illusion of the outer path, that we have talked about so many times, where you think that by doing a certain outer practice, you will automatically one day have shed the ego or the outer self.

They are still waiting for that moment to happen. You even see some people who have started this course with this dream that when they have finished the course, there will be this big "poof" and they will now be home free. Some of these people will be disappointed by coming to my last lesson and realizing it did not happen, it did not happen automatically.

You also see some people who go into a form of denial where they start looking at certain signs. As they climb up towards the 96th level, they recognize that they have made progress. They have overcome some of the things they had a number of years ago when they first started the path. They now begin to believe that they are advanced students. They have reached a certain level. Some of these people may even come to a point where they declare themselves to be ego-free or enlightened, or however their spiritual thought system defines the end goal of the path. You see throughout the spiritual, New Age, ascended master community, some people who go into this state of denial where now they actually believe that they no longer have an outer self or an ego but it is based on them denying what they have left.

I am seeking to help you avoid going into this denial, so you accept that you do have an outer self and you will have an outer self with you until you ascend. Therefore, by accepting this, you can make peace with that fact, you can make peace with yourself that you are a perfectly acceptable ascended master student even though you have an outer self left. We never actually said that we expected you to be free of the outer self while you are in embodiment. This you can make peace with. When you have made peace with this, you can build on it.

Making peace with matter

Naturally, I have a somewhat broad agenda for this lesson. Now, I did earlier talk about the hatred of the Mother, the hatred of the matter realm, of feeling that the matter realm is your enemy and is resisting you and so forth and so on. When you make peace with the fact that you do not have to be perfect in order to be acceptable to the ascended masters, then you can also make the shift of realizing that the earth or the matter realm does not have to be perfect in order for you to feel at peace with being here.

In other words, some of you are avatars who have come from a natural planet where matter is far less dense than it is on earth. Some of you are the inhabitants of the earth who have a certain inner memory of what it was like before the earth descended to its current density. You have a sense that things should not be the way they are. You need to make a shift here where you realize that, yes, of course, it is quite possible to have a higher state than what you currently have on earth. Of course, we of the ascended masters are gradually, slowly moving the planet towards that state. You are, of course, here to help with that.

You do not help us move the planet to a higher state if you are resisting the state that is here right now. If you are resisting what is here right now, you are subconsciously saying: "I can't be the Christ as long as the planet is this dense, I can't express my spiritual potential as long as the planet has these terrible manifestations." This is the illusion of focusing on outer things and it has caused many spiritual students to actually go into this detour (that I talked about earlier) where they now seek to use force to change other people or outer conditions.

This brings us to the point where you need to recognize here that planet earth is at a certain level of density right now. The collective consciousness has a certain density, a certain level of chaos and turmoil, a certain level of entropy, as you would say in thermodynamics. You need to accept that this is the current condition. You do not accept that it is permanent, that it will remain that way. You accept that you will make peace with current conditions. You will accept that these conditions not only make it possible for you to express Christhood but they actually are ideal for the expression of your Christhood. What is Christhood? We have said it many times: "Christhood is not some ideal condition, it is not a state of mind that can only be expressed in ideal conditions."

Look at Jesus when he walked the earth 2,000 years ago in Palestine. A very dark, a very dense area with a very, very dense collective consciousness, much more dense than most of you have grown up in, in this lifetime. Yet he still expressed Christhood because what is Christhood? It is that you challenge status quo, so no matter what status quo is, you can challenge it. You might even say that the lower status quo is, the easier it is to challenge it. This does not mean it is easy to express Christhood but it is certainly possible and this is what you need to accept. You need to accept that even though the earth has a certain density right now, it is still possible for you to fulfill the goals that you defined in your Divine plan because those goals were made with the awareness of the current density of matter. You did not define an *unrealistic* goal for yourself, you defined a *realistic* goal. In order to manifest that realistic goal, you need to accept that it is possible to manifest it, even with conditions as they are right now.

You also need to, then, start looking at your outer desires, your outer expectations. You need to recognize that many of these outer desires (that you might have carried with you from past lifetimes, that you might have adopted in childhood or that you might have formulated after you found a spiritual teaching, even an ascended master teaching), these desires are not realistic. They are based on this dream of being home free, of somehow finding a way to be on earth and be untouched by what is happening on earth. You need to recognize here that some of these desires are simply unrealistic and you need to let them go.

Your expectations of what should be

When you do that, you can make another shift. You can recognize that, truly, the biggest hindrance to you manifesting something on earth (manifesting, as I have said, a better material lifestyle, manifesting your Divine plan, manifesting balance or harmony between your spiritual and material life), the biggest hindrance to manifesting these goals is your expectations—your expectations of how things *should* be.

If you have an expectation that is built by the outer self and that expectation contradicts the goals in your Divine plan, then as long as you hold on to that expectation with your conscious mind, it will block the manifestation of your Divine plan. You will not be able to accept that the goals in your Divine plan descend to the physical level. Therefore, you will subconsciously block them, and many spiritual people have done this.

This means you now have to re-think what you may have read from these books that talk about how to manifest what you want. They will, for example, tell you if you are making a treasure map to be very, very specific. If you want to manifest a certain house, you have to be very specific of what it should have. You may even find an exact picture of what it should look like and be as specific as possible. What I am telling you now is to make a switch in your mind where you make your mind fluid, you make your expectations fluid.

You look at yourself and you look at: "Do I have certain goals and do I have a certain idea of how these goals should be fulfilled and how do I feel about them?" You might do the exercise of saying: "Okay, here are my goals, if I now was told by an authority figure that they absolutely could not be manifest, how would I react to that?"

If you would feel this very strong reaction, almost like a compulsory reaction, a sense of panic that these goals could not be manifest, then you know that these goals and expectations are based on the outer self. They come from the outer self, which cannot handle loss. Once the outer self has decided on a goal or an expectation, then anything short of the complete fulfillment of it would be experienced as a loss by the outer self. If you can identify this reaction in yourself, you know this comes from the outer self and that is when you need to take a look at these goals and expectations and realize that they just need to go.

You need to see that it is a particular internal spirit or outer self that is holding on to these goals and you need to let that self die. You will not be free of that self by fulfilling the goal, it would just create another goal for you, it would move the goalpost. You will be free of it only when you let that spirit die. You need to liquefy your expectations.

What they will also tell you in all of these precipitation books is that you need to formulate the goal, then you need to focus on it every day on a regular basis. You need to be very strong, very unmoved in your determination and your willpower, that you want this goal to manifest. You need to use your willpower to *will* it into manifestation.

No peace through force

Now, I am *not* telling you that what these books and courses are saying is a lie. It is perfectly possible to manifest things the way they describe, but it has nothing to do whatsoever with Christhood. Therefore, if you want to manifest things that way, you *can*. That is why I have said that you can come to the 96th level and you can start using your powers of mind to manifest certain things. You can do this, it is possible and people have done it.

It will not take you higher than the 96th level, which means you will eventually start going lower and become more and more self-focused. You can actually go all the way down to the lowest level possible on earth. You can, for that matter, go into the fallen consciousness. You see here that what I am telling you is to realize that you have risen to a certain level of consciousness, you have acquired certain abilities of the mind and you can use these outer techniques to manifest certain things that you want. What I desire to see, of course, is that instead of manifesting these outer desires, expectations and goals, you are manifesting what is in your Divine plan. In order to do that, you need to let go of these outer expectations and goals. You need to surrender them.

How will you attain peace at this level? Not by continuing to use your willpower and force your goals into manifestation. Even if you manifest a certain goal, there will just be another goal. This means that you can continue indefinitely using your willpower to force things into manifestation. You will not be at peace because as long as you are using force, you cannot be at peace at the same time. It is simply impossible to use force and be at peace. Of course, my beloved, if you cannot be at peace, you cannot be free, which is the 7th level of initiation and the one that will bring you, not only to the 96th level but put you on the path that brings you above the 96th level.

How can you be at peace? You cannot be at peace through force. You can only – and I say ONLY with capital letters – be at peace through surrender.

A higher way of manifesting

You may notice that there is a certain self in you that has a reaction to this statement. It might feel that you can never manifest something without being determined and using willpower, especially on a dense planet like earth. That is right! If you are at a certain level of consciousness, the only way to manifest something is to use strong willpower and force it into manifestation. By making a shift and rising above that level of consciousness, it is possible to manifest things that are in your Divine plan. Not necessarily what is in your outer self but certainly what is in your Divine plan. Now, how can you do this?

Well, you can consider which self it is that you want to manifest through. When you are using force, you are using the outer self. It is not really that you are manifesting only by the outer self, but you are manifesting *through* the outer self and the vision of the outer self. There are fallen beings who have been cut off from their I AM Presences. They can manifest only by using the energies that are already brought into the physical spectrum and they can manifest certain things that can be impressive to most people. You, of course, have not been cut off from your I AM Presence so you will not be manifesting exclusively by using the energies that are already in the material realm, although you will also be using them if you are doing it in a forceful way.

You will actually take some of the energies from your I AM Presence and you will use those to manifest the goals of the outer self. This is why, what has been called the left-handed path, can be so seductive. You see, you rise to a certain level and you have a greater connection to your I AM Presence. Therefore, you also have less identification with the outer self. You are able to actually use your willpower and force the light of your I AM Presence into the matrix defined by your outer self and therefore manifest these outer goals.

Now, of course, as you do this, what will happen is that gradually the amount of light flowing from your I AM Presence will be reduced. This is a safety mechanism to prevent you from making more and more karma and becoming more and more identified with the outer self, therefore going into a downward spiral. The light from your I AM Presence will be reduced. This could be a wakeup call and it has been for some people. When they felt they no longer had the power to manifest, they started wondering why and then they actually switched back to the true path.

The left-handed path

Others have gone a different route. They have continued on the left-handed path. Now, they have started using the energies that are already in the material realm to continue manifesting what they want. This is possible and there will come a certain point where, if you do this, you will become a disciple of one of the fallen beings who will teach you how to use what has been called black magic to manifest what you desire.

You see, you start out by using the light from your I AM Presence, then when it is no longer strong enough to manifest what you desire, you shift into using the energy that is already in the material realm. This, of course, means that you have to steal that energy from other people, and that puts you into an endless spiral of seeking to manipulate and control other people. When you do not go into this situation, you have to come to this point where you recognize that you do not want to manifest anything through the outer self. That means you have to go through a period where you are deliberately surrendering the goals, the desires and the expectations of the outer self. You give up the goals because with the outer self you can learn to recognize its goals. They will often have the dream of some ultimate state, some ultimate state of riches, some ultimate sexual experience, some ultimate spiritual experience. It is always extreme. It is always more than before. It is always some ultimate state. That is why it becomes a never-ending spiral, a never-ending quest for more and more conquest.

You can come to recognize these goals and then you surrender them. You can surrender this goal for an ultimate sexual experience without having to give up sex completely (although you may give it up for a time, if you so feel). The point is, there comes a phase here where the key to moving higher is to surrender, let go—surrender, surrender, surrender.

This really means that you go into a phase where you start realizing that although you can manifest certain desires through the outer self, you do not want to do this. Some of you (in fact, *all* of you) will have this temptation in some form but some of you will have it in a very concrete form. You will be faced with a situation where you could see that you could manifest your dream house by using force. You choose instead to surrender it, to surrender the dream of the dream house. What you will find is that sometimes this means that for a time, you will not have a dream house or any house.

Then, there may come a time where there will be another house that will manifest, which is not exactly like your dream house but it still facilitates the progression of your Divine plan in a better way than your dream house could have done. If you had forced that dream house into manifestation, there would have been certain strings attached. It would have required a certain amount of energy, time and attention from you. This means you would not have anything left over for other things, including aspects of your Divine plan. You begin to become more discerning of how you spend the time and energy so you do not spend it on the needs of the outer self to the point where it takes away from the fulfillment of your Divine plan.

Inner or outer desires

You can then also begin to make a shift that Jesus demonstrated when he himself said 2,000 years ago: "I can of my own self do nothing." As you can see, based on what I have told you, this requires some more explanation. Of course, Jesus could have done something out of his own self, meaning his outer self. He could have done some things with the level of consciousness he had. He could have manifested many things with his outer self. What he was really saying is: "I don't want to do anything out of my own self." He also said: "It is the Father within me—he doeth the works," meaning: "It is the I AM Presence and the higher vision of my Divine plan that is deciding what is to be manifest in my life."

You come to a point where you need to face this evaluation where you say: "Do I want the will of my outer self to decide what is going to be manifest in my life or do I want a higher will, my I AM Presence, the choices I made when I formulated my Divine plan to determine what is going to be manifest in my life?" This is what requires surrender. You surrender to that higher will. You say, as Jesus: "Not my will but thine be done." This does not mean that there is some God in heaven that is the ultimate control freak that is seeking to control you. What you are submitting to is not an *external* will. It is your own *internal* will that you used when you formulated your Divine plan.

Your outer self will, of course, say that you are submitting to an external will because to the outer self, your higher will is external. Really, to you, as the Conscious you, it is the will of the outer self that is external. The outer self is seeking to force its will upon you, contrary to what you actually chose when you were in that higher state of clarity when you formulated your Divine plan. You see, it is a matter of making that switch: "What do I truly desire?"

Really, you could say that it is a matter of what kind of experience do you desire to have for the rest of your lifetime? This is where we get into, we might say (from a certain perspective, at least), the major obstacle that people face on earth, the major challenge that people face on earth and it is the challenge of ownership.

The challenge of ownership

Look at this planet! Step back and look at this planet. Look at all the chaos, look at all the turmoil, look at all the changes: natural disasters, earthquakes, storms, wars, all of these things that are constantly uprooting people, destroying their homes, destroying entire cities. Is this really a planet where you want to explore all the avenues of ownership? Is it really wise to put yourself in a state of mind where you are driven by the desire to own something?

Take the dream house again. There is nothing wrong with living in a house that is comfortable, but do *you* own the house or does *the house* own you? This is the challenge faced on earth in a sense. You can own things on earth, yes you can, but there is always a price to be paid. It requires a certain amount of attention, time and energy. I am not even talking about money, although it also often requires money to own something. It requires your attention and in order to maintain what you have, once you have it, that also requires attention.

The question is: "What kind of experience do you want for the rest of your life?" Do you want the experience of having something, of owning something, or do you want the experience of growing? You understand, do you not, that ownership is still-stand and growth is movement. We have talked about flowing with the River of Life. You are not flowing with the River of Life by owning something. It does not mean you cannot own something and flow with the River of Life—but only if what you own does not own you. As long as you desire ownership, you will not be at peace on a planet like earth—it cannot be done. There will always be some threat you can imagine, and I can assure you that when you own something you do not want to lose, you will be able to imagine all kinds of threats that could take it away from you.

This messenger some time ago watched a documentary on TV about billionaires. He realized that if you believed everything that was said in there, all other people should feel sorry for the billionaires because it was so difficult for them to deal with having so much money. He, of course, laughed at this but there is a truth there, in the sense that the more people have, the more what they have, has them. The more they are owned by their possessions, the more energy and attention they spend on worrying about either accumulating more or not losing what they have. For many people, there comes a point where they have accumulated as much as they desired to have when they started. Now, they become worried about not losing it. This, of course, will not facilitate your growth towards the goals in your Divine plan.

Shedding the ownership self

You need to look at this, realize this is an outer self. It is very strong on this planet because the momentum in the collective consciousness is very, very strong—but what are you here for? You are here to raise yourself above the collective consciousness and thereby help raise the collective consciousness.

Of course, at this level of initiation you can shed this self. You can realize that you do not want to manifest the goals of the outer self and you do not want to manifest anything through the outer self. You do not want to manifest anything through force. How can you, then, manifest anything? Many people who have read these traditional books on manifestation will say: "Well, how can I manifest anything if I don't use force and will power, if I am not focused and if I am not focusing my energy? You are telling me to let go of all the goals and desires, to not be specific, to liquefy my mind and expectations. How can I then manifest anything?"

Well, my beloved, there was a wise man, some 2,500 years ago, who talked about the Middle Way. I am not telling you not to use any kind of will power or any kind of focus or any kind of determination. I am telling you to shift your focus away from the outer self and tune in to your Divine plan. I am actually also telling you to liquefy your mind and expectations, at least for a time, because it will take some time to let go of these expectations from the outer self. You need to go into an interim period where you are willing to sort of let things float, just float randomly on the surface of the water, letting the current take you.

You see, my beloved, there is a way to make decisions with the outer mind where you use willpower or you focus on a goal and you become very determined. You are, so to speak, pushing aside any opposition to the fulfillment of your goal. There is also another way where you let go of these outer desires and you go into the state that Jesus described: "Not my will but thine be done."

In other words, you are not saying you do not want anything to manifest in your life. You are just saying you do not want the will of the outer self to manifest. You want the higher will that you yourself defined when you formulated your Divine plan. You are willing to wait for that to happen. You are willing to *let* it happen, to let it unfold. You are willing to go into a state of mind where you think that you are not actually manifesting anything. You are not *forcing* anything into manifestation. You are *letting it drop* into manifestation.

Letting things manifest

You have, in the Arab world, the saying that an orange drops in your turban. You are sitting under an orange tree and an orange naturally drops. This is a state of mind that you are capable of going into at this level. You are not seeking to force the Ma-ter Light to give you what your outer self wants. You are giving the Ma-ter Light space to manifest what you, with your higher will, decided you wanted. You are allowing your higher desires to descend into physical manifestation instead of blocking them with all of these outer expectations. Do you see? It is possible to manifest through the forceful approach of the outer self. The alternative is to take what will at first (or at least to the outer self) seem like a passive approach—but it is not passive. It is simply reconnecting to your Divine plan and allowing that to manifest.

You see my beloved, many of the people who go into these courses and books about manifestation, they often do it from a state of lack because there is something they want. Often, it is money. They do not have enough money, they want to manifest this money and now they take these courses and they solidify this outer desire. Then, they use all of their willpower and determination to push it into the higher realms. They may not know about the three higher bodies as you do. Nevertheless, they are seeking – from the conscious level – to push into the emotional, mental and identity realm. When you do this from the conscious level, you first have to push into the emotional, then you have to push into the mental, then you have to push into the identity realm. Once you have pushed it into the identity realm, the impulse may actually turn around and start descending again.

The problem is, you only have a certain amount of energy available as you are sending that impulse into the emotional realm. There may be all kinds of turmoil in your emotional body that you have not resolved and that creates resistance. The energy wave that you are sending out with the conscious mind creates all kinds of interference patterns with the diffused and chaotic energies in your emotional body. By the time it reaches the mental, it is not only weakened, it may also be somewhat distorted. Again, you have different chaotic conditions, unresolved beliefs in your mental body so by the time it reaches the identity body, it is again diffused. You may again be unclear in your identity body who you really are, what you really want and so, again, there is a reduction and a distortion. By the time the impulse actually turns around and starts descending again, it has already been changed and reduced in strength.

Many, many people do this. They spend a certain amount of time because they get very enthusiastic about reading these books that promise them all kinds of things. They spend a certain amount of time and energy on it and then nothing happens. They sit there, not knowing why nothing has manifested or they give up on the whole thing, maybe even give up on the spiritual path because they were not really on the spiritual path, they were just looking for a quick fix. Or they may even have a situation where part of their goal manifests and now they really think this is the way to manifest everything. They try again and there comes a point where they realize it does not work. It is not working.

What I am asking you do to, is to do something different. I am asking you to let go of all the outer things and just be willing to float, to flow with the River of Life, to let life take you in whatever direction it wants to take you. What you are doing, then, is you are reaching up for what you already defined in your Divine plan. That means you are bypassing whatever resistance there may be from the outer self in your emotional, mental and lower identity bodies. You are going right to the source of what you formulated before you took embodiment. Then, you are connecting to that and you are willing to let that be manifest even if you currently do not see what it is, even if it is not in alignment with the outer expectations you had built at a certain point. You are willing to surrender those expectations and say: "Not my outer will be done but my higher will be done, whatever that will is. Come what may, I am going to accept it, I am going to receive it and I am going to be grateful for whatever I receive."

Manifestation through surrender

There are many people who have actually manifested something but it was not exactly what their outer selves wanted. They did not feel it was enough or they rejected it outright. There are people who have manifested certain opportunities but it was not what they ideally wanted so they did not go into it. Therefore, they missed a growth opportunity that they had defined in their Divine plans. I am asking you to, at this point, be willing to be liquid, be willing to let go of these very fixed images you have of how your life should unfold. Reconnect to that higher will that is your own will, that you had when you were not looking through the density of your four lower bodies.

This is an act of surrender that truly can bring you to a state of peace because you accept certain things. You accept the omega aspect of manifesting something on earth, which is that the earth is a certain density or that people have their free will, the collective consciousness is at a certain level. This sets limitations for what you can manifest. You cannot necessarily manifest the ideal condition you can envision because of all of these outer conditions. What you can always manifest is what facilitates your growth to a higher level of consciousness. That is the omega—making peace with things the way they are and making the best of it instead of complaining that things are not ideal.

The alpha aspect is that you go beyond the desires of the outer self. You reconnect to the higher desires that you yourself had before you took embodiment. You allow those to manifest and you accept that this is good enough, this is the opportunity you want and you will embrace it. You will make the best possible use of it and you will focus on growing from it instead of owning something.

There is a very important concept that Jesus actually expressed some time ago in a dictation where he said that we of the ascended masters are like used car salesmen who use the bait-and-switch technique. People are in such a low state of consciousness when they have not found the spiritual path that they have all kinds of dreams and desires. We have to give them something that they can relate to, that they can accept and that can motivate them to start the path. Then, of course, when they get higher on the path, we have to switch them into realizing that their initial desires were not realistic, and now, hopefully, they can adopt a higher desire that will put them on the path so they can continue towards the 144th level.

It is the exact same thing here. It is inevitable that when people start this course, they have certain desires, certain expectations and they are not the highest possible. How could they be at the 48th level of consciousness? How could you have a realistic expectation of what the spiritual path is about at the 48th level? You cannot. Other Chohans have mentioned the same thing. It is very important, now at this level, that you really come to the point where you look at these unrealistic expectations and you let them go.

Making peace with being imperfect

You especially need to make peace with the fact that you will not come to some ultimate state of enlightenment or cosmic consciousness (or whatever you want to call it) as long as you are in physical embodiment. You will have elements of the human consciousness with you until you ascend. You will see people on earth who will dispute this claim. Some will say it is an entirely false teaching. Some will say: "Well, surely Jesus or the Buddha or this guru or that guru or the next guru, manifested enlightenment." Well, that depends on how you define enlightenment. If you define enlightenment as being completely free of the outer self, then nobody has attained that state until right before they ascended. Jesus did not attain it until he was hanging on the cross and gave up the ghost, the final aspect of the outer self, the final expectation of the outer self.

You see here that, certainly, you could say that when you reach a certain level of consciousness, you have risen far above the 48th level, and therefore, you are more enlightened than you were. The problem is that you have seen people on earth who have declared themselves to be a guru and be enlightened or so forth. Now, they have begun to believe that they no longer need to look in the mirror. They do not need to look at the beam in their own eye because they have no more beam, they have no more ego left, they have no more outer self. This means that from that point on, they are not growing. What I am trying to give you is the realistic sense that you will need to be looking in the mirror, you will need to be growing, you will need to be overcoming things, you will need to surrender things, and you will need to let certain things die for as long as you are in embodiment. That is the only way you are going to make it to the 144th level and your ascension.

14 | Overcoming the things that take your peace

Do you think it was any different for me, my beloved? I had to do the exact same thing to qualify for my ascension. So did Jesus, so did Gautama, so did Master MORE, so did Kuthumi, so did Mother Mary, so did all of the people who have ascended from earth. We have all walked the path that we are teaching you how to walk. The difference is, most of us did not have ascended teachers, at least not that we were consciously aware of or that we were able to read a teaching, but you do. It is my hope that you will make use of that outer teaching and make that switch, make the switches I have talked about in this lesson so that you can be prepared to make the even bigger switch that I will talk about in my next lesson, which I look forward to giving you.

15 | INVOKING MANIFESTATION THROUGH SURRENDER

In the name I AM THAT I AM, Jesus Christ, I call to my I AM Presence to flow through the I Will Be Presence that I AM and give this invocation with full power. I call to Saint Germain to help me experience how to manifest through surrender. Help me overcome all desires to own something in this world, including ...

[Make personal calls]

Part 1

1. I make peace with the fact that as long as I remain in embodiment, I will have elements of the outer self.

> O Saint Germain, you do inspire,
> my vision raised forever higher,
> with you I form a figure-eight,
> your Golden Age I co-create.
>
> **O Saint Germain, what love you bring,**
> **it truly makes all matter sing,**
> **your violet flame does all restore,**
> **with you we are becoming more.**

2. I give up the dream that one day I will reach a level of consciousness where I will be "home free" or reach an ultimate level of spiritual attainment.

> O Saint Germain, what Freedom Flame,
> released when we recite your name,
> acceleration is your gift,
> our planet it will surely lift.
>
> **O Saint Germain, what love you bring,**
> **it truly makes all matter sing,**
> **your violet flame does all restore,**
> **with you we are becoming more.**

3. I recognize that I will have an element of the outer self with me as long as I am in embodiment. I accept this and I make peace with it.

> O Saint Germain, in love we claim,
> our right to bring your violet flame,
> from you Above, to us below,
> it is an all-transforming flow.

15 | Invoking manifestation through surrender

> O Saint Germain, what love you bring,
> it truly makes all matter sing,
> your violet flame does all restore,
> with you we are becoming more.

4. Because I am not identified with the outer self, the outer self does not really matter anymore. It is not running my life so it does not really matter.

> O Saint Germain, I love you so,
> my aura filled with violet glow,
> my chakras filled with violet fire,
> I am your cosmic amplifier.

> O Saint Germain, what love you bring,
> it truly makes all matter sing,
> your violet flame does all restore,
> with you we are becoming more.

5. The outer self I have left is not preventing me from fulfilling the goals I have set in my Divine plan. I can outplay some desires of the outer self and it does not detract from my Divine plan.

> O Saint Germain, I am now free,
> your violet flame is therapy,
> transform all hang-ups in my mind,
> as inner peace I surely find.

> O Saint Germain, what love you bring,
> it truly makes all matter sing,
> your violet flame does all restore,
> with you we are becoming more.

6. I see that I have certain desires, certain experiences I would like to have and I do not feel that I have had quite enough of those experiences. It is possible to continue to walk the path, still seeking to fulfill those desires but doing so in a balanced manner that does not disturb the progression of my Divine plan.

> O Saint Germain, my body pure,
> your violet flame for all is cure,
> consume the cause of all disease,
> and therefore I am all at ease.
>
> **O Saint Germain, what love you bring,**
> **it truly makes all matter sing,**
> **your violet flame does all restore,**
> **with you we are becoming more.**

7. I make peace with the fact that I will continue to have an outer self. It may affect the way I look at life and it may pull me into seeking to fulfill certain desires. I am aware that this is okay as long as it does not disturb the progression of my Divine plan.

> O Saint Germain, I'm karma-free,
> the past no longer burdens me,
> a brand new opportunity,
> I am in Christic unity.
>
> **O Saint Germain, what love you bring,**
> **it truly makes all matter sing,**
> **your violet flame does all restore,**
> **with you we are becoming more.**

8. I am accepting that I have an outer self, but I am not accepting that this will never change. I am constantly monitoring myself and my reactions. I realize that for each level of consciousness, I am going to have to see a particular illusion of the outer self and let it go.

> O Saint Germain, we are now one,
> I am for you a violet sun,
> as we transform this planet earth,
> your Golden Age is given birth.
>
> **O Saint Germain, what love you bring,**
> **it truly makes all matter sing,**
> **your violet flame does all restore,**
> **with you we are becoming more.**

9. There is an inner spirit, there is a certain self that I need to let die. I am monitoring this constantly—not that I am imbalanced about it, I am just being aware. I am monitoring my own reactions but I am not disturbed by it.

> O Saint Germain, the earth is free,
> from burden of duality,
> in oneness we bring what is best,
> your Golden Age is manifest.
>
> **O Saint Germain, what love you bring,**
> **it truly makes all matter sing,**
> **your violet flame does all restore,**
> **with you we are becoming more.**

Part 2

1. I am not feeling that I am imperfect or not good enough because I have this outer self. I accept myself for who I am right now. I accept that I am at a certain level of the path and that it is simply natural, inevitable for me to have a certain outer self.

> O Saint Germain, you do inspire,
> my vision raised forever higher,
> with you I form a figure-eight,
> your Golden Age I co-create.
>
> **O Saint Germain, what love you bring,**
> **it truly makes all matter sing,**
> **your violet flame does all restore,**
> **with you we are becoming more.**

2. I will not go into a state of denial and believe that I no longer have an outer self or an ego. I accept that I do have an outer self and I will have an outer self with me until I ascend.

> O Saint Germain, what Freedom Flame,
> released when we recite your name,
> acceleration is your gift,
> our planet it will surely lift.
>
> **O Saint Germain, what love you bring,**
> **it truly makes all matter sing,**
> **your violet flame does all restore,**
> **with you we are becoming more.**

3. By accepting this, I make peace with that fact. I make peace with myself that I am a perfectly acceptable ascended master student even though I still have an outer self.

> O Saint Germain, in love we claim,
> our right to bring your violet flame,
> from you Above, to us below,
> it is an all-transforming flow.
>
> **O Saint Germain, what love you bring,**
> **it truly makes all matter sing,**
> **your violet flame does all restore,**
> **with you we are becoming more.**

4. When I make peace with the fact that I do not have to be perfect in order to be acceptable to the ascended masters, then I make the shift of realizing that the earth or the matter realm does not have to be perfect in order for me to feel at peace with being here.

> O Saint Germain, I love you so,
> my aura filled with violet glow,
> my chakras filled with violet fire,
> I am your cosmic amplifier.
>
> **O Saint Germain, what love you bring,**
> **it truly makes all matter sing,**
> **your violet flame does all restore,**
> **with you we are becoming more.**

5. I realize that it is possible to have a higher state than what we currently have on earth, but I will not resist the state that is here right now.

O Saint Germain, I am now free,
your violet flame is therapy,
transform all hang-ups in my mind,
as inner peace I surely find.

O Saint Germain, what love you bring,
it truly makes all matter sing,
your violet flame does all restore,
with you we are becoming more.

6. If I am resisting what is here right now, I am subconsciously saying: "I can't be the Christ as long as the planet is this dense, I can't express my spiritual potential as long as the planet has these terrible manifestations."

O Saint Germain, my body pure,
your violet flame for all is cure,
consume the cause of all disease,
and therefore I am all at ease.

O Saint Germain, what love you bring,
it truly makes all matter sing,
your violet flame does all restore,
with you we are becoming more.

7. This is the illusion of focusing on outer things and it has caused many spiritual students to go into the detour where they seek to use force to change other people or outer conditions.

O Saint Germain, I'm karma-free,
the past no longer burdens me,
a brand new opportunity,
I am in Christic unity.

**O Saint Germain, what love you bring,
it truly makes all matter sing,
your violet flame does all restore,
with you we are becoming more.**

8. I recognize that planet earth is at a certain level of density right now. The collective consciousness has a certain density. I accept that this is the current condition. I do not accept that it is permanent, that it will remain that way, but I make peace with current conditions.

O Saint Germain, we are now one,
I am for you a violet sun,
as we transform this planet earth,
your Golden Age is given birth.

**O Saint Germain, what love you bring,
it truly makes all matter sing,
your violet flame does all restore,
with you we are becoming more.**

9. I accept that these conditions not only make it possible for me to express Christhood, but they actually are ideal for the expression of my Christhood because Christhood is challenging status quo.

O Saint Germain, the earth is free,
from burden of duality,
in oneness we bring what is best,
your Golden Age is manifest.

**O Saint Germain, what love you bring,
it truly makes all matter sing,
your violet flame does all restore,
with you we are becoming more.**

Part 3

1. I accept that even though the earth has a certain density right now, it is still possible for me to fulfill the goals that I defined in my Divine plan because those goals were made with the awareness of the current density of matter.

O Saint Germain, you do inspire,
my vision raised forever higher,
with you I form a figure-eight,
your Golden Age I co-create.

**O Saint Germain, what love you bring,
it truly makes all matter sing,
your violet flame does all restore,
with you we are becoming more.**

2. I did not define an *unrealistic* goal for myself, I defined a *realistic* goal. In order to manifest that realistic goal, I accept that it is possible to manifest it, even with the conditions as they are right now.

O Saint Germain, what Freedom Flame,
released when we recite your name,
acceleration is your gift,
our planet it will surely lift.

**O Saint Germain, what love you bring,
it truly makes all matter sing,
your violet flame does all restore,
with you we are becoming more.**

3. I look at my outer desires, my outer expectations. I recognize that many of these outer desires are not realistic. They are based on this dream of being home free, of somehow finding a way to be on earth and be untouched by what is happening on earth. I recognize that these desires are unrealistic and I let them go.

O Saint Germain, in love we claim,
our right to bring your violet flame,
from you Above, to us below,
it is an all-transforming flow.

**O Saint Germain, what love you bring,
it truly makes all matter sing,
your violet flame does all restore,
with you we are becoming more.**

4. The biggest hindrance to me manifesting the goals in my Divine plan is my expectations—my expectations of how things *should* be.

O Saint Germain, I love you so,
my aura filled with violet glow,
my chakras filled with violet fire,
I am your cosmic amplifier.

> O Saint Germain, what love you bring,
> it truly makes all matter sing,
> your violet flame does all restore,
> with you we are becoming more.

5. If I have an expectation that is built by the outer self, and that expectation contradicts the goals in my Divine plan, then as long as I hold on to that expectation with my conscious mind, it will block the manifestation of my Divine plan.

O Saint Germain, I am now free,
your violet flame is therapy,
transform all hang-ups in my mind,
as inner peace I surely find.

> O Saint Germain, what love you bring,
> it truly makes all matter sing,
> your violet flame does all restore,
> with you we are becoming more.

6. I will not be able to accept that the goals in my Divine plan descend to the physical level. I will subconsciously block them.

O Saint Germain, my body pure,
your violet flame for all is cure,
consume the cause of all disease,
and therefore I am all at ease.

> O Saint Germain, what love you bring,
> it truly makes all matter sing,
> your violet flame does all restore,
> with you we are becoming more.

7. I am making a switch in my mind where I make my mind fluid, I make my expectations fluid.

> O Saint Germain, I'm karma-free,
> the past no longer burdens me,
> a brand new opportunity,
> I am in Christic unity.

> **O Saint Germain, what love you bring,**
> **it truly makes all matter sing,**
> **your violet flame does all restore,**
> **with you we are becoming more.**

8. When I look at my goals and see a compulsory reaction, a sense of panic that these goals could not be manifest, then I know that these goals and expectations are based on the outer self. They come from the outer self, which cannot handle loss.

> O Saint Germain, we are now one,
> I am for you a violet sun,
> as we transform this planet earth,
> your Golden Age is given birth.

> **O Saint Germain, what love you bring,**
> **it truly makes all matter sing,**
> **your violet flame does all restore,**
> **with you we are becoming more.**

9. When I identify this reaction in myself, I know this comes from the outer self. I see that it is a particular internal spirit or outer self that is holding on to these goals and I let that self die. I will be free only when I let that spirit die and I liquefy my expectations.

O Saint Germain, the earth is free,
from burden of duality,
in oneness we bring what is best,
your Golden Age is manifest.

**O Saint Germain, what love you bring,
it truly makes all matter sing,
your violet flame does all restore,
with you we are becoming more.**

Part 4

1. I recognize that I have risen to a certain level of consciousness, I have acquired certain abilities of the mind and I can use certain outer techniques to manifest the things that I want.

O Saint Germain, you do inspire,
my vision raised forever higher,
with you I form a figure-eight,
your Golden Age I co-create.

**O Saint Germain, what love you bring,
it truly makes all matter sing,
your violet flame does all restore,
with you we are becoming more.**

2. Instead of manifesting these outer desires, expectations and goals, I will focus on manifesting what is in my Divine plan. I let go of these outer expectations and goals. I surrender them.

15 | Invoking manifestation through surrender

> O Saint Germain, what Freedom Flame,
> released when we recite your name,
> acceleration is your gift,
> our planet it will surely lift.
>
> **O Saint Germain, what love you bring,**
> **it truly makes all matter sing,**
> **your violet flame does all restore,**
> **with you we are becoming more.**

3. I will not attain peace by continuing to use my willpower to force my goals into manifestation. As long as I am using force, I cannot be at peace. It is impossible to use force and be at peace.

> O Saint Germain, in love we claim,
> our right to bring your violet flame,
> from you Above, to us below,
> it is an all-transforming flow.
>
> **O Saint Germain, what love you bring,**
> **it truly makes all matter sing,**
> **your violet flame does all restore,**
> **with you we are becoming more.**

4. How can I be at peace? I cannot be at peace through force. I can ONLY be at peace through surrender.

> O Saint Germain, I love you so,
> my aura filled with violet glow,
> my chakras filled with violet fire,
> I am your cosmic amplifier.

> **O Saint Germain, what love you bring,**
> **it truly makes all matter sing,**
> **your violet flame does all restore,**
> **with you we are becoming more.**

5. I will no longer manifest through the outer self and the vision of the outer self. I will no longer take the energies from my I AM Presence and use them to manifest the goals of the outer self. I reject the left-handed path.

> O Saint Germain, I am now free,
> your violet flame is therapy,
> transform all hang-ups in my mind,
> as inner peace I surely find.

> **O Saint Germain, what love you bring,**
> **it truly makes all matter sing,**
> **your violet flame does all restore,**
> **with you we are becoming more.**

6. I do not want to manifest anything through the outer self. I am deliberately surrendering the goals, the desires and the expectations of the outer self. I give up the goals of the outer self that always aim for some ultimate state.

> O Saint Germain, my body pure,
> your violet flame for all is cure,
> consume the cause of all disease,
> and therefore I am all at ease.

> O Saint Germain, what love you bring,
> it truly makes all matter sing,
> your violet flame does all restore,
> with you we are becoming more.

7. I recognize these goals and I surrender them. The key to moving higher is to surrender, let go—surrender, surrender, surrender.

> O Saint Germain, I'm karma-free,
> the past no longer burdens me,
> a brand new opportunity,
> I am in Christic unity.

> O Saint Germain, what love you bring,
> it truly makes all matter sing,
> your violet flame does all restore,
> with you we are becoming more.

8. Although I *can* manifest certain desires through the outer self, I do not want to do this. I choose to surrender the dream of the outer self.

> O Saint Germain, we are now one,
> I am for you a violet sun,
> as we transform this planet earth,
> your Golden Age is given birth.

> O Saint Germain, what love you bring,
> it truly makes all matter sing,
> your violet flame does all restore,
> with you we are becoming more.

9. I am discerning of how I spend my time and energy so I do not spend it on the needs of the outer self to the point where it takes away from the fulfillment of my Divine plan.

> O Saint Germain, the earth is free,
> from burden of duality,
> in oneness we bring what is best,
> your Golden Age is manifest.

> **O Saint Germain, what love you bring,**
> **it truly makes all matter sing,**
> **your violet flame does all restore,**
> **with you we are becoming more.**

Part 5

1. I do not want to do anything out of my own self. It is the I AM Presence and the higher vision of my Divine plan that is deciding what is to be manifest in my life.

> O Saint Germain, you do inspire,
> my vision raised forever higher,
> with you I form a figure-eight,
> your Golden Age I co-create.

> **O Saint Germain, what love you bring,**
> **it truly makes all matter sing,**
> **your violet flame does all restore,**
> **with you we are becoming more.**

15 | *Invoking manifestation through surrender*

2. I do not want the will of my outer self to decide what is going to be manifest in my life. I want a higher will, my I AM Presence, the choices I made when I formulated my Divine plan to determine what is going to be manifest in my life.

> O Saint Germain, what Freedom Flame,
> released when we recite your name,
> acceleration is your gift,
> our planet it will surely lift.

> **O Saint Germain, what love you bring,**
> **it truly makes all matter sing,**
> **your violet flame does all restore,**
> **with you we are becoming more.**

3. I surrender to that higher will and I say as Jesus: "Not my will but thine be done." What I am submitting to is not an external will. It is my own internal will that I used when I formulated my Divine plan.

> O Saint Germain, in love we claim,
> our right to bring your violet flame,
> from you Above, to us below,
> it is an all-transforming flow.

> **O Saint Germain, what love you bring,**
> **it truly makes all matter sing,**
> **your violet flame does all restore,**
> **with you we are becoming more.**

4. My outer self will say that I am submitting to an external will because to the outer self, my higher will is external. To me, as the Conscious you, it is the will of the outer self that is external.

O Saint Germain, I love you so,
my aura filled with violet glow,
my chakras filled with violet fire,
I am your cosmic amplifier.

**O Saint Germain, what love you bring,
it truly makes all matter sing,
your violet flame does all restore,
with you we are becoming more.**

5. The outer self is seeking to force its will upon me, contrary to what I actually chose when I was in that higher state of clarity when I formulated my Divine plan.

O Saint Germain, I am now free,
your violet flame is therapy,
transform all hang-ups in my mind,
as inner peace I surely find.

**O Saint Germain, what love you bring,
it truly makes all matter sing,
your violet flame does all restore,
with you we are becoming more.**

6. The kind of experience I desire to have for the rest of my lifetime is to be free of the need for ownership that comes from the outer self.

O Saint Germain, my body pure,
your violet flame for all is cure,
consume the cause of all disease,
and therefore I am all at ease.

> **O Saint Germain, what love you bring,**
> **it truly makes all matter sing,**
> **your violet flame does all restore,**
> **with you we are becoming more.**

7. This is not a planet where I want to explore the avenues of ownership. Is it not wise to put myself in a state of mind where I am driven by the desire to own something.

> O Saint Germain, I'm karma-free,
> the past no longer burdens me,
> a brand new opportunity,
> I am in Christic unity.

> **O Saint Germain, what love you bring,**
> **it truly makes all matter sing,**
> **your violet flame does all restore,**
> **with you we are becoming more.**

8. I can own things on earth, but there is always a price to be paid. It requires my attention and in order to maintain what I have, once I have it, that also requires attention.

> O Saint Germain, we are now one,
> I am for you a violet sun,
> as we transform this planet earth,
> your Golden Age is given birth.

> **O Saint Germain, what love you bring,**
> **it truly makes all matter sing,**
> **your violet flame does all restore,**
> **with you we are becoming more.**

9. I do not want the experience of having something, of owning something. I want the experience of growing. Ownership is still-stand and growth is movement.

> O Saint Germain, the earth is free,
> from burden of duality,
> in oneness we bring what is best,
> your Golden Age is manifest.
>
> **O Saint Germain, what love you bring,**
> **it truly makes all matter sing,**
> **your violet flame does all restore,**
> **with you we are becoming more.**

Part 6

1. I am not flowing with the River of Life by owning something. I can own something and flow with the River of Life—but only if what I own does not own *me*.

> O Saint Germain, you do inspire,
> my vision raised forever higher,
> with you I form a figure-eight,
> your Golden Age I co-create.
>
> **O Saint Germain, what love you bring,**
> **it truly makes all matter sing,**
> **your violet flame does all restore,**
> **with you we are becoming more.**

2. As long as I desire ownership, I will not be at peace on a planet like earth—it cannot be done. There will always be some threat that could take what I own away from me.

> O Saint Germain, what Freedom Flame,
> released when we recite your name,
> acceleration is your gift,
> our planet it will surely lift.
>
> **O Saint Germain, what love you bring,**
> **it truly makes all matter sing,**
> **your violet flame does all restore,**
> **with you we are becoming more.**

3. I realize the desire for ownership comes from an outer self that is very strong in the collective consciousness. I am here to raise myself above the collective consciousness and thereby help raise the collective consciousness.

> O Saint Germain, in love we claim,
> our right to bring your violet flame,
> from you Above, to us below,
> it is an all-transforming flow.
>
> **O Saint Germain, what love you bring,**
> **it truly makes all matter sing,**
> **your violet flame does all restore,**
> **with you we are becoming more.**

4. At this level of initiation, I can shed this self. I do not want to manifest the goals of the outer self and I do not want to manifest anything through the outer self. I do not want to manifest anything through force.

> O Saint Germain, I love you so,
> my aura filled with violet glow,
> my chakras filled with violet fire,
> I am your cosmic amplifier.
>
> **O Saint Germain, what love you bring,**
> **it truly makes all matter sing,**
> **your violet flame does all restore,**
> **with you we are becoming more.**

5. I shift my focus away from the outer self and I tune in to my Divine plan. I liquefy my mind and expectations. I am willing to let things float for a time, floating randomly on the surface of the water, letting the current take me.

> O Saint Germain, I am now free,
> your violet flame is therapy,
> transform all hang-ups in my mind,
> as inner peace I surely find.
>
> **O Saint Germain, what love you bring,**
> **it truly makes all matter sing,**
> **your violet flame does all restore,**
> **with you we are becoming more.**

6. There is a way to make decisions where I let go of the outer desires and I go into the state that Jesus described: "Not my will but thine be done."

> O Saint Germain, my body pure,
> your violet flame for all is cure,
> consume the cause of all disease,
> and therefore I am all at ease.

**O Saint Germain, what love you bring,
it truly makes all matter sing,
your violet flame does all restore,
with you we are becoming more.**

7. I am not saying I do not want anything to manifest in my life. I am saying I do not want the will of the outer self to manifest. I want the higher will that I myself defined when I formulated my Divine plan.

O Saint Germain, I'm karma-free,
the past no longer burdens me,
a brand new opportunity,
I am in Christic unity.

**O Saint Germain, what love you bring,
it truly makes all matter sing,
your violet flame does all restore,
with you we are becoming more.**

8. I am willing to wait for that to happen. I am willing to *let* it happen, to *let* it unfold. I am willing to go into a state of mind where I am not forcing anything into manifestation. I am letting it drop into manifestation.

O Saint Germain, we are now one,
I am for you a violet sun,
as we transform this planet earth,
your Golden Age is given birth.

> **O Saint Germain, what love you bring,**
> **it truly makes all matter sing,**
> **your violet flame does all restore,**
> **with you we are becoming more.**

9. I am going into a state of mind where I am not seeking to force the Ma-ter Light to give me what my outer self wants. I am giving the Ma-ter Light space to manifest what I, with my higher will, decided I wanted.

> O Saint Germain, the earth is free,
> from burden of duality,
> in oneness we bring what is best,
> your Golden Age is manifest.

> **O Saint Germain, what love you bring,**
> **it truly makes all matter sing,**
> **your violet flame does all restore,**
> **with you we are becoming more.**

Part 7

1. I am allowing my higher desires to descend into physical manifestation instead of blocking them with all of these outer expectations. This is not a passive approach. I am reconnecting to my Divine plan and allowing that to manifest.

> O Saint Germain, you do inspire,
> my vision raised forever higher,
> with you I form a figure-eight,
> your Golden Age I co-create.

15 | *Invoking manifestation through surrender*

**O Saint Germain, what love you bring,
it truly makes all matter sing,
your violet flame does all restore,
with you we are becoming more.**

2. I let go of all the outer things and I am willing to float, to flow with the River of Life, to let life take me in whatever direction it wants to take me. I am reaching up for what I already defined in my Divine plan.

O Saint Germain, what Freedom Flame,
released when we recite your name,
acceleration is your gift,
our planet it will surely lift.

**O Saint Germain, what love you bring,
it truly makes all matter sing,
your violet flame does all restore,
with you we are becoming more.**

3. I am bypassing the resistance from the outer self in my emotional, mental and lower identity bodies. I am going right to the source of what I formulated before I took embodiment.

O Saint Germain, in love we claim,
our right to bring your violet flame,
from you Above, to us below,
it is an all-transforming flow.

**O Saint Germain, what love you bring,
it truly makes all matter sing,
your violet flame does all restore,
with you we are becoming more.**

4. I am connecting to that and I am willing to let that be manifest, even if I currently do not see what it is, even if it is not in alignment with the outer expectations I have built.

> O Saint Germain, I love you so,
> my aura filled with violet glow,
> my chakras filled with violet fire,
> I am your cosmic amplifier.
>
> **O Saint Germain, what love you bring,**
> **it truly makes all matter sing,**
> **your violet flame does all restore,**
> **with you we are becoming more.**

5. I am willing to surrender those expectations and say: "Not my outer will be done but my higher will be done, whatever that will is. Come what may, I am going to accept it, I am going to receive it and I am going to be grateful for whatever I receive."

> O Saint Germain, I am now free,
> your violet flame is therapy,
> transform all hang-ups in my mind,
> as inner peace I surely find.
>
> **O Saint Germain, what love you bring,**
> **it truly makes all matter sing,**
> **your violet flame does all restore,**
> **with you we are becoming more.**

6. I am willing to be liquid, I am willing to let go of these fixed images of how my life should unfold. I reconnect to the higher

will that is my own will, that I had when I was not looking through the density of my four lower bodies.

> O Saint Germain, my body pure,
> your violet flame for all is cure,
> consume the cause of all disease,
> and therefore I am all at ease.

> **O Saint Germain, what love you bring,**
> **it truly makes all matter sing,**
> **your violet flame does all restore,**
> **with you we are becoming more.**

7. This is an act of surrender that brings me to a state of peace. I accept the omega aspect of manifesting something on earth, which is that the earth has a certain density that sets limitations for what I can manifest. I can always manifest what facilitates my growth to a higher level of consciousness.

> O Saint Germain, I'm karma-free,
> the past no longer burdens me,
> a brand new opportunity,
> I am in Christic unity.

> **O Saint Germain, what love you bring,**
> **it truly makes all matter sing,**
> **your violet flame does all restore,**
> **with you we are becoming more.**

8. The alpha aspect is that I go beyond the desires of the outer self. I reconnect to the higher desires that I myself had before I took embodiment. I allow those to manifest and I accept that this is good enough, this is the opportunity I want and I

embrace it. I make the best possible use of it and I will focus on growing from it instead of owning something.

> O Saint Germain, we are now one,
> I am for you a violet sun,
> as we transform this planet earth,
> your Golden Age is given birth.

> **O Saint Germain, what love you bring,**
> **it truly makes all matter sing,**
> **your violet flame does all restore,**
> **with you we are becoming more.**

9. I make peace with the fact that I will not come to some ultimate state of enlightenment as long as I am in physical embodiment. I will need to be looking in the mirror, I will need to be growing, I will need to be overcoming things, I will need to surrender things, and I will need to let certain things die for as long as I am in embodiment. That is the only way I am going to make it to the 144th level and my ascension.

> O Saint Germain, the earth is free,
> from burden of duality,
> in oneness we bring what is best,
> your Golden Age is manifest.

> **O Saint Germain, what love you bring,**
> **it truly makes all matter sing,**
> **your violet flame does all restore,**
> **with you we are becoming more.**

Sealing:

In the name of the Divine Mother, I fully accept that the power of these calls is used to set free the River of Life, so it can outpicture the perfect vision of Christ for my own life, for all people and for the planet. In the name I AM THAT I AM, it is done! Amen.

16 | WHEN MATTER AND YOU DO NOT MATTER

I AM the Ascended Master Saint Germain, and for this seventh and final initiation at my retreat, I wish to take this in a slightly different direction. I said in a previous discourse that you need to come to a point where "*matter* does not matter." For this seventh initiation, you need to come to a point where *you* do not matter.

The gravitational force

Now, monitor yourself when you hear or read this statement: "*You* do not matter." What is the reaction you feel in yourself? This will give you some idea that there is a self in you that wants to matter, that *needs* to matter, perhaps even has an obsessive-compulsive need to matter, to make a difference.

Now, what have we told you is the goal of the initiations you go through between the 48th and the 96th level? It is to raise yourself above the pull of the mass consciousness. You may liken this to the force of gravity. In a sense, the mass consciousness acts like a gravitational force that seeks to pull everyone down to what we might call the lowest common denominator—which is not necessarily the lowest but it is the average level of the collective consciousness. Certainly, there is a range within the collective where there are some people that are lower, some people that are higher but there is a certain average, and the gravitational force of the mass consciousness seeks to pull everyone down at least to that average level.

In order to rise above this and walk the spiritual path, you have to pull yourself free from that gravitational pull. It is something that requires a certain amount of determination, will power, a certain amount of momentum and "go." We might even say that it requires a certain amount of struggle. Although what the other Chohans have attempted to help you come to, is the point where you break free of the sense of struggle. You no longer feel you are struggling against the mass consciousness.

How do you break free of the collective consciousness, the mass consciousness? We are on a planet called earth, which has a very high density of matter and a very strong collective consciousness that is at a fairly low level, compared to the level of Christhood. It does require quite an effort, quite a determination, to break free. Now, if you compare this to what it takes to break free from the force of gravity, you will see that if this is done the traditional way, you build a rocket and it has to have a huge motor. It has to have a lot of fuel so that as it burns, that fuel can push the rocket up to where it is finally free from the gravitational pull of the earth and can now go into orbit. When a spaceship is in orbit, there is no force pulling it back down to earth. It is literally orbiting in a certain orbit around the planet and can keep doing so almost indefinitely. There is no longer any effort required.

16 | When matter and you do not matter

What I seek to help you accomplish with these seven levels of initiation in my course, is to get you to a point where you (so to speak) have reached an orbit where you are free of the gravitational pull of the mass consciousness. Now, contrary to a spaceship, this does not mean that I want you to stay at that level indefinitely. I do not want you to keep going around and around at this level of consciousness. I want you, of course, to continue to grow towards the 144th level.

Nevertheless, there can come that point where you have reached a certain orbit and now, at least to some degree, the prince of this world comes and has nothing in you. In other words, if we define the prince of this world as the collective consciousness, the collective consciousness has nothing in you whereby it can pull you back. Now, this does not mean that another prince of this world, namely the fallen beings, will not have something in you. They will have something in you, to some degree, until the 144th level, although there will, of course, come that point where you start seeing through all of their schemes. Therefore, you are, for all practical purposes, not fooled into being pulled into them anymore.

Going into orbit

What I am saying here is that there can come that point where you are now in orbit, you have launched yourself so high above the collective consciousness that you can go into an orbit where you are not in danger of sliding back down. This, of course, is the point I want you to get to as a result of following these many levels of initiation, in this entire course of the seven rays. What will it take for you to go into orbit and be free of the gravitational pull of the mass consciousness? You know from a rocket that you have a huge rocket that sits on the ground but it is not just one rocket—it has several levels. It has a huge booster motor that is meant to take it up to a certain height and then what does the rocket do? Well, it separates itself from that motor, that whole unit, that bottom level and it just lets it fall back to earth.

What have you done to raise yourself from the 48th to the 96th level? You have used a vehicle and that vehicle is a self. The self is made up of several internal spirits, as we have talked about during this course. It is really more than an internal spirit and that is why I prefer to call it a self because a self can have different layers. An internal spirit has one narrowly focused program. It is like a program on your computer that is designed to do a very specific task, such as, for example, a calculator or an email program. This is an internal spirit, it has a specific task, a specific programming. A self can be more complex, can have different elements, different levels, even different internal spirits, even different selves.

You have built a self that was the vehicle you used to go from the 48th to the 96th level. Again, there is no blame here. This is what we all had to do to raise ourselves above the collective consciousness. You need to recognize here that if you are to go *above* the 96th level and if you are to pass the crucial initiation of the 96th level, that self needs to go. You need to let it drop from you and let it fall back down to earth. How can you do this?

The self for which matter matters

You can do this only by accepting, by pondering on my statement that: "*You* do not matter." What is the "you" that does not matter? It is precisely that "you," that self that you used as your vehicle to get to the 96th level. That self is very much

16 | When matter and you do not matter

a self that reacts to matter. It is created in reaction to matter, or rather the state of matter as it is seen through the collective consciousness.

I have made quite the effort to help you see that there is a difference between what science would call the *objective* reality and the *perceived* reality. In other words, there is what we can call an "objective reality," in the sense that this is the state of the earth that was created by the Elohim. Then, there is what we could call a "subjective perception" of reality, which is the collective consciousness. The collective consciousness has a specific view of matter. It was the collective consciousness that created the current density of matter. Therefore, the collective consciousness cannot overcome the current density of matter. Even Albert Einstein said: "You cannot overcome a problem with the same consciousness that created the problem."

How do you overcome the current density of matter? Only by reaching for something higher, which is the Christ consciousness. At the 48th level of consciousness, you can reach beyond that level to get something that is a step higher. *That* is an element of the Christ consciousness that then takes you to the 49th level. You can continue to do this until you reach the 96th level. You need the Christ, the Christ consciousness, that universal awareness. You need that to get from the 48th to the 96th level. At each level, you are receiving a gift from the universal Christ consciousness or from the individualized consciousness through an ascended master, your own Christ self and so on.

You cannot pull yourself up by your own bootstraps. You cannot go from the 48th to the 96th level without receiving something from the Christ. What does that mean when you go above the 96th level? Of course, you still need to receive something from the Christ to get to the 144th level. For each of the levels above the 96th, you need to receive a gift from the

Christ, but over the 96th you have the potential to shift into accepting that the Christ is not an *external* force that comes to you from without. It becomes an *internal* force that comes to you from within. This means that you also become more of an instrument for the Christ to express itself and help other people. You shift from the external view of the external savior to the internal Christ that you begin to embody in greater and greater measure as you approach the 144th level.

The self that is anti-christ

My concern here is that you pass the initiation at the 96th level, which is that you begin to embody Christ instead of seeing it as an external force. You need to recognize here that the self that you have built to take you to the 96th level cannot do this. It cannot make the shift and see Christ as an internal force, an internal reality. It will always see Christ as external and it will always see matter as external. It will always see other people as external and it will see the gravitational force of the collective consciousness as an external force resisting it.

You could say that this self that you have built is based on resisting. It is based on struggling against opposition, struggling against something that resists your progress. That is why I have talked about coming to that point where you surrender so that, instead of forcing yourself forward, you are open to receiving. You are open to letting things unfold even if you do not see them clearly with your outer conscious mind.

There are spiritual students, whether they were in an ascended master teaching or other teachings, who have reached the 96th level but they have not understood what I and the other Chohans have prepared you to understand. They have not grasped what we have prepared you to grasp. They have not grasped the need to let this self die. You see my beloved, we all need a motivation to walk the spiritual path. We all need to make an effort to rise above the collective consciousness and we need a motivation for doing so.

When you started at the 48th level, you had some dream, some desire, some motivation that propelled you to even start this course. As you have gone through the course, you may have changed that motivation somewhat. You still may have elements of what we might call a "human" motivation, a human ambition, a human desire to be special, to have special powers, to be able to do what no one else can do. It can take many, many forms individually.

You need to make an effort here to look at what are the elements of motivation in this outer self. Then, you need to be willing to openly acknowledge that you have this because if you do not openly acknowledge it, you cannot let it go. The people who fail the initiation at this level, it is because they are not willing to admit that they have a certain element of human motivation. Perhaps they have pride. Perhaps they have a desire to feel better than others. Perhaps they have a desire to be able to manifest some miraculous thing, like Jesus did, that people cannot deny, whatever it may be.

It is always revolving around this outer self that wants to have some kind of reward for all the struggle it feels it has gone through to propel you to the 96th level. Do you begin to see what I am saying here? This self has been your vehicle for getting to the 96th level. As such, it has served a valid purpose but the self has a mind of its own. Built into this self is a motivation. You have the old drawing of a carrot dangling on a stick in front of the donkey who is pulling the cart, thinking it will one day catch up to the carrot. That is essentially the situation of this outer self. It has pulled your carriage, your wagon, your cart from the 48th to the 96th level. It thought it would one day catch up to the carrot. It would one day reach the carrot and get its reward.

The self that wants a reward

What you need to come to grips with here at this level, this seventh level of initiation at my retreat, is that the outer self will never get its reward if you continue on the path of Christhood. There is no reward for the outer self, there never has been, there never will be. Human beings have over time created many fantasy images of how there is a certain reward. We have seen ascended master students who thought, for example, that they would reach a certain level where suddenly several ascended masters would appear to them, take them through some final initiation ceremony and then they would be endowed with whatever they had imagined.

This is not going to happen. As long as you have that ambition, we cannot even approach you because it would only reinforce the outer self. As long as you want to be acknowledged by us, we must stay away from you because it is the only opportunity we have for helping you avoid being trapped in the outer self. There are students, as I said, who have come to this level and they have been driven by this desire for a reward. They have been so attached to the desire for this reward that they could not let go of the outer self. What did they do then? They started using the powers of mind that they had developed up until the 96th level in order to try to give themselves that reward here on earth.

You will see that even Jesus talked about how you can have your reward on earth or your reward in heaven—and you *can!* Within the Law of Free Will it is perfectly allowed that you can raise yourself to the 96th level because you are seeking a certain reward. Then, you have to decide: "Do I now want to come up where I seek a higher reward (which is my ascension) or do I want the reward that I had in mind while I was climbing to the 96th level?" If you want the reward that you had in mind, in the outer mind, in the human self, then you can use your powers to seek to get that here on earth. You have seen people who have done this. They have reached the 96th level and now they have tried to set themselves up as some kind of guru or leader. They have attempted to create a following who would give them the recognition and make them feel so special and who would follow them blindly into whatever adventures they have gone into.

Now again, it is not that this is necessarily unlawful in terms of the Law of Free Will. It is certainly not Christhood. I desire those of you who are willing to step up to the path of Christhood. What will it take for you? Well, it will take, of course, that you take an honest look at this outer self and the carrot that it has been using to pull the cart of your four lower bodies up to the 96th level—and then you let it go. You realize that this was not the highest motivation. It was not even the highest reward you could have and you find a way to let it go.

It is not about you

Now, this messenger went through this initiation quite a few years ago. For a period of several years, whatever he went through, whatever situations he encountered, his motto was: "It's not about me. It is not about me!" What he did with this was that he gradually separated himself from that human self until it did not have any pull on him. He got to the point where he was not doing what he was doing based on this motivation of the outer self. It no longer mattered. The outer self simply did not matter. Now, of course, you may say: "Is telling you this enough to help you get over this outer self?" No, it is not necessarily but we, of course, have not intended to leave you with nothing. Even though this lesson concludes the course, we have, over the last couple of years, brought forth teachings that you can start using immediately upon completion of this course. These teachings start with the book "My Lives." It continues with the other books that are building on it that talk about the primal self, that talk about how (whether you are an avatar or one of the original inhabitants of the earth) you developed a certain self that was reactionary to the fallen beings.

Of course, the real way to overcome the outer self is to look at this primal self and stop reacting, stop reacting to the fallen beings, to the majority of human beings, to the conditions of matter. You are not reacting to all of these external conditions. You get yourself to a point where you are free of these reactionary patterns so that your life is not a constant Ping-Pong match where something sends a ball at you, and you feel you have to send it back because you feel you have to react.

My beloved, the self, the outer self, that you used from the 48th to the 96th level functions the same way as the primal self. In fact, the primal self is part of this outer self. These selves, they always have a problem that they see on earth, a problem that has to be solved the way the self sees it. How is that problem going to be solved? Well, the self projects at you that *you* have to do something to solve the problem. It also projects that the problem can only be solved by other people changing. In other words, you are in this constant push-and-pull because you feel you have to do something to change other people.

Of course, other people are not willing to change so you also feel you can never really accomplish your goal. You are powerless to accomplish your goal because you are always waiting for other people or some external conditions to change. This is essentially what this reactionary self or conglomerate of selves puts you into. It puts you into this waiting position where you are always waiting for something. Going above the 96th level means that you start letting go of all this reactionary self, all of these reactionary selves. You start letting them go so that you are not reacting to anything on earth. You are not waiting for anything, you are looking at: "What can I do right now, what can I do in my outer situation to improve, to rise to a higher level of consciousness?"

You cannot wait for Christhood

It is not a matter of outer conditions or other people doing anything. As long as you are trapped in thinking that your happiness, or your peace of mind, or your spiritual growth, or the expression of your Christhood depends on certain outer conditions or other people, then you are not the Christ in action. You cannot express anything. You will be waiting and you will be thinking: "When this or that outer condition is fulfilled, then I can express my Christhood."

As I have said (and as we have said many times), there are no ideal conditions for expressing Christhood. Christhood is challenging status quo. In a sense, whatever condition you are facing, is the ideal condition for challenging that status quo and expressing something higher and *that* is Christhood. When you start doing that in whatever situation you are in, you will gradually build a momentum and then conditions will change. Conditions will not change until you start using the conditions you have, accepting them as the perfect opportunity to express Christhood. You start where you are, you make the best of it, you transcend it, you express something higher—*that* is how you get to the next step up.

Then, you get to the next step up and as you go step-by-step-by-step, there comes those points where you can now look back and say you have really covered quite a distance. You covered that distance by taking one small step at a time, by always working with the situation you were in. Whereas the people who have in their minds that once they have covered that big distance, then they can be the Christ—well, they will never get there.

We have before talked about the old Greek philosopher Zeno who came up with the paradox of how you can come from point A to point B. You first have to go to the halfway point. Then, you go to the halfway point of the remaining distance and you keep dividing the remaining distance into two parts. You always go to the halfway point, which means you never arrive—this is the human consciousness. You are, in a sense, not even saying: "I will go to the halfway point." You are looking at the mountain and saying: "When the mountain comes to me, then I'll be the Christ." It is not going to happen on a planet like earth. For that matter, it is not going to happen on a natural planet either, but you do not expect that on a natural planet.

Missing the point at the 96th level

There is a gap here (and Master MORE has given teachings on the gap and overcoming the gap in these other books I talked about). The gap is that those of you who have reached the 96th level, you have reconnected to your intuitive knowledge that there is something better. If you are an avatar, you know how life was on a natural planet. If you are an original inhabitant of the earth, you have a sense of what the earth was like before the fallen beings came here. You know there is an ideal condition and you know the earth is far from that ideal condition. If you are allowing the outer self to use this to say that when the ideal condition is fulfilled on earth, then you can be the Christ on earth, well, my beloved, then you are completely missing the point—you are *completely* missing the point. It is possible, although it may be shocking to you, to reach the 96th level and still have completely missed the point because you are still too identified with this outer self that brought you here. You are not willing to give up this sense of the reward that you are supposed to get. Again, there is *no* reward! Whatever the outer self imagined would be your reward for climbing to the 96th level, was a complete fantasy. It had no reality to it.

Does that mean it was wrong? No! Does it mean it was useless? No! Not if it gave you a motivation to continue climbing. My beloved, if you will go back and read these books again, study these books again, you will see that from Master MORE and forward, all of us have attempted to help you start dis-identifying with that outer self. Not to the point where you suddenly lost all connection to it because then you would not have a vehicle to carry you on. We have attempted to help you gradually stop identifying with it, overcome these desires and imaginations of the outer self. There is one thing we could not help you overcome at lower levels, and that was the very core of your motivation for walking the path. You see, what is the very core of that motivation, my beloved. What is the outer self? It is a *reactionary* self, it reacts to something on earth. The outer self imagines that when you reach the 96th level and receive your reward, that reward will give you some kind of recognition here on earth because that is the only kind of reward that the outer self can imagine.

The core of the outer self

The core of this outer self is that it desires some kind of recognition or position (but it is essentially the same thing) on earth, meaning from other people, from the institutions of society, whatever you have. That is the core of this outer self. It wants a reward on earth. I cannot make this choice for you, I cannot pass this initiation for you. That is why I have to end this course, not only my own section of it but the section of all of us Chohans, I have to end this course by leaving you at a crossroads. I have set before you life and death. *We* have set before you life and death.

You are standing now at a fork in the road. If you choose the one side of continuing to seek a reward on earth, then our efforts to put you on the path of Christhood have failed. This is a risk that we know and that we are willing to take. The path is not mechanical. We cannot guarantee a result. We *cannot* guarantee a result. We are ascended masters and we will not influence your mind or your free will.

Now, if you take the other fork in the road, you will put yourself on the path to Christhood. You can then use the tools and teachings that we have given, and we have given numerous teachings on the path to Christhood through this messenger. There are, of course, other teachings out there that you can use if you desire. Then, you can gradually start climbing. I am not saying, again, that there will come a "poof," and your outer self is gone all at once. Again, it is something you overcome one step at a time. You might say to some degree that, as we have said before, you will have elements of the outer self with you until you ascend. You could say that the path from the 96th to the 144th level is the path of overcoming that outer self step-by-step.

Giving up the reward

Nevertheless, what I am telling you is that there can come a point where, with your outer mind, you make peace with the fact that there will never be a reward on earth for climbing the spiritual path. The only reward for the spiritual path is your ascension, meaning your reward is in heaven by being in the ascended consciousness. I can assure you that once you are in the ascended consciousness and know the contrast, the difference between the ascended and the unascended state of consciousness, it will be the ultimate reward. This, of course, is a statement that might mean very little to you if you are still identified with that outer self that so compulsively wants that reward on earth.

Again, is it about you or is it about something else? If it is about you, you will take that fork in the road and seek to build some kind of acknowledgment here on earth, some kind of position. If you take the other road, you will let go of this desire to be recognized on earth. It does not mean that you could not be recognized but you are not desiring it, you are not wanting it. You are not keeping in your mind that one day this should happen. You are letting it go, you are letting the self die. The self always projects there is a problem, for example recognition, you need to have a certain recognition on earth. Well, what does it mean that you are recognized on earth? It means that other people must see you and see you as being special and acknowledge you in some way as being special.

Well, that means that *they* have to change, right? They have to use *their* free will to acknowledge you. This is something that is beyond *your* free will. You cannot make the choice to make other people choose to acknowledge you. You cannot change that with your free will. You can change it with your unfree will, with the will of the outer self. You can seek to force them, even though you may not call it force, you may seek to force them to acknowledge you. That is not your *free* will, you are now going into the left-handed path, using black magic to influence the minds of other people. You can do this and gain recognition.

If this is your desire, then I can only say: "Go that route and then when you (later in this lifetime or in a future lifetime) come to the point where you have had enough of it, then come back to me and I will seek to help you from that point on." If you go that route, then no ascended master can really help you. You may think we do but it is not the real ascended masters but the false hierarchy of those who pretend to be ascended masters.

The choice between life and death

You see, my beloved, I have given you a path forward. There are tools you can use, there are books you can use, but as much as it may shock you, I must leave you without any kind of reward, any finality. I am not leaving you in a particular state where you have passed the initiation. I am leaving you at the point where you now have the awareness of the initiation you are facing.

As I said, I cannot choose for you, and even if I could, I would not do so because it would not, of course, further *your* growth. You grow by making the choice from within because you come to the point of resolution where you are not making this choice with the outer mind. I know that there are many students who will be at this point and who will react and say: "I am choosing with the outer mind to walk the path of Christhood. I am going to take all these books, I'm going to study them, I'm going to do the invocations and I'm going to make it." You see, my beloved, you cannot actually walk the path of Christhood through the outer mind. You can walk from the 48th to the 96th level with the outer mind—that is what I have been telling you. You cannot go beyond the 96th level with the outer mind. The decision to enter the path of Christhood, of course, you can make it with the outer mind and think you are entering the path, but the decision that brings you onto the path must come from within. It is not a *willed* decision, it is a *spontaneous*, inner decision. It is not something you can force. You cannot *make* it happen. You can *let* it happen by using the tools to resolve these primal selves and other selves that are pulling you away from the decision, that are pulling you into solving a problem.

Now, in a sense we could say that: "How have you looked at the spiritual path so far?" The outer self that brought you from the 48th to the 96th level has looked at it in a very distinct way: "The spiritual path is a problem that I must solve. There is an initiation and in order to pass the initiation I have to know something, I have to see something, I have to understand something. There's a problem I need to solve." This has been valid from the 48th to the 96th level but above the 96th level it is no longer valid. It is not going to take you even to the 97th level.

Giving up the problem-solving self

You need to switch your entire approach to the path where you realize it is not a matter of solving a problem. It is a matter of stopping yourself from trying to solve problems. It is a matter of letting it happen. Why is this so? What have we talked about? The big problem on earth is the consciousness of separation created by the fallen beings through the consciousness of duality. You have the illusion that you are a separate being, everybody is a separate being, everybody is looking out for themselves, looking out for number one, trying to get what they can get.

That is essentially where the mass consciousness is at right now, although certainly in some countries there has developed more of a common sense of humanity. Nevertheless, there is still separation. Now, you have a mass consciousness where people see themselves as separate individuals that are often fighting against each other. They also see themselves as having certain groups and if you belong to a group, you have to follow that group. If you belong to the one group, you have to hate those of the other group and so on.

In order to pull yourself out from that whole struggle, what do you have to do? Well, you obviously have to see yourself as being separate from the people in the group where you grew up, even all those in the mass consciousness. What is it you are doing to get from the 48th to the 96th? You are building a self that sees itself as being separated from the people who are in the mass consciousness. This is natural. Again, no blame here, this is just what you have to do, but you are not going to get beyond the 96th level by using this self because what is the path of Christhood?

The path of Christhood is overcoming the illusion of separation and coming to see that behind all of the phenomena on earth (all of the matter, all of the consciousness, the duality consciousness, the consciousness of separation) is an underlying state of oneness, the oneness of all life. All life is one, there is no separation. In a sense, you could say that to get to the 96th level, you have to build a strong individualistic self. To get to the ascended state, you have to break down that self. Step-by-step from the 48th to the 96th level, you are building a self and then you need to switch. Now, step-by-step, from the 97th to the 144th level, you are dismantling that self. You are dismantling the self that sees itself as separated. When you come to the point where you can let the final element of that self go, that is when you go into the state of oneness that is the ascension.

You have now done everything you want to do as a separate self in an unascended sphere, not even on earth but in an unascended sphere in general. You have done everything you wanted to do as a separate being. You can let that final element of the separate self go and ascend. Obviously, you are not at that point at the 96th level but you are at the point where you can begin to realize that this is what you need to do. You need to dismantle, step-by-step this separate self. As you do that, the reward is that you come to feel a greater and greater oneness.

In the beginning, this may be a little bit difficult. What are you going to feel one with? Obviously, not all of these other people that you have just made such an effort to pull yourself away from. Not the fallen beings either. I suggest that you start by focusing (and this is again what we have given you many tools and teachings on) on seeking oneness with your I AM Presence, which is within yourself.

If it is easier for you, then focus on seeking oneness with one particular ascended master. It does not have to be me, whomever is closest to your heart. Then, as you go higher, you may start feeling a certain oneness with other spiritual people, although it may be difficult for you to find other spiritual people at that level of consciousness. There may be some you can find and you can start building a sense of oneness with them.

Be careful here because it cannot be, what we have seen in so many spiritual movements, where you build this elitist sense that: "Oh, we are the most advanced students on the planet, therefore we are better than others." This is not Christhood, this is not oneness. You can build a oneness with each other but not by being higher than everybody else. As you go higher in Christhood, you begin to actually build that sense of oneness with all life. Again, you could say that you are separating yourself from the mass consciousness to get to the 96th level but as you get closer to the 144th level, you are not pulled in, you are not in danger of being pulled into the mass consciousness. Therefore, you can start feeling a sense of oneness with all people, with all life.

I could go on indefinitely but we have already given enough teachings in other books. Therefore, I again need to leave you, not with a sense of finality, not with a sense that you have *passed* the final initiation of this course but that you are *facing* the final initiation of this course. I have set before you life and death—*choose life!*

17 | INVOKING FREEDOM FROM THE SELF THAT MATTERS

In the name I AM THAT I AM, Jesus Christ, I call to my I AM Presence to flow through the I Will Be Presence that I AM and give this invocation with full power. I call to Saint Germain to help me overcome the self that desperately wants to matter. Help me overcome all desires for some kind of reward on earth, including …

[Make personal calls]

Part 1

1. There is a self in me that wants to matter, that needs to matter, that has an obsessive-compulsive need to matter, to make a difference.

> O Saint Germain, you do inspire,
> my vision raised forever higher,
> with you I form a figure-eight,
> your Golden Age I co-create.
>
> **O Saint Germain, what love you bring,**
> **it truly makes all matter sing,**
> **your violet flame does all restore,**
> **with you we are becoming more.**

2. The goal of this course is to help me rise above the collective consciousness and go into orbit where I am not in danger of sliding back down.

> O Saint Germain, what Freedom Flame,
> released when we recite your name,
> acceleration is your gift,
> our planet it will surely lift.
>
> **O Saint Germain, what love you bring,**
> **it truly makes all matter sing,**
> **your violet flame does all restore,**
> **with you we are becoming more.**

3. In order to go from the 48th to the 96th level of consciousness, I have built a self that is like a rocket that has pulled me above the gravitational force of the mass consciousness.

> O Saint Germain, in love we claim,
> our right to bring your violet flame,
> from you Above, to us below,
> it is an all-transforming flow.

**O Saint Germain, what love you bring,
it truly makes all matter sing,
your violet flame does all restore,
with you we are becoming more.**

4. The challenge I now face is that this self cannot take me above the 96th level. Therefore, I need to separate myself from it and let it die, let it fall back to earth.

O Saint Germain, I love you so,
my aura filled with violet glow,
my chakras filled with violet fire,
I am your cosmic amplifier.

**O Saint Germain, what love you bring,
it truly makes all matter sing,
your violet flame does all restore,
with you we are becoming more.**

5. I accept the statement that: "I do not matter." The "I" that does not matter is the "I," the self, that I used as my vehicle to get to the 96th level.

O Saint Germain, I am now free,
your violet flame is therapy,
transform all hang-ups in my mind,
as inner peace I surely find.

**O Saint Germain, what love you bring,
it truly makes all matter sing,
your violet flame does all restore,
with you we are becoming more.**

6. That self is very much a self that reacts to matter. It is created in reaction to matter, or rather the state of matter as it is seen through the collective consciousness.

> O Saint Germain, my body pure,
> your violet flame for all is cure,
> consume the cause of all disease,
> and therefore I am all at ease.

> **O Saint Germain, what love you bring,**
> **it truly makes all matter sing,**
> **your violet flame does all restore,**
> **with you we are becoming more.**

7. The collective consciousness has a specific view of matter. It was the collective consciousness that created the current density of matter. Therefore, the collective consciousness cannot overcome the current density of matter.

> O Saint Germain, I'm karma-free,
> the past no longer burdens me,
> a brand new opportunity,
> I am in Christic unity.

> **O Saint Germain, what love you bring,**
> **it truly makes all matter sing,**
> **your violet flame does all restore,**
> **with you we are becoming more.**

8. I overcome the current density of matter only by reaching for something higher, which is the Christ consciousness.

> O Saint Germain, we are now one,
> I am for you a violet sun,
> as we transform this planet earth,
> your Golden Age is given birth.
>
> **O Saint Germain, what love you bring,
> it truly makes all matter sing,
> your violet flame does all restore,
> with you we are becoming more.**

9. At each level, I am receiving a gift from the universal Christ consciousness or from the individualized consciousness through an ascended master or my Christ self. I cannot pull myself up by my own bootstraps.

> O Saint Germain, the earth is free,
> from burden of duality,
> in oneness we bring what is best,
> your Golden Age is manifest.
>
> **O Saint Germain, what love you bring,
> it truly makes all matter sing,
> your violet flame does all restore,
> with you we are becoming more.**

Part 2

1. I shift into accepting that the Christ is not an *external* force that comes to me from without. It is now an *internal* force that comes to me from within.

O Saint Germain, you do inspire,
my vision raised forever higher,
with you I form a figure-eight,
your Golden Age I co-create.

**O Saint Germain, what love you bring,
it truly makes all matter sing,
your violet flame does all restore,
with you we are becoming more.**

2. I shift from the external view of the external savior to the internal Christ that I begin to embody in greater and greater measure as I approach the 144th level.

O Saint Germain, what Freedom Flame,
released when we recite your name,
acceleration is your gift,
our planet it will surely lift.

**O Saint Germain, what love you bring,
it truly makes all matter sing,
your violet flame does all restore,
with you we are becoming more.**

3. I am determined to pass the initiation at the 96th level, which is that I begin to embody Christ instead of seeing it as an external force.

O Saint Germain, in love we claim,
our right to bring your violet flame,
from you Above, to us below,
it is an all-transforming flow.

17 | Invoking freedom from the self that matters

**O Saint Germain, what love you bring,
it truly makes all matter sing,
your violet flame does all restore,
with you we are becoming more.**

4. I recognize that the self that I have built to take me to the 96th level cannot do this. It cannot make the shift and see Christ as an internal force, an internal reality. It will always see Christ as external and it will always see matter as external. It will always see other people as external and it will see the gravitational force of the collective consciousness as an external force resisting it.

O Saint Germain, I love you so,
my aura filled with violet glow,
my chakras filled with violet fire,
I am your cosmic amplifier.

**O Saint Germain, what love you bring,
it truly makes all matter sing,
your violet flame does all restore,
with you we are becoming more.**

5. The self that I have built is based on resisting. It is based on struggling against opposition, struggling against something that resists my progress.

O Saint Germain, I am now free,
your violet flame is therapy,
transform all hang-ups in my mind,
as inner peace I surely find.

**O Saint Germain, what love you bring,
it truly makes all matter sing,
your violet flame does all restore,
with you we are becoming more.**

6. I am at the point where I surrender so that instead of forcing myself forward, I am open to receiving. I am open to letting things unfold, even if I do not see them clearly with my outer conscious mind.

O Saint Germain, my body pure,
your violet flame for all is cure,
consume the cause of all disease,
and therefore I am all at ease.

**O Saint Germain, what love you bring,
it truly makes all matter sing,
your violet flame does all restore,
with you we are becoming more.**

7. I grasp the need to let this self die. When I started at the 48th level, I had some dream, some desire, some motivation that propelled me to start this course.

O Saint Germain, I'm karma-free,
the past no longer burdens me,
a brand new opportunity,
I am in Christic unity.

**O Saint Germain, what love you bring,
it truly makes all matter sing,
your violet flame does all restore,
with you we are becoming more.**

17 | Invoking freedom from the self that matters

8. I still have elements of a human motivation, a human ambition, a human desire to be special, to have special powers, to be able to do what no one else can do. I am willing to see what form this takes for me individually.

> O Saint Germain, we are now one,
> I am for you a violet sun,
> as we transform this planet earth,
> your Golden Age is given birth.
>
> **O Saint Germain, what love you bring,**
> **it truly makes all matter sing,**
> **your violet flame does all restore,**
> **with you we are becoming more.**

9. I am willing to look at the elements of motivation in this outer self. I am willing to openly acknowledge that I have this because if I do not acknowledge it, I cannot let it go. I am willing to admit that I have a certain element of human motivation.

> O Saint Germain, the earth is free,
> from burden of duality,
> in oneness we bring what is best,
> your Golden Age is manifest.
>
> **O Saint Germain, what love you bring,**
> **it truly makes all matter sing,**
> **your violet flame does all restore,**
> **with you we are becoming more.**

Part 3

1. The outer self wants to have some kind of reward for all the struggle it feels it has gone through to propel me to the 96th level. The self has a mind of its own and its own motivation.

> O Saint Germain, you do inspire,
> my vision raised forever higher,
> with you I form a figure-eight,
> your Golden Age I co-create.
>
> **O Saint Germain, what love you bring,**
> **it truly makes all matter sing,**
> **your violet flame does all restore,**
> **with you we are becoming more.**

2. The outer self has pulled me from the 48th to the 96th level, and it thought it would one day get its reward.

> O Saint Germain, what Freedom Flame,
> released when we recite your name,
> acceleration is your gift,
> our planet it will surely lift.
>
> **O Saint Germain, what love you bring,**
> **it truly makes all matter sing,**
> **your violet flame does all restore,**
> **with you we are becoming more.**

3. I grasp and accept that the outer self will never get its reward if I continue on the path of Christhood. There is no reward for the outer self, there never has been, there never will be.

17 | Invoking freedom from the self that matters

> O Saint Germain, in love we claim,
> our right to bring your violet flame,
> from you Above, to us below,
> it is an all-transforming flow.

> **O Saint Germain, what love you bring,**
> **it truly makes all matter sing,**
> **your violet flame does all restore,**
> **with you we are becoming more.**

4. I surrender all of the fantasy images of how there is a certain reward. I surrender all desire for the ascended masters to appear to me and take me through some final initiation ceremony that endows me with special powers.

> O Saint Germain, I love you so,
> my aura filled with violet glow,
> my chakras filled with violet fire,
> I am your cosmic amplifier.

> **O Saint Germain, what love you bring,**
> **it truly makes all matter sing,**
> **your violet flame does all restore,**
> **with you we are becoming more.**

5. I surrender all attachment to this desire for a reward and I let go of the outer self. I will not use the powers of mind that I had developed up until the 96th level in order to try to give myself the reward here on earth.

O Saint Germain, I am now free,
your violet flame is therapy,
transform all hang-ups in my mind,
as inner peace I surely find.

**O Saint Germain, what love you bring,
it truly makes all matter sing,
your violet flame does all restore,
with you we are becoming more.**

6. I come up where I seek a higher reward, which is my ascension. I surrender the reward that I had in mind while I was climbing to the 96th level.

O Saint Germain, my body pure,
your violet flame for all is cure,
consume the cause of all disease,
and therefore I am all at ease.

**O Saint Germain, what love you bring,
it truly makes all matter sing,
your violet flame does all restore,
with you we are becoming more.**

7. I am willing to step up to the path of Christhood. I take an honest look at this outer self and the carrot that it has been using to pull the cart of my four lower bodies up to the 96th level—and then I let it go.

O Saint Germain, I'm karma-free,
the past no longer burdens me,
a brand new opportunity,
I am in Christic unity.

17 | Invoking freedom from the self that matters

**O Saint Germain, what love you bring,
it truly makes all matter sing,
your violet flame does all restore,
with you we are becoming more.**

8. I realize that this was not the highest motivation. It was not even the highest reward I could have, and I let it go.

O Saint Germain, we are now one,
I am for you a violet sun,
as we transform this planet earth,
your Golden Age is given birth.

**O Saint Germain, what love you bring,
it truly makes all matter sing,
your violet flame does all restore,
with you we are becoming more.**

9. I shift away from self-focus, and whatever situations I encounter, my motto is: "It's not about me. It is not about me!"

O Saint Germain, the earth is free,
from burden of duality,
in oneness we bring what is best,
your Golden Age is manifest.

**O Saint Germain, what love you bring,
it truly makes all matter sing,
your violet flame does all restore,
with you we are becoming more.**

Part 4

1. I gradually separate myself out from the human self until it does not have any pull on me. I am not doing what I am doing based on this motivation of the outer self. It no longer matters. The outer self simply does not matter.

> O Saint Germain, you do inspire,
> my vision raised forever higher,
> with you I form a figure-eight,
> your Golden Age I co-create.

> **O Saint Germain, what love you bring,**
> **it truly makes all matter sing,**
> **your violet flame does all restore,**
> **with you we are becoming more.**

2. The real way to overcome the outer self is to stop reacting, stop reacting to the fallen beings, to the majority of human beings, to the conditions of matter. I am not reacting to all of these external conditions.

> O Saint Germain, what Freedom Flame,
> released when we recite your name,
> acceleration is your gift,
> our planet it will surely lift.

> **O Saint Germain, what love you bring,**
> **it truly makes all matter sing,**
> **your violet flame does all restore,**
> **with you we are becoming more.**

3. I will use the tools to get myself to a point where I am free of these reactionary patterns so that my life is not a constant Ping-Pong match where something sends a ball at me, and I feel I have to send it back because I feel I have to react.

> O Saint Germain, in love we claim,
> our right to bring your violet flame,
> from you Above, to us below,
> it is an all-transforming flow.

> **O Saint Germain, what love you bring,**
> **it truly makes all matter sing,**
> **your violet flame does all restore,**
> **with you we are becoming more.**

4. The outer self, that I used from the 48th to the 96th level, has a problem that it sees on earth, a problem that has to be solved the way the self sees it. The self projects at me that I have to do something to solve the problem.

> O Saint Germain, I love you so,
> my aura filled with violet glow,
> my chakras filled with violet fire,
> I am your cosmic amplifier.

> **O Saint Germain, what love you bring,**
> **it truly makes all matter sing,**
> **your violet flame does all restore,**
> **with you we are becoming more.**

5. The self also projects that the problem can only be solved by other people changing. It puts me in this constant push and

pull because I feel I have to do something to change other people.

> O Saint Germain, I am now free,
> your violet flame is therapy,
> transform all hang-ups in my mind,
> as inner peace I surely find.

> **O Saint Germain, what love you bring,**
> **it truly makes all matter sing,**
> **your violet flame does all restore,**
> **with you we are becoming more.**

6. This makes me powerless to accomplish my goal because I am always waiting for other people or some external conditions to change. This reactionary self puts me into this waiting position where I am always waiting for something.

> O Saint Germain, my body pure,
> your violet flame for all is cure,
> consume the cause of all disease,
> and therefore I am all at ease.

> **O Saint Germain, what love you bring,**
> **it truly makes all matter sing,**
> **your violet flame does all restore,**
> **with you we are becoming more.**

7. Going above the 96th level means that I start letting go of this reactionary self, all of these reactionary selves. I start letting them go so that I am not reacting to anything on earth. I am not waiting for anything, I am looking at: "What can I do

right now, what can I do in my outer situation to improve, to rise to a higher level of consciousness?"

> O Saint Germain, I'm karma-free,
> the past no longer burdens me,
> a brand new opportunity,
> I am in Christic unity.

> **O Saint Germain, what love you bring,**
> **it truly makes all matter sing,**
> **your violet flame does all restore,**
> **with you we are becoming more.**

8. As long as I am trapped in thinking that my happiness, my peace of mind, my spiritual growth, or the expression of my Christhood depends on certain outer conditions or other people, then I am not the Christ in action. I cannot express anything.

> O Saint Germain, we are now one,
> I am for you a violet sun,
> as we transform this planet earth,
> your Golden Age is given birth.

> **O Saint Germain, what love you bring,**
> **it truly makes all matter sing,**
> **your violet flame does all restore,**
> **with you we are becoming more.**

9. There are no ideal conditions for expressing Christhood. Christhood is challenging status quo. Whatever condition I am facing, is the ideal condition for challenging that status quo and expressing something higher—and *that* is Christhood.

O Saint Germain, the earth is free,
from burden of duality,
in oneness we bring what is best,
your Golden Age is manifest.

**O Saint Germain, what love you bring,
it truly makes all matter sing,
your violet flame does all restore,
with you we are becoming more.**

Part 5

1. I will start doing that in whatever situation I am in, and then conditions *will* change. Conditions will not change until I start using the conditions I have, accepting them as the perfect opportunity to express Christhood.

O Saint Germain, you do inspire,
my vision raised forever higher,
with you I form a figure-eight,
your Golden Age I co-create.

**O Saint Germain, what love you bring,
it truly makes all matter sing,
your violet flame does all restore,
with you we are becoming more.**

2. I start where I am, I make the best of it, I transcend it, I express something higher—that is how I get to the next step up.

17 | Invoking freedom from the self that matters

> O Saint Germain, what Freedom Flame,
> released when we recite your name,
> acceleration is your gift,
> our planet it will surely lift.
>
> **O Saint Germain, what love you bring,**
> **it truly makes all matter sing,**
> **your violet flame does all restore,**
> **with you we are becoming more.**

3. I know there is an ideal condition and I know the earth is far from that ideal condition. I will not allow the outer self to use this to say that when the ideal condition is fulfilled on earth, *then* I can be the Christ on earth.

> O Saint Germain, in love we claim,
> our right to bring your violet flame,
> from you Above, to us below,
> it is an all-transforming flow.
>
> **O Saint Germain, what love you bring,**
> **it truly makes all matter sing,**
> **your violet flame does all restore,**
> **with you we are becoming more.**

4. I am no longer identified with this outer self that brought me here. I am willing to give up this sense of the reward that I am supposed to get.

> O Saint Germain, I love you so,
> my aura filled with violet glow,
> my chakras filled with violet fire,
> I am your cosmic amplifier.

**O Saint Germain, what love you bring,
it truly makes all matter sing,
your violet flame does all restore,
with you we are becoming more.**

5. I accept that there is no reward! Whatever the outer self imagined would be my reward for climbing to the 96th level, was a complete fantasy. It had no reality to it.

O Saint Germain, I am now free,
your violet flame is therapy,
transform all hang-ups in my mind,
as inner peace I surely find.

**O Saint Germain, what love you bring,
it truly makes all matter sing,
your violet flame does all restore,
with you we are becoming more.**

6. I am looking at the very core of my motivation for walking the path. The outer self is a reactionary self, it reacts to something on earth. The outer self imagines that when I reach the 96th level and receive my reward, that reward will give me some kind of recognition here on earth because that is the only kind of reward that the outer self can imagine.

O Saint Germain, my body pure,
your violet flame for all is cure,
consume the cause of all disease,
and therefore I am all at ease.

**O Saint Germain, what love you bring,
it truly makes all matter sing,
your violet flame does all restore,
with you we are becoming more.**

7. The core of the outer self is that it desires some kind of recognition or position, meaning from other people or from the institutions of society.

O Saint Germain, I'm karma-free,
the past no longer burdens me,
a brand new opportunity,
I am in Christic unity.

**O Saint Germain, what love you bring,
it truly makes all matter sing,
your violet flame does all restore,
with you we are becoming more.**

8. The ascended masters cannot make this choice for me. They cannot pass this initiation for me. I accept that I am standing at a crossroads and Saint Germain has set before me life and death.

O Saint Germain, we are now one,
I am for you a violet sun,
as we transform this planet earth,
your Golden Age is given birth.

**O Saint Germain, what love you bring,
it truly makes all matter sing,
your violet flame does all restore,
with you we are becoming more.**

9. I do *not* choose the one side of continuing to seek a reward on earth. I choose to take the other fork in the road and put myself on the path to Christhood.

> O Saint Germain, the earth is free,
> from burden of duality,
> in oneness we bring what is best,
> your Golden Age is manifest.

> **O Saint Germain, what love you bring,**
> **it truly makes all matter sing,**
> **your violet flame does all restore,**
> **with you we are becoming more.**

Part 6

1. With my outer mind, I make peace with the fact that there will never be a reward on earth for climbing the spiritual path. The only reward for the spiritual path is my ascension, meaning my reward is in heaven by being in the ascended consciousness.

> O Saint Germain, you do inspire,
> my vision raised forever higher,
> with you I form a figure-eight,
> your Golden Age I co-create.

> **O Saint Germain, what love you bring,**
> **it truly makes all matter sing,**
> **your violet flame does all restore,**
> **with you we are becoming more.**

17 | Invoking freedom from the self that matters

2. It is not about me. I let go of this desire to be recognized on earth. I am not desiring it; I am not wanting it. I am not keeping in my mind that one day this should happen. I am letting it go; I am letting the self die.

> O Saint Germain, what Freedom Flame,
> released when we recite your name,
> acceleration is your gift,
> our planet it will surely lift.
>
> **O Saint Germain, what love you bring,**
> **it truly makes all matter sing,**
> **your violet flame does all restore,**
> **with you we are becoming more.**

3. The self always projects there is a problem, for example that I need to have a certain recognition on earth. Being recognized on earth means that other people must see me as being special and acknowledge me as being special.

> O Saint Germain, in love we claim,
> our right to bring your violet flame,
> from you Above, to us below,
> it is an all-transforming flow.
>
> **O Saint Germain, what love you bring,**
> **it truly makes all matter sing,**
> **your violet flame does all restore,**
> **with you we are becoming more.**

4. This is something that is beyond my free will. I cannot make the choice to make other people choose to acknowledge me.

O Saint Germain, I love you so,
my aura filled with violet glow,
my chakras filled with violet fire,
I am your cosmic amplifier.

**O Saint Germain, what love you bring,
it truly makes all matter sing,
your violet flame does all restore,
with you we are becoming more.**

5. I will not seek to force them to acknowledge me. I will *not* go into the left-handed path, using black magic to influence the minds of other people. This is not my desire.

O Saint Germain, I am now free,
your violet flame is therapy,
transform all hang-ups in my mind,
as inner peace I surely find.

**O Saint Germain, what love you bring,
it truly makes all matter sing,
your violet flame does all restore,
with you we are becoming more.**

6. I am making the choice from within because I am at the point of resolution where I am not making this choice with the outer mind.

O Saint Germain, my body pure,
your violet flame for all is cure,
consume the cause of all disease,
and therefore I am all at ease.

17 | Invoking freedom from the self that matters

**O Saint Germain, what love you bring,
it truly makes all matter sing,
your violet flame does all restore,
with you we are becoming more.**

7. I cannot walk the path of Christhood through the outer mind. I can walk from the 48th to the 96th level with the outer mind, but I cannot go beyond the 96th level with the outer mind.

O Saint Germain, I'm karma-free,
the past no longer burdens me,
a brand new opportunity,
I am in Christic unity.

**O Saint Germain, what love you bring,
it truly makes all matter sing,
your violet flame does all restore,
with you we are becoming more.**

8. The decision to enter the path of Christhood comes from within. It is not a willed decision, it is a spontaneous, inner decision. It is not something I can force. I cannot *make* it happen. I can *let* it happen by using the tools to resolve these outer selves that are pulling me away from the decision, that are pulling me into solving a problem.

O Saint Germain, we are now one,
I am for you a violet sun,
as we transform this planet earth,
your Golden Age is given birth.

**O Saint Germain, what love you bring,
it truly makes all matter sing,
your violet flame does all restore,
with you we are becoming more.**

9. I let the self die that looks at the spiritual path as a problem that I must solve. I switch my entire approach to the path and I realize it is not a matter of solving a problem. It is a matter of stopping myself from trying to solve problems. It is a matter of letting it happen.

O Saint Germain, the earth is free,
from burden of duality,
in oneness we bring what is best,
your Golden Age is manifest.

**O Saint Germain, what love you bring,
it truly makes all matter sing,
your violet flame does all restore,
with you we are becoming more.**

Part 7

1. The big problem on earth is the consciousness of separation created by the fallen beings through the consciousness of duality. People see themselves as separate individuals that are fighting against each other.

17 | Invoking freedom from the self that matters

> O Saint Germain, you do inspire,
> my vision raised forever higher,
> with you I form a figure-eight,
> your Golden Age I co-create.
>
> **O Saint Germain, what love you bring,**
> **it truly makes all matter sing,**
> **your violet flame does all restore,**
> **with you we are becoming more.**

2. In order to pull myself out from that struggle, I have to see myself as being separate from the people in the group where I grew up, even all those in the mass consciousness.

> O Saint Germain, what Freedom Flame,
> released when we recite your name,
> acceleration is your gift,
> our planet it will surely lift.
>
> **O Saint Germain, what love you bring,**
> **it truly makes all matter sing,**
> **your violet flame does all restore,**
> **with you we are becoming more.**

3. From the 48th to the 96th level, I am building a self that sees itself as being separated from the people who are in the mass consciousness. This is natural, but I am not going to get beyond the 96th level by using this self.

> O Saint Germain, in love we claim,
> our right to bring your violet flame,
> from you Above, to us below,
> it is an all-transforming flow.

**O Saint Germain, what love you bring,
it truly makes all matter sing,
your violet flame does all restore,
with you we are becoming more.**

4. The path of Christhood is overcoming the illusion of separation and coming to see that behind all of the phenomena on earth is an underlying state of oneness, the oneness of all life. All life is one, there is no separation.

O Saint Germain, I love you so,
my aura filled with violet glow,
my chakras filled with violet fire,
I am your cosmic amplifier.

**O Saint Germain, what love you bring,
it truly makes all matter sing,
your violet flame does all restore,
with you we are becoming more.**

5. In order to get to the 96th level, I have to build a strong individualistic self. To get to the ascended state, I have to break down that self. Step-by-step from the 48th to the 96th level, I am building a self and then I need to switch. Now, step-by-step, from the 97th to the 144th level, I am dismantling that self.

O Saint Germain, I am now free,
your violet flame is therapy,
transform all hang-ups in my mind,
as inner peace I surely find.

17 | Invoking freedom from the self that matters

**O Saint Germain, what love you bring,
it truly makes all matter sing,
your violet flame does all restore,
with you we are becoming more.**

6. I am dismantling the self that sees itself as separated. When I come to the point where I can let the final element of that self go, *that* is when I go into the state of oneness that is the ascension.

O Saint Germain, my body pure,
your violet flame for all is cure,
consume the cause of all disease,
and therefore I am all at ease.

**O Saint Germain, what love you bring,
it truly makes all matter sing,
your violet flame does all restore,
with you we are becoming more.**

7. I realize that I need to dismantle, step-by-step this separate self. As I do that, the reward is that I come to feel a greater and greater oneness with my I AM Presence, which is within myself.

O Saint Germain, I'm karma-free,
the past no longer burdens me,
a brand new opportunity,
I am in Christic unity.

**O Saint Germain, what love you bring,
it truly makes all matter sing,
your violet flame does all restore,
with you we are becoming more.**

8. I will not go into the temptation to feel I am better than other people. I will build a sense of oneness with all life. I begin to feel a sense of oneness with all people, with all life.

O Saint Germain, we are now one,
I am for you a violet sun,
as we transform this planet earth,
your Golden Age is given birth.

**O Saint Germain, what love you bring,
it truly makes all matter sing,
your violet flame does all restore,
with you we are becoming more.**

9. Saint Germain, I vow to pass the final initiation of this course and use all of the tools available to me to put myself firmly on the path of Christhood. *I choose life!*

O Saint Germain, the earth is free,
from burden of duality,
in oneness we bring what is best,
your Golden Age is manifest.

**O Saint Germain, what love you bring,
it truly makes all matter sing,
your violet flame does all restore,
with you we are becoming more.**

Sealing:

In the name of the Divine Mother, I fully accept that the power of these calls is used to set free the River of Life, so it can outpicture the perfect vision of Christ for my own life, for all people and for the planet. In the name I AM THAT I AM, it is done! Amen.

www.ingramcontent.com/pod-product-compliance
Lightning Source LLC
Chambersburg PA
CBHW031721230426
43669CB00007B/202